BECKETT AT 80 / BECKETT IN CONTEXT

Beckett at 80/

NEW YORK ✦ OXFORD ✦

Beckett in Context

Edited by
ENOCH BRATER

OXFORD UNIVERSITY PRESS ♛ 1986

OXFORD UNIVERSITY PRESS

Oxford   New York   Toronto
Delhi   Bombay   Calcutta   Madras   Karachi
Petaling Jaya   Singapore   Hong Kong   Tokyo
Nairobi   Dar es Salaam   Cape Town
Melbourne   Auckland

and associated companies in
Beirut   Berlin   Ibadan   Nicosia

Published by Oxford University Press, Inc.
200 Madison Avenue, New York, New York 10016

Library of Congress Cataloging-in-Publication Data
Main entry under title:
Beckett at 80/Beckett in context.
Includes index.
1. Beckett, Samuel, 1906–   —Criticism and interpretation—
Addresses, essays, lectures.   I. Brater, Enoch.
II. Title: Beckett at eighty/Beckett in context.
PR6003.E282Z5715   1986   848'.91409   85-21523
ISBN 0-19-504001-5

Excerpts from Samuel Beckett's published works are reprinted
with the kind permission of Grove Press, Inc., New York,
and John Calder (Publishers) Ltd., London. Excerpts from *Waiting for Godot,
Endgame, Happy Days, Krapp's Last Tape, Ends and Odds*
and *Collected Shorter Plays of Samuel Beckett* by Samuel Beckett
are reprinted by permission of Faber & Faber Ltd., London.

2 4 6 8 10 9 7 5 3 1
Printed in the United States of America

For Liz

Acknowledgments

Most of the essays published here were originally presented as part of a lecture series sponsored by the University of Michigan during the academic year 1984–85 to mark the playwright's eightieth birthday on April 13, 1986. At the university the project was jointly sponsored by the LSA Enrichment Fund, the School of Music, the Horace H. Rackham School of Graduate Studies, and the Department of English Language and Literature. Four people made that series possible: Peter O. Steiner, Paul C. Boylan, Alfred S. Sussman, and John R. Knott. Four others helped it run smoothly: Gail R. Stander, Marilyn Abramson, Andrew Cerniski, and E. Karen Clark. To Mary B. Price, the able administrative assistant and ally who saw it all through, I wish to express a special debt of gratitude. I must do that as well to William P. Sisler, my sympathetic and enthusiastic editor at Oxford University Press, who believes, as I do, that now that Beckett is eighty, it is time to put Beckett in context.

Ann Arbor, Michigan   **E.B.**
April 1986

Acknowledgments

Contents

BECKETT AT 80 / BECKETT IN CONTEXT

Introduction: The Origins of a Dramatic Style

ENOCH BRATER

The year 1986 marks the eightieth anniversary of Samuel Beckett's birth, but in terms of theater experience it marks something else as well: the maturing of an authentic style that in so many ways has come to represent the drama in our time. After Ibsen, after Strindberg, after Chekhov, Shaw, Pirandello, and Brecht, there is one figure whose place onstage rests secure in the panoply of the great modernist tradition. "Béquet, Béquet," the hysterical spectator cries out in the unpublished and unperformed *Eleuthéria* of 1947, "ça doit être un juif groenlandais matiné d'auvergnat," though the world now knows that the background in this case is pure Anglo-Irish, not Jewish; the native language, Irish-English, not the King's and certainly not the acquired French of Beckett's own Jacques Moran. Critics are likely to ponder forever the road Beckett has traveled—from Foxrock, an affluent suburb of Dublin, to the Left Bank of Paris and international, even Nobel, acclaim—and an eightieth birthday seems a particularly apposite occasion to do so. Yet what we are likely to know best about this writer is the voice which speaks to us so hauntingly in his work: "What tenderness in these little words, what savagery."

How Beckett came to write for the stage is another of those imponderable questions. Any study of his early writing, the precocious and often derivative manuscripts of the thirties through the mid-forties, can be counted on to memorialize Beckett as a struggling young writer of prose and, even before that, of poetry. In *More Pricks Than Kicks*, the collection of short stories based on a jettisoned project for a much longer work entitled *Dream of Fair to Middling Women*, the anxiety of Joyce's influence is so great that it everywhere threatens to undermine the integrity of this otherwise ambitious fictional enterprise. In *Murphy*, the novel published by Routledge in 1938 through the generous intercession of Herbert Read, Beckett makes a tentative leap into an imaginative and highly rhetorical verbal landscape of his own. From its opening line, the narration is beginning to sound a lot less like Joyce; the discourse is beginning to sound a lot more like Beckett: "The sun shone, having no alternative, on the nothing new." Hiding out from the Nazis in Roussillon, a small village near Apt, in the Vaucluse, Beckett worked for two years on another novel, which might have been called *Poor Johnny Watt*, a four-part invention reflecting the catastrophe of war and the irrationality of a world gone mad. "When I was working on *Watt*," Beckett said in 1983, "I felt the need to create for a smaller space, one in which I had some control of where people stood or moved, above all of a certain light. I wrote *Waiting for Godot*."

Beckett's statement—made some forty years on, concerning the frustration of the years 1942–44, which he spent waiting in the south of France—belies what can only be described as a continuing fascination with language as a vehicle not so much intended to be read as spoken. Every reader of Beckett's prose feels the compulsion to read it aloud. The turn of phrase is, in fact, a turn to dialogue, the proper language of the stage. *Mercier and Camier*, one of the first prose undertakings in French (translated into English in 1974 by the author), is in this regard merely a dress rehearsal for the return-the-ball-once-in-a-way of *Waiting for Godot*:

> You keep me waiting, said Mercier.
> On the contrary, said Camier.
> I arrived at nine five, said Mercier.
> And I at nine fifteen, said Camier.
> You see, said Mercier.
> Waiting, said Camier, and keeping waiting can only be with reference to a pre-arranged terminus.

And only fictional moments before:

Don't look, said Mercier.

The sound is enough, said Camier.

True, said Mercier.

After a moment of silence Mercier said:

The dogs don't trouble you?

Why does he not withdraw? said Camier.

He cannot, said Mercier.

Why? said Camier.

One of nature's little gadgets, said Mercier, no doubt to make insemination double sure.

They begin astraddle, said Camier, and finish arsy-versy.

What would you? said Mercier. The ecstasy is past, they yearn to part, to go and piss against a post or eat a morsel of shit, but cannot. So they turn their backs on each other. You'd do as much, if you were they.

Delicacy would restrain me, said Camier.

And what would you do? said Mercier.

Feign regret, said Camier, that I could not renew such pleasure incontinent.

After a moment of silence Camier said:

Let us sit us down, I feel all sucked off.

Mercier and Camier requires only minor adjustment to change the lines assigned to its "pseudocouple" into the rhythm of stage dialogue. Fine-tuning the cues would require, of course, removing what Beckett calls in his first footnote to *Watt* "the plethoric reflexive pronoun after say," an excision which had admittedly saved that novel "much valuable space . . . that otherwise would have been lost." Yet even before the polite little canters of Mercier, Camier, and Watt, Beckett's fictional stylists format their encounters in specifically dialogic shape. Puns and other sophisticated play on words need to be heard, not scanned silently on a page. Celia, Murphy's "doxy," is a transcendent *s'il y a*, and jokes run as follows: "Why did the barmaid champagne? Because the stout porter bitter." We read—and as we read we listen. Little, then nothing, may be left to tell, but along the way Beckett has us play the dual parts of Reader and Listener that he will make far more explicit in *Ohio Impromptu.* Belacqua Shuah, the principal figure in "Yellow," one of the ten pieces in *More Pricks Than Kicks,* sounds like this in an interior monologue we are so very much tempted to exteriorize, to turn into a soliloquy: "Was it to be laughter or tears? It came to the same thing in the end, but which was it to be now? It was too late to arrange for the luxury of both." "What the hell," he cries out in the next few paragraphs, "did anything matter anyway!"

Standing stock still, thinking aloud, or moving about from place to place in one of those "funambulistic" staggers Watt has made so famous, Beckett's characters are, above all, talkers. Everywhere in the fiction we hear their voices. "She had a somewhat hairy face," Molloy says of Ruth (or was her name Edith?), "or am I imagining it, in the interests of the narrative?" "Don't be tormenting yourself," he *does* go on, "man or woman, what does it matter?" Malone can be similarly conversational: "What tedium, and I thought I had it all thought out. If I had the use of my body I would throw it out of the window." In *The Unnamable*, finally, there are no things but things voiced: "Silence once broken will never again be whole." The move to the actual stage lines of Gogo and Didi may be "a relief," as Beckett has said on more than one occasion, but it is also so natural and predictable—though one might not have predicted it at the time— that it hardly seems like a shift at all. What it required from Beckett was merely the need for "a little help," what *Watt* calls "a little understanding."

The essayists gathered together in this volume address themselves to some of the fundamental questions raised by Beckett's assumption of the dramatic mantle. This collection links, through association, a distinguished group of well-known Beckett specialists with several critics who have not necessarily focused their attention on this subject before. The attempt has been to open up the field to a much wider range of response than that usually found in anthologies of Beckett criticism. This symposium, therefore, establishes both a context and a precedent for thinking about Beckett's use of dramatic convention. Each essay offers its own perspective, most often centering its argument on a specific work and sustaining a distinct theoretical environment. The discussions here include historical appreciations, semiotic and structural applications, and performance possibilities based on the actual experiences of making theater happen. That the writers included here often appear to be engaged in a dialogue with one another is a fitting tribute to that climate of spontaneity so many audiences continue to find in Beckett's theater. Their discussions serve to remind us once again that what we celebrate in Beckett is ourselves, our own awareness not only of what drama is but also of what, given the right place and time, it might very well become.

Beckett's first attempt at playwriting, if we can indeed speak of it as such, was the sophomoric French skit called *Le Kid* (subtitled a "Cornelian nightmare"), which he coauthored at Trinity in 1931 with an exchange student from Paris, Georges Pelorson. In period costume but wearing a bowler hat, Beckett himself played the part of the swashbuckling Don Diègue, with an umbrella as improvised prop for a sword. The interlude's title is as much homage to Hollywood as it is parody of neoclassicism. *The Kid*, with Charlie Chaplin in the featured role, was the popular silent film of the twenties, which launched Jackie Coogan as an adorable child star. After *Le Kid* the college newspaper called Beckett an "exhausted aesthete" and wished "he would explain his explanations." No exegesis, however, was offered, and none is to be found in his next dramatic venture, the aborted *Human Wishes*, which dates from 1937. Inspired by Dr. Johnson's relationship with Mrs. Thrale, this fragment is set in "a room in Bolt Court. Wednesday, April 4th, 1781. Evening." The work was never finished and was not produced until March 1984, when its one scene was given a platform performance by a student group at the University of Texas at Austin in conjunction with the conference "Translating Beckett/Beckett Translating." In 1947 Beckett put aside yet another manuscript, *Eleuthéria*, certainly the most commented on unpublished work in his canon. Suffice it to say that this extravaganza takes place in three acts on three consecutive days. Its simultaneous set is filled with a cast of seventeen characters, including a glazier, a man of science and another of letters, an Oriental torturer, and a Spectator from the audience, who comments on the unfolding action. This play, whose hero, Victor Krap, is joined onstage by figures with the impossible names Meck, Piouk, and fiancée Olga Skunk, has never been performed. The stage, as Friedrich Dürrenmatt's Edgar says to Alice in *Play Strindberg*, "has had a narrow escape." Witness a sample from the activities of these vaudevillians:

MR. KRAP: Have a cigar.
DR. PIOUK: Thank you.
MR. KRAP: Yes thank you or no thank you?
DR. PIOUK: I don't smoke.
　　　　　(*Silence*)

MRS. MECK ⎱
MRS. PIOUK ⎰   (Together): I . . .

MRS. MECK: Oh, I beg your pardon. You were going to say?
MRS. PIOUK: Oh, nothing. Go on.
             (*Silence*)

Ruby Cohn will speak more formally here about the circumstances of producing *En attendant Godot* a few years later, but something about the artistic climate of Paris must be held partially responsible for its succès d'estime. When Beckett arrived there from Dublin years before as *lecteur d'anglais* at the prestigious Ecole Normale Supérieure, he was a shy, lanky, impressionable young man armed with a letter of introduction from Con Leventhal. To him Paris represented not just Joyce but all that was French, avant-garde, and possible in the arts. How much of this Beckett absorbed can only be conjectured, but certainly the theater he found there offered a fare quite different from what he had been accustomed to at the Abbey, where his own hero Murphy met an ignominious end. By the twenties and thirties, the Dadaists and the surrealists, the constructivists and the futurists, had long made their mark on the pocket theaters of the Left Bank. It was here that Tristan Tzara's *The Gas Heart* (a play whose dramatis personae include Mouth, prefiguring *Not I*), Jean Aurenche and Jean Anouilh's exuberant *Humulus the Mute*, Jean Cocteau's *The Wedding on the Eiffel Tower*, and, even earlier, Guillaume Apollinaire's *The Breasts of Tiresias* were first introduced to a very puzzled world. It was here, too, that Antonin Artaud, Roger Blin's mentor, did his visionary directing and that American movies began to be seriously discussed as "film." Though Beckett arrived too late on the scene to witness the more sensational rites such experimentation would so willingly embrace (the bruitism, the manifestations, the happenings, the self-posing, the automatic writing, the chance compositions, and the Dada excursions to nowhere in particular), "the air," to quote from *Godot*, was "full of [their] cries"— so full that they had even been heard in Dublin. But Beckett's opportunity to play a minor part in the Paris avant-garde would come in 1932, when Edward Titus published a special number of his magazine *This Quarter*. Guest-edited by André Breton, the volume was designed to acquaint the English-speaking world with the Paris surrealists. Titus printed Breton's important essay "Surrealism: Yesterday To-day and Tomorrow," which repeated almost verbatim key passages from his revolutionary manifestos, as well as the film script for *An Andalusian Dog*, Buñuel's collaboration with Dali. Beckett's translations of works by René Crevel, Paul Eluard, Benjamin Péret, Tristan Tzara, and André Breton appeared side by side with reproductions of drawings by Man Ray, Yves Tanguy, and Giorgio de Chirico. In his introduction, Titus, whose publication in English predates Herbert Read's landmark study of surrealism by several years, singled out Beckett's contributions for special acknowledgment: "His rendering of the Eluard and Breton poems in particular is characterizable only in superlatives." This commendation earned a place for Beckett's short story "Dante and the Lobster" in the December issue, where it appeared with selections from e. e. cummings and Allen Tate.

War and occupation would temporarily put Paris on hold as a center for artistic frenzy, but the city Beckett returned to soon after liberation offered him a unique challenge and a special opportunity. It was now possible to graft the recent experience of Europe—both the hideousness of history and its philosophical implications—onto the not-so-new ideas about theater that had already been established before the war. Art, theater art, could now be produced without the capital letter A. Beckett's development of Dada into Didi is, therefore, clear, precise, almost, historically speaking, "inevitable." For Beckett does not come from nowhere: he is very much a writer of his time, shaped by the forces of his time to speak to the new audience of his time. It is now possible, because Beckett is a respectable octogenarian, to look back on his long, productive career, to desentimentalize it, and to see it for what it so obviously is: a major breakthrough in the evolution of dramatic form. In the pages which follow, John Russell Brown and Normand Berlin, after registering their own initial responses to the work, discuss the dimensions of its dramaturgical and aesthetic framework; Michael Goldman and Martin Esslin draw us into its thematic presuppositions; Charles Lyons and Andrew Kennedy explore its relation to dramatic convention; Bernard Beckerman and Katharine Worth consider its rich domain of sound and stage silence; Keir Elam develops its language of signs; James Knowlson uses the resources of the Beckett Archive at Reading, England, to pinpoint the work's crucial link to technology and

the playwright's use of different media; and Thomas Whitaker, re-
turing us to the initial charge of Ruby Cohn's essay, studies the impact Beckett has had on the generation of playwrights who follow.
Taken together, these essays illuminate the variety and significance of
Beckett's lifelong achievement, "a raid on the inarticulate" that has
revolutionized the theater in our time.

I
Retrospectives

Growing (Up?) with *Godot*

RUBY COHN

Beckett's most loyal director, the late Alan Schneider, wrote that *Waiting for Godot* "is no longer a play, but a condition of life."[1] My modest intention is to examine it as a play, a script for performance, but I hope that the condition of life will seep through. Like many others, I was a student when I discovered *Godot*. Like many others, I continue to be educated by that tragicomedy written in French in 1949, translated by its author into English in 1954, and now available in over twenty languages. (The Grove Press paperback edition has sold about a million and a half copies.)

Let us review its origin. Between Beckett's postwar return to Paris, in 1945, and 1950, he wrote continuously, filling many cheap notebooks with his execrable handwriting. Although he now looks back nostalgically at that momentum, it was not unbroken even then. At an impasse in his fiction, between *Malone meurt* and *L'Innommable*, later translated as *Malone Dies* and *The Unnamable*, Beckett penned his second play. *En attendant Godot* flows across the pages with few changes and few hesitations. Beckett's manuscript—in a soft-cover, graph-paper notebook—reveals the work's fluidity. The play begins— in French—not with a title or character list, but with the setting: "A country road. A tree." Then a scenic direction describes an old man trying to take off his shoe when another old man enters. The name Vladimir evidently occurred to Beckett as soon as the second old man addressed himself in his opening speech, but when the shoe-preoccupied first old man replied, he was designated as "Levy," and he remained Levy through act 1; only at the beginning of act 2 did Beckett baptize Levy as Estragon, a plant of the wormwood family, whose name comes to European languages from the Arabic. Back in act 1, when Pozzo and Lucky first appear, the manuscript designates them as a very large man and a small one. The large man introduces himself almost at once as the friends are wondering whether he is Godot: "I present myself: Pozzo," which, he does not reveal, is Italian for "well." Lucky's name erupts only when Pozzo explains that his menial has first refusal of his discarded chicken bones: ". . . in theory the bones go to Lucky." (In print, Lucky's name is not mentioned at this point.) So the international flavor of the characters—Slavic Vladimir, Italian Pozzo, English Lucky, French Estragon—emerged in the process of writing.

In the *Godot* notebook, the bravura piece, Lucky's monologue, is scribbled in a block on three unpunctuated pages, with no sign of the three-part division that Beckett would later point out to actors—indifferent heaven, dwindling man, and earth a wilderness. After composing the monologue, Beckett apparently backtracked to note on a verso page of the manuscript the reactions of Lucky's onstage audience.

Opening act 2, Vladimir sings Beckett's translation of an old German ballad also familiar to Brecht. The three-hat routine, adapted from the Marx Brothers' *Duck Soup*, substitutes for a now unreadable—at least by me—Vladimir/Estragon exchange. Before the act 2 arrival of Pozzo and Lucky, Beckett's doodles—odd little men—intrude into the writing. Evidently, Beckett's momentum was winding down like that of Vladimir and Estragon.

Once the manuscript was titled and typed by Beckett in January 1949, it was offered to, and refused by, several Paris theater managers (along with an earlier Beckett play, the still unpublished *Eleuthéria*). Finally, it attracted an unknown actor/director, Roger Blin, who never dreamed that his own immediate delight in *Godot* would be widely shared, for Blin was accustomed to the near empty houses that yawned at his productions of Synge and Strindberg. And these playwrights had not stripped drama quite so bare as Beckett.

Blin and Beckett, two tall, lean, laconic men, were mutually sympathetic and formed a reserved friendship that lasted throughout Blin's life. (He died on January 20, 1984.) Before rehearsals began, Beckett wrote Blin: "Now that we have embarked on this dirty joke together, I think that we can address each other in the familiar form." At the time of Blin's death, he was preparing to act in a one-man Beckett show. In 1949, however, Blin's theater was going bankrupt. Nevertheless, he rehearsed odd scenes of *Godot* in odd places with odd actors for the sheer pleasure of hearing the rhythms. He submitted the script of *Godot* for a French government grant toward production of a first play, and fortunately poet/playwright Georges Neveux was on the selection committee. Three years after the play was completed, in January 1952, Neveux wrote Blin: "Dear Roger Blin, you are absolutely right in wanting to perform *Waiting for Godot*. It is an astonishing play; I needn't tell you that I am fiercely for it."[2] So fiercely that the Blin/Beckett enterprise received 500,000 old francs. It sounds like a lot, but it was something like $1,500, enabling Blin to pay for a few posters, a roll of tickets, rudimentary lights, bowler hats, and a month's rent for the Théâtre Babylone. In Blin's fifth production, he paid his actors about $15 a week, but he drew no salary for directing. In 1982 Blin reminisced:

The play struck me as so rich and unique in its nudity that it seemed to me improper to question the author about its meaning. Nor did I ask myself questions about it; during three years of rehearsal my major concerns were traps, false trails, allusions. . . . First the trap of the circus. . . . After that farcical trap, the tearful trap, especially for Vladimir. . . . I know that there are different levels in *Godot*, but the desired magic can be attained only by first dealing fully with the most immediately human level. For the characters, I took as springboard their physical defects, real or implied. Beckett heard their voices, but he couldn't describe his characters to me. [He said:] "The only thing I'm sure of is that they're wearing bowler hats."[3]

Casting was a problem for Blin, and contracts were not drawn up until a few weeks before opening. Pierre Latour as childlike, lovable Estragon had earlier acted with Blin, but the director chose a contrasting Vladimir from cabaret. Lucien Raimbourg offered comic scope with his mobile face, agile body, and carefully enunciated slang—no tearful trap there. Moreover, Raimbourg was accustomed to the disjunctive numbers of cabaret without the trained French actor's desire to build a character toward a big scene, and this was a decided asset in performing *Godot*. Unfailingly good-tempered about a role he did not try to analyze in a play he did not try to analyze, Raimbourg often bicycled across Paris after a Left Bank rehearsal so as to perform in a midnight cabaret near the Bastille. Later he toured many countries in *Godot* and played other roles in the theater of the absurd. Of the original cast of *Godot*, he alone returned to Vladimir as late as 1970, and a reviewer paid him this tribute: "The character will be marked forever by his broken, hopping walk, his nasal ramblings of an old clown, and in his eye a question mark, the image of the whole play."[4] Perhaps that image was in Beckett's mind when he attended Raimbourg's funeral in 1975. But in 1952, Blin exploited Raimbourg's vivacity. The nimble comedian literally ran circles around the stolid Estragon/Latour. Yet small Raimbourg was protective of the larger Latour, making comic absurdity of Vladimir's question as to whether he was heavier than Estragon. Only after casting Vladimir and Estragon and pacing their verbal volleys did Blin concentrate on Pozzo and Lucky. Again, he wanted contrast within the couple; he chose a heavyset Pozzo to his own Lucky, but, two weeks before the opening, Pozzo found a more remunerative role. Blin had no choice, knowing the play by heart, but to enact Pozzo himself while persuading his friend Jean Martin to be Lucky. "A one-line part," Blin teased Martin, who has proved to be lucky because Martin is the only member of the original cast who is still alive.

From the moment the cast was assembled, the actors rehearsed in bowlers. Blin stole his father's wedding jacket for Vladimir/Raimbourg, and he draped it over a loose celluloid white collar and bedraggled black tie. Estragon/Latour wore baggy trousers belted by a rope, endowing him with a lovable Chaplinesque quality. Shirtless, he sported a pea coat and a once-white scarf, jauntily knotted. Blin hid Lucky/Martin's slim frame in a long stiff scarlet jacket trimmed with gold braid, such as footmen wore in the eighteenth century, but his dark tight trousers were too short, revealing his bare calves. Lucky's mouth was a scarlet gash in a chalk-white face, with dark circles rendering the eyes stark and protuberant. Capped by the indispensable bowler, the white hair of Lucky's wig fell grotesquely to his shoulders. Martin found the worn valise in a garbage can.

A landed squire, Pozzo/Blin patterned his own costume on pictures of English John Bull. He wore a checked MacFarlane, with a cape broadening his thin frame, and he amplified his girth with a hidden pillow over which stretched a velvet vest with a diamond pattern. His bowler was gray in contrast to the black of the other three. All four actors wore their costumes with style in this unlocalized desert.

What Blin as director achieved in that first *Godot* was a rare feeling of ensemble. Cabaret was entering postwar Paris theater, so that audiences were not startled by the rhythmic sallies of Vladimir and Estragon, and yet this banter was not sustained. During long pauses it seemed as though the actors had forgotten their lines. What was new was the eruption of a master/slave pair into cabaret patter. The first Pozzo/Lucky entrance smacked of circus—the driving hand delayed by the long rope connecting the two men. An overburdened Lucky could be milked for farce, but not if he had to fall *offstage* when Pozzo jerked the rope. And once Pozzo/Blin asserted his cruel presence, the effect was too disturbing for cabaret. Why were these two couples in the same play? Later Blin explained that he intended surprise in the Pozzo/Lucky entrances, but what he achieved was dislocation.

Vladimir and Estragon at first seem like twins, but they gradually diverge, like hat and boot. Active Vladimir is faithful to the rendezvous whereas inactive Estragon keeps announcing his departure. Pozzo and Lucky at first seem antonymic, but they are finally twinned in picaresque impotence. What Blin's production conveyed was the interdependence of all humanity on a pocket stage—especially in act 2, when the four men are sprawled on the ground before rising one by one, more or less helped by one another.

I estimate that some fifty thousand people saw Blin's first production of *Godot*, including tours, and today almost everyone who was in Paris between January 5, 1953, and October 30, 1954, claims to have seen it. But I really did. I had never heard of Beckett. I knew none of the background I have just sketched. Unlike Blin, I *did* ask questions about the play, and I read reviews. In a later play, *Rough for Radio II*, Beckett would write: "Ah those old spectres from the days of . . . reviewing, they lie in wait for one at every turn." I, on the contrary, had to ferret most of them out of the dusty, uncomputerized Bibliothèque de l'Arsenal.

Thirty critics accepted the invitation to see the production before the public opening, as was customary then in Paris. The cold, rainy afternoon of January 4, 1953, did not look like a bright dawn of new theater. In the year that was just beginning, Les Editions de Minuit, Beckett's newly acquired French publisher, would sell 125 copies of the play, and yet Blin's production would last through that year (not continuously) and beyond. People wanted to see, not read, the tragicomedy—nearly three hours of plotless performance.

Contrary to later legend, the reviewers were kind. It is noteworthy that thirty people agreed to attend *Godot*, as compared, for example, to the handful present just a few months earlier at Arthur Adamov's *The Parody* or Eugène Ionesco's *The Chairs*. To be sure, the most powerful theater critic of Paris, Jean-Jacques Gautier of *Le Figaro*, was absent, but "a reasonable percentage" of those who came wrote reviews. The earliest I found closed with regret that the brilliant play and remarkable interpretation would probably attract only a coterie audience.[5] The most mistaken review states: "This unusual work by the American novelist seems to be inspired by the miserable condition of famished tramps hunted down by farmers, who abound in the South of the United States."[6] One reviewer explained that Godot was "happiness, eternal life, the ideal and unattainable quest of all men."[7] Another critic rejoiced: "Samuel Beckett is a subversive spirit; you can't image how comforting that is."[8] Some dozen reviews in the daily papers ranged from tolerant to enthusiastic, and the weeklies followed suit. One of them closed wittily: "Samuel Beckett paints boredom without boring us, sleep without putting us to sleep, despair with merriment, and he mocks theater theatrically."[9] Not surprisingly—at least it doesn't surprise me—the American Paris *Herald* was harshest: ". . . dramatically *En attendant Godot* does not hang together very well and is repetitious and rather clumsy in making its points."[10] Not a whisper as to what those points might be.

With monthly publications came the first meditated criticism of *Godot*. The then unknown *nouveau romancier* Alain Robbe-Grillet dismisses guesses about the identity of Godot as God, the social order, death, silence, the self. He clarifies: "Godot is the person awaited by two tramps" who are *there* before us onstage. Suddenly, the theater reveals that the human condition is *to be there*, as Heidegger affirmed. Further, Robbe-Grillet writes: "Didi and Gogo will be there again the next day, and the next, and the day after that . . . without future, without past, irremediably there."[11] After this praise from the

budding novelist came enthusiasm from France's two most successful playwrights of the time, Jean Anouilh and Armand Salacrou, the
former calling *Godot* "a vaudeville sketch of Pascal's *Pensées* as
played by the Fratellini clowns."[12]

Toward the end of *Godot*'s run at the Théâtre Babylone it was
seen by American director Alan Schneider, who wrote:

My French is just good enough to get me in and out of the American
Express. Yet through the entire performance I sat alternately spellbound
and mystified, knowing something terribly moving was taking place on
that stage. When the highly stylized "moon" suddenly rose and night
"fell" at the end of the first act, I didn't have to understand French in
order to react. And when, at the beginning of the second act, the once-
bare tree reappeared with little green ribbons for leaves, that simple representation of rebirth affected me beyond all reason. Without knowing exactly what, I knew that I had experienced something unique and
significant in modern theater. *Godot* had me in the beginnings of a grip
from which I have never escaped.[13]

Someone in Paris was evidently reading the reviews, for *En attendant Godot* was advertised in 1954 as "a metaphysical drama unfolding under the tinsel of farce." Certainly, Didi and Gogo look as
though they belong in farce, silent films, or vaudeville. Most of their
gestures are familiar in those genres. The play opens with an old
mime of farce; Estragon struggles to take off a tight shoe. Later he
speaks with full mouth, uses one lung as a bellows, interrupts an escape to retrieve a carrot, mimics Lucky as carrier and as dancer, starts
to tell a dirty joke, loses his balance, tries to hide behind a skeletal
tree, and finally drops his trousers. In spite of superior sophistication,
Vladimir is also a creature of farce; he leaves his fly unbuttoned,
laughs painfully, smiles suddenly, spits with disgust at Estragon's
stinking shoe, stuffs his pockets with miscellaneous rubbish, minces
like a model; he, too, imitates Lucky as carrier and dancer. Together
the two friends take gorilla postures, huddle in exaggerated fright,
examine one another as objects; they pose as scouts on the lookout,
or they juggle hats. They manipulate their respective props, shoe and
hat, identically. They tug at Estragon's rope belt, which breaks and
nearly topples them.

All these familiar physical gags unmask Beckett as an observant
student of farce, but he is an original master of verbal dynamics, and

his dialogue seems at times to listen to itself. "Let's make a little conversation," urges Estragon in act 1, and in act 2: "That's the idea, let's ask each other questions." "That's the idea, let's abuse each other." "That's the idea, let's contradict each other." Even "back to back," the two comedians patter on. Afraid of silence, they angrily command one another to finish a phrase. Perhaps Lucky is so obsessed with tennis because that is the game that eludes him. He obeys Pozzo's commands, but not even once in a way does he return the verbal ball, as Didi and Gogo unbeatably do.

The first audiences laughed at how hard it was for them to do so, but subsequent audiences, as criticism accumulated, acknowledged how lightly the comedians wore their erudition. The Bible threads through their discourse—not only the conundrum of the two thieves damned or saved, where the visual imagery reinforces the verbal references to Christ crucified between two thieves, but there are also snatches from *Proverbs* (hope deferred . . .), *Revelations* (the last moment), *Matthew* (the wind in the reeds; one brother among sheep and the other among goats), *Genesis* (Cain and Abel), *Kings* or *Elijah* (a little cloud). And Estragon claims to have spent a lifetime comparing himself to Christ.

Less plentiful is the classical residue—Atlas, who is the brother (not the son) of Jupiter; Pan; caryatids. Vladimir quotes a Latin phrase—*Memoria praeteritorium bonarum*. In the original French text, Vladimir claims his name is Catullus, and he subverts Heraclitus. Fainter are the reminiscences of Shakespeare—Lucky's homage to divine Miranda, Vladimir's abridgments of Hamlet's "Words, words, words" and of Hamlet's most celebrated line to "*that* is the question." In act 2, the Pozzo/Lucky couple seems to illustrate Gloucester's line: "'Tis the times' plague, when madmen lead the blind." And four men on a bare stage recall the heath scene of *Lear*. The erstwhile poet Estragon quotes Shelley in English: "Pale for weariness." Two small figures dwarfed in the immensity of the moonscape resemble those in a Caspar David Friedrich painting.

Bert States has written gracefully: ". . . if we were to walk back along the mythic road on which *Godot* takes place, we would encounter numerous shapes from scriptural, historical, and literary memory which might be called ancestors of the scene enacted before us."[14] Perhaps "analogues" would be more accurate than "ancestors." Early reviewers derived *Godot* from Artaud, Joyce, Kafka. Suzanne

Aron in 1955 and, independently, Eric Bentley in 1956 seized on Balzac's *Faiseur* of 1851, in which characters await the arrival of a M. Godeau, and the French novelist Marcel Jouhandeau has also written of M. Godeau. Other names on that mythic road belong to French writers preoccupied with death: Ronsard, Bossuet, Pascal, Baudelaire. The Japanese critic Yasunari Takahashi expands on the fortuitous similarities between Beckett and the Ghost No play. Eugène Ionesco equates Beckett with Job. Classicists cite the relevance of *Godot* to Greek tragedy; and medievalists, to both mysteries and moralities. Dante hovers over all of Beckett's work. Names and phrases of *Godot* have passed into popular currency, from Beckett's own rumored uneasiness at flying in a plane whose pilot was Captain Godeau to a recent headline on the financial page of *Le Monde*, "En attendant Godot," where Godot proves to be a metaphor for lower American interest rates. The culinary column of New York's *Village Voice* appears under the byline of a pseudonymous Vladimir Estragon, and a publisher of Italian art books is actually named Pozzo.

Beckett himself has drawn on *Godot* in his subsequent works. The name Pozzo occurs insidiously in Text 5 for Nothing: "Why did Pozzo leave home, he had a castle and retainers." Pozzo's toast, "Happy days," becomes the title of a major Beckett play, and the word "enough," often repeated in *Godot*, becomes the title of Beckett's 1967 story. In 1956 the master/servant couple move to center stage in *Endgame* whereas the landscape of the void nourishes the 1961 play *Happy Days*. Lucky's stones become the bedrock for the suicide of *Eh Joe*. A frail tree takes form in *Act Without Words 1*, and carrots reappear in *Act Without Words 2*. Comparably contrasting members of a couple are the spine of *Act Without Words 2* and of both *Roughs for Theatre*. Pozzo's line about birthing astride of a grave is differently vivified in *Breath* and *A Piece of Monologue*. Estragon tries calling Pozzo several names "to hit on the right one sooner or later," and Mouth in *Not I* tries words to "hit on it in the end." In the BBC production of . . . *but the clouds* . . . , the single character wears the bowler hat so prevalent in *Godot*, and, returned from roaming the roads, he busies himself with the very "nothing" that has to be done in *Godot*. Lucky's final word "unfinished" applies to Hamm's chronicle, Clov's departure, Mouth's monologue. *Godot*'s several references to its audience prove to be the germ of Beckett's theatereality of the late plays.

The late play, Ghost Trio, of 1975 is haunted by Godot even though there is only one lonely protagonist and the awaited presence is feminine: "He will now think he hears her." Ghost Trio's original title was Tryst, a poetic synonym for an appointment, and the visible character is no saint, but he, too, keeps his appointment, and he too is disappointed. The television figure peers not into twilight but into dark night; like Didi and Gogo, this figure counterpoints gesture against words. As in Godot, a boy arrives in Ghost Trio. Although the television play's boy does not speak, he apparently bears the same message: "Boy shakes head faintly"—twice, as in the two acts of Godot.

Didi and Gogo grow more inventive as they grow more anxious in act 2 of Godot. The converse is true of the solitary man of Ghost Trio. In what Beckett calls Pre-Action, words address the television viewer, describing the scene we see, a room resembling that of Beckett's post-Godot plays. In the action proper, fewer words accompany the movement of the protagonist, virtually instructing him. In the Re-action only nonverbal sounds punctuate the repetition of his movements, and it is the Re-action that most resembles Godot, where energy is more evidently entropic.

Ghost Trio not only parallels Waiting for Godot. It metaphorizes the movement of Beckett's dramatic art: from dialogue toward silence, from verbal to formal music, from diachronic action to a near coalescence of Pre-action, Re-action, and actual theatereality (convergence of what we see with what we hear about). For all the vestigial concentration of Ghost Trio, however, it will not mirror Godot in containing a cosmos and a history of theater.

I have skipped through Godot's lexicon of farce—what Roger Blin called the trap of farce. But I think that the trap lies in limiting the play to farce and its exploitation of shoe, hat, and rope. At the same time, what Blin called the tearful trap is present in the residue of tragedy—a Pozzo blind and prescient like the prophet Tiresias, a divine messenger despite a truncated message, a reduced Chorus that speaks for the polis ("all mankind is us"), and the deus that never descends from the mechane. In act 1 Pozzo blusters like a hero, classical or Shakespearean, but by act 2 he falls, a literal de casibus casualty. In act 2 four characters grovel on the ground, even as in naturalism, a category to which turnips, carrots, radishes, and bones also belong. And yet Godot spurns naturalism, for its setting is a void; its time, indefinite; and its action, at once plotless and repetitive. Two trajectories cross; tramps and travelers are staples of realistic drama, but they meet in this play without rhyme or reason, and they separate without growing "wiser, richer, more conscious of one's blessings," as Pozzo brags unconvincingly.

In its own rebellion against realism, *Waiting for Godot* enfolds some of its dramatic predecessors: nothing so elaborate as Strindberg's *A Dream Play* or *The Ghost Sonata*, and yet the air of *Godot* is dense with dreams and ghosts. Beckett's play illustrates one of Pirandello's titles—to each his own truth; the quality of the Didi/ Gogo dialogue hints at another title—tonight it's improvisation. Thornton Wilder was enthusiastic about *Godot*, which also dramatizes life lived by the skin of our teeth. In *Jumpers*, Tom Stoppard's unpleasant academic explodes: "Wham bam! Thank you Sam!" in homage to Sam Beckett, from whom Stoppard borrowed whole sequences of *Rosencrantz and Guildenstern Are Dead*. Harold Pinter has been candid about Beckett's impact on him, and he always sends the older playwright his newly completed manuscripts. Pinter's very first play, *The Birthday Party*, seems to me to owe a debt to *Godot* from the vaudeville pair Goldberg and McCann to an offstage Monty, the whole blending the comic into the cosmic. Peter Handke's springboard in *Kaspar* is the biography of nineteenth-century Kaspar Hauser, the prisoner taught language in his late teens, but the way language manipulates its learner recalls Lucky.

A few American playwrights have leaned lightly on *Godot*: Edward Albee dramatizes the contrasting members of a couple in *Zoo Story* and *Who's Afraid of Virginia Woolf?* Tennessee Williams's *Out-Cry* is set in an entropic theater in an unnamed country, which recalls Beckett. And Sam Shepard has confessed to me that he admires Beckett, an echo of whom I hear in the patter of two would-be cowboys of *Cowboys #2* and in the extraordinary word duel of *Tooth of Crime*.

Waiting for Godot is Beckett's most resonant play. After *Godot* it was theatrically viable to perform a deeply serious and playful play. After *Godot* plots could be minimal; expositions, expendable; characters, contradictory; settings, unlocalized; and dialogue, unpredictable. Blatant farce could jostle tragedy; obscenity could pun on the sacred. One actor could recite a ten-minute monologue, and another be mute; or the same actor could be both monologuist and mute.

Delicate verse lines could mourn the humanist tradition—like leaves, like ashes—while the stage showed the crueltly of that tradition—a charnel house! In *Waiting for Godot*, Beckett honed our perceptions to what was before us onstage while inviting our imaginations to roam the stars, as well as this earthly bog. Vladimir is accurate in his boast: "We're inexhaustible."

NOTES

1. See Alan Schneider, " 'Any Way You Like, Alan': Working with Beckett," *Theatre Quarterly* 5:19 (September–November 1975), 27.
2. *Le Nouvel Observateur*, September 26, 1981.
3. Ibid.
4. *Le Monde*, March 18, 1970.
5. Marc Beigbeder in *Revue théâtrale*, January 5, 1953.
6. G. Joly, in *L'Aurore*, January 6, 1953.
7. Sylvain Zegel, in *Libération*, January 7, 1953. Reprinted in *Samuel Beckett: The Critical Heritage*, edited by Lawrence Graver and Raymond Federman (London: Routledge & Kegan Paul, 1979), pp. 88–89.
8. Guy Dumur, in *Combat*, January 12, 1953.
9. Claude Jamet, in *France réelle*, January 23, 1953.
10. American Paris *Herald*, February 13, 1953.
11. *Critique*, 9 (February 1953), 108–14.
12. *Arts-Spectacles* 400 (February 27, 1953), 1.
13. *Chelsea Review*, September 1958. Reprinted in *The Critical Heritage*, pp. 3–20.
14. *The Shape of Paradox* (Berkeley: University of California Press, 1978), p. 71.

Beckett and the Art of the Nonplus

JOHN RUSSELL BROWN

When I read Waiting for Godot for the first time, in 1955, I was nonplussed; but, nevertheless, after a couple of years, I began to plan a production of the play. Peter Hall's presentation in London had not encouraged me because its mixture of music hall acts, meaningful statements, and slow-moving narrative had shown me other values than those which had disturbed and silenced me. Nor did the lively discussion that followed that first production do more than widen the context in which I felt insecure because the critics were concerned mostly with the text's obvious and detachable symbols.

After reading only a few pages, I had known that I had been "appalled." This had been suggested by the very first stage direction and the words that follow:

> Estragon, sitting on a low mound, is trying to take off his boot.
> He pulls at it with both hands, panting. He gives up, exhausted, tries again.
> As before.
> Enter Vladimir.
> ESTRAGON: (giving up again). Nothing to be done.
> VLADIMIR: (advancing with short, stiff strides, legs wide apart).
> I'm beginning to come round to that opinion. All my life I've tried to put it from me, saying, Vladimir, be reason-

able, you haven't yet tried everything. And I resumed the
struggle.
(*He broods, musing on the struggle* . . .)[1]

That was not how characters were introduced in the plays I knew at
that time. The interchange of words seemed accidental, and only one
of the two speakers seemed to hear the other. And how could the
one who listened know what was meant by the one who spoke? Still
more strange was the opening stage direction: how long would all
this quiet business take to enact? *"Panting"* is not an action established in a brief moment. *"Exhausted"* is not a direction to put into
effect easily, and again it takes time. And *why* should the boot fail to
move? What obstacle did Estragon encounter, if any? I asked these
ordinary, practical questions and became more sure that I had lost
my bearings.

Only a few minutes into the play came a passage which caught my
imagination more deeply and still holds it after I have seen numerous actors in numerous productions, all embodying the author's text
and directions in their own ways:

ESTRAGON: It hurts?
VLADIMIR: Hurts! He wants to know if it hurts!
ESTRAGON: (*pointing*). You might button it all the same.
VLADIMIR: (*stooping*). True (*He buttons his fly.*) Never neglect the
little things of life.
ESTRAGON: What do you expect, you always wait till the last moment.
VLADIMIR: (*musingly*). The last moment . . . (*He meditates.*) Hope
deferred maketh the something sick, who said that?
ESTRAGON: Why don't you help me?
VLADIMIR: Sometimes I feel it coming all the same. Then I go all
queer. (*He takes off his hat, peers inside it, feels about
inside it, shakes it, puts it on again*). How shall I say? Relieved and at the same time . . . (*he searches for the
word*) . . . appalled. (*With emphasis.*) AP-PALLED.
(*He takes off his hat again, peers inside it.*) Funny. (*He
knocks on the crown as though to dislodge a foreign body,
peers into it again, puts it on again.*) Nothing to be done.
(*Estragon with a supreme effort succeeds in pulling off his
boot. He looks inside it, feels about inside it, turns it up-
side down, shakes it, looks on the ground to see if anything
has fallen out, finds nothing, feels inside it again, staring
sightlessly before him.*) Well?

ESTRAGON: Nothing.
VLADIMIR: Show.
ESTRAGON: There's nothing to show.
VLADIMIR: Try and put it on again.
ESTRAGON: (*examining his foot.*). I'll air it for a bit.
VLADIMIR: There's man all over for you, blaming on his boots the
faults of his feet. (*He takes off his hat again, peers inside
it, feels about inside it, knocks on the crown, blows into
it, puts it on again.*) This is getting alarming. (*Silence.
Vladimir deep in thought, Estragon pulling at his toes.*)

The direction for "*Silence*" after "This is getting alarming" is the
first of many such in the play and in subsequent plays by Beckett.
Soon in *Godot* there are six silences within the space of fourteen
lines; and elsewhere, five within ten lines. Besides there are many
more silences which are only implied, for example:

VLADIMIR: I get used to the muck as I go along.
ESTRAGON: (*after prolonged reflection*). Is that the opposite?

This stage direction for Estragon also calls forth a particular kind of
"*silence.*"

Most alarming or appalling are silences which are followed by
words or actions that have little or no continuity from what precedes
them: the characters have become nonplussed until something accidental happens—perhaps Estragon's boot comes off—or some new
topic for talk rises without apparent connection as if welling up from
the subconscious of the character or possibly of the author. After
Vladimir's "This is getting alarming," the next words are his: "One
of the thieves was saved. (*Pause.*) It's a reasonable percentage.
(*Pause.*) Gogo." His mind has moved at a tangent, for reasons un-
stated: old worries or old consolations have surfaced, claiming the
effort of speech, and make play for present consolation by means of
attempted communication.

At the end of each act, Vladimir and Estragon seem ready to accept silence and attempt nothing more. They stay stock-still at the
end of their dramatic lives without further recourse to speech or
movement; their act is finished, played out if not completed:

ESTRAGON: . . . We weren't made for the same road.
VLADIMIR: (*without anger*). It's not certain.

ESTRAGON: No, nothing is certain.
Vladimir slowly crosses the stage and sits down beside Estragon.
VLADIMIR: We can still part if you think it would be better.
ESTRAGON: It's not worth while now.
Silence.
VLADIMIR: No, it's not worth while now.
Silence.
ESTRAGON: Well, shall we go?
VLADIMIR: Yes, let's go.
They do not move.

Curtain

The words of the last two speeches of act 2 are the same as these at the end of act 1; only the speakers are now switched round, Vladimir making the suggestion that they should go, while his introductory "Well" is followed by a question mark and not a comma. The other difference is that the two speakers have been thinking more extensively about suicide and the possibility that Godot might appear: the identical words cover, or present, a different set of concerns; they work now within a different structure of thought and feeling. And still there is no more to say or do.

At one time I was almost sure that Vladimir and Estragon stayed together at the end of each act because they had sensed, in these last moments, that what they needed above all else was each other's company. But I think now that this interpretation sentimentalizes the play. Although actors can relish and communicate the bond that holds the two characters together, the business of making this narrative apparent in performance slows down the action, creating rhythms of behavior that require more time than the rhythms of the spoken text and the patience of audiences will permit. I have sat through a sentimental production of *Wating for Godot* that lasted well over three and a half hours.

I suspect that both characters have spoken during each act, "in such a place, and in such a world," all that they "can manage, more than they could" and that this is why the play ends. Here I have adapted Beckett's comments about the main characters of *Endgame*[2] to explain those of *Waiting for Godot* because I suspect that the action of both dramas is to draw its characters into a position where no more is possible. If each other's company has helped to bring them this far, their sense of this can take them no further; the end of the play is no occasion to celebrate togetherness, and actors should not be encouraged to take time along the way to respond too hopefully to each other's presence or moments of verbal agreement.

Waiting for Godot is not about the relationship of its characters or the story of their lives, and it does not state any theme or argument. It is rather a presentation of how these characters have been set in motion and speech by their author, on "A country road," with "A tree," at "Evening" on two successive days. Thus, the action of the play is the action of its author's mind at a certain place and time in our present world, given certain dramatis personae as postulates: it is no more, and it seems to be no less.

This dramaturgy holds attention by discrete disciplines, by the economy with which each item of stage reality speaks for itself. In one sense, Anton Chekhov's The Cherry Orchard also presents its characters as its author's mind directs, and story and argument are only a small part of its appeal; and it, too, finishes with silence. Bur Firs, the character onstage, together with the visible reality in which he is placed, is not sufficient to bring the play to a close. The audience is forced to think of other realities as well—and the consequences of events for other lives and other times:

> FIRS: [of Gaev] Gone off in his light overcoat. (Sighs anxiously.) I should have seen to it. . . . Oh, these youngsters. (Mutters something which cannot be understood.) My life's gone just as if I'd never lived. . . . (Lies down.) I'll lie down a bit. No strength left. Nothing's left. Nothing. Ugh, you—nincompoop! (Lies motionless.) A distant sound is heard, which seems to come from the sky, the sound of a breaking string, slowly dying away, melancholy. It is followed by silence, broken only by the sound of an axe striking a tree far away in the orchard.
>
> Curtain.[3]

The oddity and particularity of Chekhov's language are in contrast to the complete simplicity of Beckett's conclusion to Waiting for Godot, where "trousers" is the only word that is not a monosyllable that could be found in a child's reading primer. Chekhov's "nincompoop," as David Magarshack's translation has it, was "silly-billy" in Michael Frayn's translation for the National Theatre in London; and before Ralph Richardson had assumed that word with the role of Firs and thus made it mysteriously and indefinably his own, there had been considerable debate about what should be spoken at this vital moment.

Chekhov's *The Three Sisters* also ends with silence, but in this earlier play the author needed more complex words and took pains to set his audience thinking about after-events:

> OLGA: (*Embraces her two sisters*). The music is so cheerful and gay, and I want to live. Dear God! Time will pass and we shall be gone forever. We shall be forgotten, and people will no longer remember our voices or our faces or how many of us there were. But our sufferings will pass into joy for those who live after us. . . . Peace and happiness will reign on earth, and we who live now will be remembered with gratitude and will be blessed. Oh, my dear, dear sisters, our lives are not finished yet. Let us live! The music is so gay, so joyful, and it almost seems that in a little while we shall know why we live and why we suffer. Oh, if only we knew . . . if only we knew!
> *The music is growing fainter and fainter;* KULYGIN, *looking happy and smiling, comes in carrying the hat and cape.* ANDREY *is wheeling the pram, in which Bobby is sitting.*
> CHEBUTYKIN: (*sings softly*). Tara-ra-boom-di-ay . . . I'm sitting in a room-di-day. . . . (*Reads his newspaper.*) It makes no difference! It makes no difference!
> OLGA: If only we knew . . . if only we knew!
>
> *Curtain.*

The sound of a departing band and the sight of a solicitous husband, together with a proud father and his guileless baby, are combined with demanding words like "gratitude," "peace," "happiness," "reign," and "suffer" and idiosyncratic ones like "Tara-ra-boom-di-ay" (which has acquired dark associations). All these devices serve to bolster up the more stark and Beckettian simplicity of "If only we knew . . . if only we knew!" But even that statement is less simple than it sounds because it has become geared into three particular and individual stories, each with a possible continuation and development.

In Beckett's plays, action is constantly arrested in silence, and it is brought to a close with unusual simplicity. So the reader or audience is left in possession of little more than what has happened at each moment in the play; no concluding summary or widening vision is provided to put the experience into a further context. At the end there is no more to say or do.

When I read *Waiting for Godot* for the first time, I found this way of writing amazing and unprecedented, and I am still of the same mind. How can Beckett lead us so convincingly to those states of consciousness, to theatrical images which are so complete in their simple elements that they haunt us insistently?

First of all, in this art of the nonplus, I would identify Beckett's ability to stay with chosen elements until each has been tested to the point of destruction. It is no accident that Estragon and Vladimir have talked throughout the play of "going" and have not managed to do so; Pozzo also had known that he "must go" and needed a great deal of encouragement before he could do so. All this earlier drama is echoed in the play's last moment: "Well? Shall we go? . . . Yes, let's go. *They do not move.*" These are characters who have moved cautiously but persistently toward the very end of their tethers. Just before the final curtain falls, they and the audience are brought sharply to a halt as these lines of thought tauten and, giving no more, hold them still and silent. No sound of a breaking string in the air, and no fall of an ax or whip offstage are relevant at that terminus. No "if" is spoken to mitigate the completeness of the moment.

The next feature of this style is its fierce exactness: no detail is unconsidered. Beckett has been observed at rehearsals mouthing the text of *Happy Days* before the actors could speak it although he did not hold a script in his hands. He could prompt more quickly than the stage manager who did hold the book. He knew the placing of a comma, which was unnecessary for making sense, but timed a speech one way rather than another. So exhaustive is his control over language that actors and directors can rely on the change from "Well," to "Well?" at the end of *Godot* with the same assurance that they would give to an exactly placed and fully explicit direction in the text of another dramatist—such as "He enters" "He shouts" or "He falls down."

Each word is used so precisely that phrases, made of common elements, are rendered uncommonly memorable. Moreover, the placing of each silence provides a moment of comparative rest in which the shape of the preceding talk becomes isolated and its self-sufficiency is recognized—like a completed unit in a musical composition. By means of a sequence of silences, the shape of a whole play begins to become apparent: rhythms are established and recognized, echoes are heard, structures are defined, and the musical form of words are perceived. By the interaction of words and silences and the absence of ordinary reassurances, the minds of an audience move backward and then forward in time and in and out of what is audible and visible. By these means it may come to comprehend and, in some degree, share the author's sense of a play's balance, of that consciousness which depends on going the whole journey and completing the necessary exploration.

Beckett has used silence, I suspect, because it is part of our lives, a necessary element of any individual's attempt to cope with an inner, uncertain self and with the disorder and the (sometimes more frightening) order which lie outside that self. But he had to force silence into the theater. It is not a natural element in those public, noisy, celebratory, holiday theaters, where the "players cannot keep counsel" but must tell all that their author knows in torrents of words and eye-catching exploits. It also seems foreign to those other theaters which delight their audiences with colorful, lively, and unlikely fantasies. But Beckett has shown that silence is also a part of the theater's birthright as it is a part of our lives. He did this by taking infinite pains and by waiting long years for a very small theater to attempt to stage *Godot* for a small audience.

Silence had been used previously only with elaborate supporting devices or only for the most fleeting effects. But Beckett has used both silence and words with such authority that today almost every dramatist follows his lead confidently. Franz Xavier Kreutz's play *The Nest*, for example, has one silence lasting over twenty minutes, during which a very repetitive job is started and completed. Silences of many kinds are common now, even in plays by authors who use theater as a means to demonstrate, argue, and persuade: so Edward Bond's Clare, in *The Fool*, is rendered incapable of speech for his last scene although he is a poet; Bond's Shakespeare, in his play *Bingo*, is introduced sitting silent for minutes on end, holding a piece of paper; Bond's Lear, in the play of that name, finishes trying to shovel earth from a great wall; and Len, in Bond's much earlier *Saved*, ends by saying nothing while he tries to mend a broken chair.

Of course, the increased use of silence in our theater is due in part to the influence of film and television, in which the camera can direct attention without the help of words. But such moments could not have been transferred to the theater so readily had not Beckett and others after him worked precisely and slowly to control silence by the simplest of means. Beckett is like a painter who reduces his palette in order to dwell on the quality of a single color, the play of light on the canvas, and even the apparent difficulty with which the paint is handled. He has refined the attention we bring to all theater representations and to ourselves.

I have spoken so far only of Beckett's use of very simple verbal elements, and before going further, I must correct one impression that this may have given. Words are not for him fixed or finite in sound or effect. He turns them over and over, as they are repeated, so that they become more polished, refined, opaque, varied, or treacherous as the play proceeds. Often speech is halted when a word seems to change its meaning as it is being spoken: I have already quoted Vladimir's "appalled," which is at once repeated with new emphasis: "AP-PALLED," capitals and a hyphen in the printed text marking the meaning which had confronted the speaker as he spoke and which now leads him to fall silent, to take off his hat and peer inside, as if something other than his own mind were responsible for uttering these sounds. He then escapes from thoughts of death with the single word "Funny," in the context no sign of pleasure. He then goes on to further silent business, knocking on the crown of the hat as if to dislodge a foreign body. Immediately before this surprise encounter with a hidden meaning, Vladimir had reached consciously toward a heightened and memorable statement, remembered from earlier days; and in his failure to recall the exact words, a new version had been forged: "Hope deferred maketh the something sick, who said that?" So even a familiar quotation is metamorphosed and given new life.

Beckett's characters breathe an air that is full of cries from former

days and different occasions, and these seem to rise into life only to
die once more, leaving the speaker stranded with nothing more to
say or do. Even when a speaker, like Lucky or Pozzo, consciously attempts to speak with eloquence or passion, the purposes of speech
can go awry or be mistaken. Words seem to turn around and achieve
either more or less than the speaker intended; the effect is often to
stop speech altogether:

ESTRAGON: . . . let us try and converse calmly, since we are incapable
of keeping silent.
VLADIMIR: You're right, we're inexhaustible.
ESTRAGON: It's so we won't think.
VLADIMIR: We have that excuse.
ESTRAGON: It's so we won't hear.
VLADIMIR: We have our reasons.
ESTRAGON: All the dead voices.
VLADIMIR: They made a noise like wings.
ESTRAGON: Like leaves.
VLADIMIR: Like sand.
ESTRAGON: Like leaves.
   Silence.
VLADIMIR: They all speak together.
ESTRAGON: Each one to itself.
   Silence.
VLADIMIR: Rather they whisper.
ESTRAGON: They rustle.
VLADIMIR: They murmur.
ESTRAGON: They rustle.
   Silence.
VLADIMIR: What do they say?
ESTRAGON: They talk about their lives.
VLADIMIR: To have lived is not enough for them.
ESTRAGON: They have to talk about it.
VLADIMIR: To be dead is not enough for them.
ESTRAGON: It is not sufficient.
   Silence.
VLADIMIR: They make a noise like feathers.
ESTRAGON: Like leaves.
VLADIMIR: Like ashes.
ESTRAGON: Like leaves.
   Long silence.
VLADIMIR: Say something!

ESTRAGON: I'm trying.
          Long silence.

These two will try to "take their *leaves*" repeatedly during the play, and they will be left thinking of doing that on the very last page. Their reasons in argument are like *dead voices*, but very much alive in their minds, coming unbidden, overnight, like the *leaves* which now hang on the single tree which diversifies and commands the stage set and which in act 1 had been leafless. Their "reasons" are like *sand*, like the sand which Lucky is said to be carrying in his bags. They are like *ashes*, and yet to be "dead is not enough for them"; and they are also like *feathers*, light and living in the air. Beckett's characters are so created that they test words in their talk, each one liable to "slip, slide or perish," becoming useless, expended and perhaps frightening in their metamorphoses. And we, in listening, find ourselves the echoing and deceptive chamber that lies hidden within our own heads as it seems to be within theirs. By removing other stimuli, Beckett has made such inner thoughts fill out the silences until those silences are more than sufficient to hold an audience. Our attention is focused on what in other plays passes without reflection or consequence.

Everything counts and holds attention. The whole of the very short *Breath* (1971) illustrates this:

CURTAIN

1. Faint light on stage littered with miscellaneous rubbish. Hold about five seconds.
2. Faint brief cry and immediately inspiration and slow increase of light together reaching maximum together in about ten seconds. Silence and hold about five seconds.
3. Expiration and slow decrease of light together reaching minimum together (light as in 1) in about ten seconds and immediately cry as before. Silence and hold about five seconds.

CURTAIN

For that short play, lasting less than a minute, several details were fixed still more precisely by Beckett in notes that are almost as lengthy as the play:

RUBBISH

No verticals, all scattered and lying.

CRY

Instant of recorded vagitus. Important that two cries be identical, switching on and off strictly synchronized light and breath.

BREATH

Amplified recording.

MAXIMUM LIGHT

Not bright. If 0 = dark and 10 = bright, light should move from about 3 to 6 and back.[4]

When I saw a performance of this play, I found that I had been totally unprepared for one effect which, when I looked again, I found indicated very clearly in the text. I had not noticed that this play opens, as well as closes, with the stage direction "*Curtain.*"

We waited in a darkened theater, about a hundred people standing close around a curved curtain. Then, in the dark, the curtain moved and made its own sound, slowly revealing the stage in its "faint light." At the end, we heard the same sound, and the faint light was removed again from sight; and in the long moment of darkness after the play—a darkness which seemed redoubled in density, after we had peered toward that "miscellaneous rubbish" in the half-light—our minds went on working, feeding on the short and teasing experience. The two instances of "*Curtain*" had become a frame for the play's central action, a device to isolate and contain. I also received the curtains as a manifestation of the play's maker, who had remained otherwise unseen and silent. We had experienced those moving curtains as the least artificial element of the entertainment (because the cries and breathing were only recorded sounds), and so they had touched us, as it were, more directly and closely. I am hardly exaggerating when I say, "I shall never forget those curtains"—at least exaggerating no more than Estragon when he says he will never forget "this carrot" and at once remembers to ask whether he and Vladimir are tied to Godot.

Beckett's alarming and invigorating carefulness; his discipline, patience, and precision; and the consciousness we have of his controlling, purposeful command enhance every element of the drama and give to each an importance beyond the ordinary. His plays seem to be full to their brims, full to the limits of the means he uses. Only with

such economy can a dramatist search out what happens when no
more can be thought honestly or presented coherently.

All this means that the burden placed on actors is more than usually
severe, but the contribution that they make is also more than usually
crucial for the success of a production. Actors for Beckett's plays must
have a technical and imaginative finesse to respond to the finesse of
the text: nothing may be slurred or ill-judged; nothing can seem
capable of being other than it is. The smallest details of performance
have to be attuned to the smallest details of the text, but, more than
that, the actors must also go beyond the text in creating living creatures to inhabit and flesh out Beckett's roles. When an actor is able
to do this, without contradictions at least and without noticeable
effort beyond what the text requires be shown, then an extraordinary
event happens because, beyond the text, the embodiment makes its
own statement in unprecedented ways. Performance reveals, without
fuss or confusion, living concomitants for Beckett's words. In both
fleeting and deep-set impressions, the singular beings of the per-
formers become absolutely present as they fulfill selflessly the technical requirements which are as rigorous and demanding as those of any
other text that I can call to mind. The outward manifestation of this
act of creation may not be large or amazing in itself in much the
same way that Beckett's verbal language may seem, before he has put
it to his own use, to be ordinary and even commonplace; but when
inhabiting these fictions, an actor becomes close to Beckett's mind,
and that brings into play the actor's most secret and most individual
responses—I think that is why the best actors of Beckett's plays become his friends and associates.

The smallest physical and vocal details are able to count, and so
small auditoriums are best for Beckett's plays. The Royal Court
Theatre is "not big," Beckett wrote, "but *Fin de partie* gains unquestionably in the greater smallness of the [Champs Elysées] Studio,"
the theater in which it was performed for the first time in Paris. In
another letter, he wrote that in the much smaller theater "the hooks
went in," and so the play worked as it had not done in its London
premiere.[5]

Good actors enjoy Beckett's plays because in them the subtlest
modifications of voice, look, posture, breathing, or even pulse rate can

become apparent and powerful. It is like discovering a new palette or a new dimension where previously it had seemed that nothing further could be done; and then these new powers are taken to the point where they, too, can achieve no more.

The success with which Beckett has taken theater toward those alarming, probing, delicate, and deeply felt moments of nonplus is evident in the flock of imitators that have pressed forward, as best they may, toward the same destination. For twelve years I was responsible for reading new scripts submitted to the National Theatre in London, and that showed me how pervasive his influence has been, not so much in direct imitation of form and substance—even the youngest or the most struggling playwrights can usually see how difficult *that* example is to follow—but in the handling of incidental exchanges when inner tensions are being established and, still more frequently, at the end of plays.

Successful, as well as neophyte, dramatists are indebted in this way. There is an exchange near the beginning of David Mamet's *The Woods*, first performed by the St. Nicholas Theater Company in Chicago in 1977, in which words are briefly arrested. Nicholas has invited Ruth to his father's old cabin near a lake, situated in Northern Michigan, and Ruth leads the talk on the day after arrival:

> RUTH: I slept so good yesterday.
> All the crickets. You know?
> With the rhythm.
> You wait.
> And you hear it.
> Chirp.
> Chirp chirp.
> Not "chirping."
> *Pause.*
> Not "*chirping*," really.
> *Birds* chirp.
> Birds chirp, don't they, Nick?
> Birds?
> NICK: Crickets, too, I think.
> RUTH: Yes?
> NICK: (*to self*): "I heard crickets chirp."
> "The crickets chirped."
> (*Aloud*). Yes.

RUTH: I thought so. What do frogs do?
NICK: They croak.
    Pause.
RUTH: I listened. All night long. They get soft at dawn.
    Maybe they go to sleep.
    Maybe the sun makes the air different and they become
    harder to hear. I don't know.[6]

The word "croak" stops the exchange like Vladimir's "AP-PALLED" or Estragon's "leaves"; for a moment, death enters Ruth's mind, and her talk is silenced until she reverts to the busy and insistent crickets. A few minutes later, Mamet indicates that this is what has happened because when the two lovers tell themselves, "Nothing lasts," Ruth suddenly, out of nowhere, remembers the croak of the frogs and then tells Nick about a threatening bear coming to the cabin.

At the end of the play, after nearly murderous fights and after Nick has tried to commit suicide, he asks Ruth to talk to him—he doesn't mind about what. She starts to retell a story from earlier in the play, but she cannot complete it. She has got to the point of nonplus, and the last moments have a Beckettian simpleness:

RUTH: Their Granma told them not to go too far.
    Or else they might get lost.
    For you must all be careful when you go into the woods.
    And they went in.
    It started to get dark.
    He said he thought that they had lost their way.
NICK: Are you all right?
RUTH: Yes.
NICK: Are you cold?
RUTH: No.
    They lay down.
    Pause.
    He puts his arms around her.
    Pause.
    They lay down in the forest and they put their arms
    around each other.
    In the dark. And fell asleep.
    Pause.
NICK: Go on.
    Pause.

RUTH: What?
NICK: Go on.
RUTH: (*to self*): Go on . . .
NICK: Yes.
    Pause.
RUTH: The next day . . .
    The lights fade.

Harold Pinter is the playwright who has pressed closest on Beckett's heels, and he has the imagination and skill to turn everything to his own uses. In the early play, *The Caretaker*, first performed in London in 1960, five years after *Waiting for Godot*, Mick and Aston meet for the second and last time in silence and then speak only one and a half words. Mick has just smashed a small statue of the Buddha, which had represented for the two brothers their scheme for Aston's rehabilitation by furnishing an empty house as both home and business proposition. At this point, Aston makes his final entry, under the scrutiny of Davies, the tramp whom he has introduced to the room as a potential companion, victim, or caretaker. After a "*silence*," a "*door bangs*," and once more there is a "*silence*" in which Mick and Davies "*do not move*":

> ASTON *comes in. He closes the door, moves into the room and faces* MICK. *They look at each other. Both are smiling, faintly.*
> MICK (*beginning to speak to* ASTON). Look . . . uh . . . He *stops, goes to the door and exits.* ASTON *leaves the door open, crosses behind* DAVIES, *sees the broken Buddha, and looks at the pieces for a moment. He then goes to his bed, takes off his overcoat, sits, takes the screwdriver and plug and pokes the plug.*
> DAVIES: I just come back for my pipe.
> ASTON: Oh yes.[7]

This last encounter, unlike those of Estragon and Vladimir or of Winnie and Willie in *Happy Days*, shows two independent courses as one silence follows another, and silent business provides all the drama.

The conclusion of *The Caretaker* shows Aston with his back to Davies, standing silent at the window, facing the garden where he intends to use his hands to build a shed made of "good wood," and then Davies takes attention as he becomes increasingly aware of being isolated; his words drop away, one after another, until his last resources are exposed and he, too, becomes silent:

> DAVIES: If you want me to go . . . I'll go. You just say the word.
> *Pause.*
> I'll tell you what though . . . them shoes . . . them shoes you give me . . . they're working out all right . . . they're all right. Maybe I could . . . get down. . . .
> ASTON *remains still, his back to him, at the window.*
> Listen . . . if I . . . get down . . . if I was to . . . get my papers . . . would you . . . would you let . . . would you . . . if I got down . . . and got my. . . .
> *Long silence.*

Curtain.

In performance this can be like a slow death. Fantasies about Sidcup and hopes of dignity ("no one has more dignity than me," Davies had asserted earlier, standing upright in his rags) have now disappeared: even a new pair of "good shoes" has not released him from dependency. But these words may also be like a coming to life, the birth of truth and independence even at the moment of despair. Davies can go no further in Pinter's mind, and the audience may sense that he has come to realize and accept this. It could be the end of caretaking, and each actor who plays the role will have to discover whether this is true for his performance in the last "*Long silence.*"

In other plays Pinter travels further. *Old Times* of 1971 ends with a long speech by Kate, the wife of Deeley and earlier friend of Anna. She has been by far the most silent of the three characters in the play and the only one who has been concerned in any sustained way with the future and with new places. Now her last speech seems unstoppable, and it is loaded with violent images. It distances her from both friend and husband. Then nothing more is said, but Kate's two adversaries move across the stage from one position to another like self-impelled pieces on a chessboard. Kate has concluded her talk to Anna like this:

> KATE: When I brought him into the room your body of course had gone. What a relief it was to have a different body in my room, a male body behaving quite differently, doing all

those things they do and which they think are good, like
sitting with one leg over the arm of an armchair. We had
a choice of two beds. Your bed or my bed. To lie in, or on.
To grind noses together, in or on. He liked your bed, and
thought he was different in it because he was a man. But
one night I said let me do something, a little thing, a little
trick. He lay there in your bed. He looked up at me with
great expectation. He was gratified. He thought I had prof-
ited from his teaching. He thought I was going to be
sexually forthcoming, that I was about to take a long
promised initiative. I dug about in the windowbox, where
you had planted our pretty pansies, scooped, filled the
bowl, and plastered his face with dirt. He was bemused,
aghast, resisted, resisted with force. He would not let me
dirty his face, or smudge it, he wouldn't let me. He sug-
gested a wedding instead, and a change of environment.
Slight pause
Neither mattered.
Pause
He asked me once, at about that time, who had slept in
that bed before him. I told him no one. No one at all.
Long silence
ANNA *stands, walks toward the door, stops, her back to
them.*
Silence
DEELEY *starts to sob, very quietly.*
ANNA *stands still.*
ANNA *turns, switches off the lamps, sits on her divan, and
lies down.*
The sobbing stops
Silence
DEELEY *stands. He walks a few paces, looks at both divans.
He goes to* ANNA's *divan, looks down at her. She is still.*
Silence
DEELEY *moves towards the door, stops, his back to them.*
Silence
DEELEY *turns. He goes towards* KATE's *divan. He sits on
her divan, lies across her lap.*
Long silence
DEELEY *very slowly sits up.*
He gets off the divan.
He walks slowly to the armchair.

> *He sits, slumped.*
> *Silence*
> *Lights up full sharply.* Very bright.
> DEELEY *in armchair.*
> ANNA *lying on divan.*
> KATE *sitting on divan.*[8]

This mysterious episode concludes a play in which the surface of dialogue has been disturbed frequently and sometimes illuminated by images and notions from earlier times. But here the greatest mystery is the figure of Kate: she sees all these silent movements, hears the footfalls, the sobbing and the breathing, and yet sits still, communicating, if at all, only with her eyes—eyes that she has fancied to be staring out into a limitless desert. In performance, Kate is by far the hardest role because in her unmoving presence violence, peace, and hope must have full, sharp, and yet fugitive life. The moment of nonplus is very protracted, so that Pinter's skeptical romanticism comes to delicate life in the silence.

I do not want to suggest that the art of the nonplus is a peculiarly twentieth-century phenomenon. I would argue, rather, that Samuel Beckett and other dramatists of our day have been tapping, in a more thorough and single-minded way than before, one of the major resources of all dramatic representations of life.

Whether they make it evident or not, all adventurous dramatists have tested their dramatis personae to the breaking point, encouraging them to live in their imaginations on the brink of extinction, "saying as much as they can, and more than they could."

Nowhere is this more evident than in the greatest and most searching works. The mad scenes of *King Lear* have been compared to twentieth-century absurdist and existentialist dramas, but I believe that this tragedy comes closest to our dramatic experiments in its very last scene, in Lear's words that have sometimes been played sentimentally and sometimes with utmost cynicism. I believe, however, that this is a Beckettian moment of "nothing more." Lear's words have the same simplicity as the concluding words in many of Beckett's plays:

> Thou'lt come no more;
> Never, never, never, never, never.

> Pray you undo this button. Thank you, sir.
> Do you see this? Look on her! Look, her lips!
> Look there! Look there! (5.3.305–9)

Earlier, a belief that Cordelia was alive had led Lear to think only of his own sorrows and the pain that others had inflicted on him. But now he reveals a desire to share whatever he has just seen or fitfully imagined. Lear ends directing attention to nothing, dependent on the response of others.

Submerged in other plays by Shakespeare—not given full representation because the noisy Elizabethan and Jacobean theaters were not fit cockpits for exposing such inward battles, but revealed to us when, taught by Beckett and other contemporaries, we look more searchingly into Shakespeare's texts—are the dramas that take the figments of an author's imagination—the embodiments of his thoughts and feelings—to the moment of nonplus. "The rest is silence," says Hamlet. Much earlier, Richard II had recognized:

> Nor I, nor any man that but man is,
> With nothing will be pleased, till he be eased,
> With being nothing. (5.5.39–43)

And so Prospero, at the very end of The Tempest, says most in saying almost nothing. He lost his daughter, he acknowledges briefly, "In this last tempest." His assembled enemies are "new to thee," he is content to tell his daughter. Later, when he has asked the assembled company to "draw near," he says absolutely nothing in greeting to any one of them. He has said "as much as he can, more than he could"; and strangely enough he has become in that last moment more free than he has ever been even as he knows that he will never be as free as Ariel, the spirit, now happy and in some ways enviable. Prospero is silent because he is free from the compulsion to speak; he is alone and unappeased, but sure that there is no more to say until the dramatic illusion is broken and the epilogue follows.

Critics have seldom noted the silence as the courtiers leave the stage in appropriate order and Prospero alone is left. But if we read or rehearse the text, attuned to such testing moments by our reading of modern dramatists, we may begin to grasp the significance of this change that has come over the commanding and loquacious magician of the enchanted island. It may be true of The Tempest, as it is of

Waiting for Godot, that the action of the play is the action of the author's mind as it works toward the place where it can reach no more.

NOTES

1. Waiting for Godot (New York: Grove Press, 1954), p. 7; (London: Faber & Faber, 1956). Subsequent references to Godot are from the Grove Press edition.
2. See Samuel Beckett, Disjecta: Miscellaneous Writings and a Dramatic Fragment, ed. Ruby Cohn (London: John Calder, 1983), p. 109.
3. All citations from Chekhov are from Four Plays, trans. David Magarshack (New York: Hill & Wang, 1969).
4. See Collected Shorter Plays of Samuel Beckett (London: Faber & Faber, 1984), p. 211. I do not know why Beckett used the Latin word vagitus; perhaps he wished to refer to both "the cry of young children" and "the bleating of young animals."
5. Disjecta, p. 108.
6. David Mamet, The Woods (New York: Grove Press, 1979), p. 3. Subsequent references to Mamet's play are from this edition.
7. Citations from The Caretaker are from The Caretaker and the Dumb Waiter (New York: Grove Press, 1961).
8. See Old Times (New York: Grove Press, 1971), pp. 72–75.

The Tragic Pleasure of
Waiting for Godot

NORMAND BERLIN

Back in 1956, when I saw the New York production of *Waiting for Godot*, I didn't know Beckett from Adam. A friend of mine had heard that a strange play was being praised by some critics and damned by others, and he thought I would like to see it, so he bought the tickets, and we went. It was the most exhilarating evening I had had in the theater until then, and it remains so after thirty years of playgoing. Something happened to me while I was watching it, and at the time—while watching it, that is—I did not know what. I'm still not altogether sure, but I've spent a lot of time trying to find out why I felt the way I did. I remember that when the curtain descended on those frozen figures, Didi and Gogo, I too remained frozen for a few seconds before I joined in the applause for the actors—Bert Lahr, who played Gogo; E. G. Marshall, who played Didi; Kurt Kasznar, as Pozzo; Alvin Epstein, as Lucky. I left the theater in a kind of daze, I remember, not because of the obscurity of the play's meaning—that special academic daze would come later—but because of the sheer purity of the presentation. Something new was happening in theater, yet something deceptively simple. A road, a tree, two men talking and waiting for someone called Godot to come. The words they spoke, common words, sang out with a remarkable clarity, and yet they touched mystery; the very simplicity of presentation seemed to elicit strongly felt emotions. Beckett was drawing an uncannily deep response from the often crazy juxtaposition of word, gesture, and silence. Like Keats, when he first looked into Chapman's Homer, I was affected by the "pure serene" of the play. Keats writes: "Then felt I like some watcher of the skies / When a new planet swims into his ken / Or like stout Cortez when with eagle eyes / He stared at the Pacific—and all his men / Looked at each other with a wild surmise / Silent, upon a peak in Darien." Something happened to me that New York evening of 1956 and, as we all know as we celebrate Beckett's eightieth birthday (which coincides with the thirtieth anniversary of that Broadway production of *Waiting for Godot*), something happened to modern drama. The play has become a touchstone, a modern classic that makes most other modern plays—and many plays not so modern—seem artistically insignificant. I left the theater that evening exhilarated; my friend left it annoyed, believing that he was the victim of an enormous hoax. Well, what was there about that evening, about that play both praised and damned, that gave me pleasure?—and that is the word I want, *pleasure*.

To answer such a question, I must first try to recall what happened at the performance, what happened to me as a spectator of a specific staging of the play on a particular night, which comes before any examination of what happens in the play, the more familiar academic and critical enterprise. What did I see and hear? What did I experience? It was a long time ago, but this is what I remember about that performance. I remember—am I reminding you of Krapp hearing his own tape?—I remember the curtain rising to Gogo's enormous and engrossing effort to take off his boot. Bert Lahr brilliantly presented a man's confrontation with an inanimate thing, his panting and his looks exhibiting pure exhaustion. His physical effort believably and inevitably led to words that rang out clearly: "Nothing to be done." I remember E. G. Marshall, as Didi, walking onstage stiffly with legs apart, and I knew the poor guy was having trouble with his groin. I remember Lahr periodically gazing in every direction, including the audience's, with hands screening his eyes, looking for something. I remember a lot of business with hats, not only Didi looking into his and tapping it but also the switching of hats and especially the hat that had to be taken off Lucky to stop his endless speech. I remember that speech—not its words, of course, but its delivery, interminable, exhausting, a tour de force by actor Alvin Epstein. And I think I remember my relief when it was over, a relief I shared with Didi and Gogo and Pozzo—and Lucky, too. I remember a lot of pacing around, a lot of movement, a lot of going around in circles but also movement across the stage, especially by Pozzo and Lucky, probably because that rope between them called attention to itself. (In a play of few props and no scenery, everything counts!) I remember the way Pozzo, whip in hand, loudly shouted "On!" to the burdened Lucky. I remember Lucky's quick and stiff dance, and Lahr's clumsy imitation of it. I remember a heap of bodies onstage, trying to get up, but stumbling. I remember Lahr eating a carrot with such eagerness and sucking the end of it so suggestively that I believed him when he said, "I'll never forget this carrot." I remember how cozily Gogo crawled up into himself to go to sleep and how tenderly Didi covered him with his own coat. I remember the buzzing of the audience in the beginning of act 2, when the three or four leaves on the previously bare tree were discovered. (This discovery by the audience came before Didi looked at the tree; after all, when a play's landscape is bare, even a leaf or two will cause a stir.) I remember Gogo's boots, left on center stage during the intermission, splayed Chaplin-style, staring at the audience as though they had become characters, too. And I'll never forgot the different ways that Bert Lahr said, "Ah!" with his finger in the air, when he was reminded that they were waiting for Godot, nor will I forget the frozen positions and glaring stares of Didi and Gogo as each act ended and the curtain descended.

That was a special evening, and as I look back on it, I realize that so much of the play's impact on me depended on its physical reality, on the gestures, on the few props (like hats and boots and carrots and rope), on the bareness of scene, on the sheer here-and-now of it. The life of the play seemed fully present to my senses, and that offered a kind of pleasure, despite the frustrations and sadnesses and pain that were dramatized. That is, the play got to me on the first level because Beckett permitted nothing to come between me and the stage. The experience was an experience in the theater—Beckett never allowing me to forget I was seeing a play—but strangely authentic as well, a kind of higher realism.

Of course, as I think back on these first impressions, as I try to perceive myself watching the play, I realize that other contexts must have helped to stir my emotions of the moment. These were the echoes produced by the physical images. How could two men wearing bowlers, two men who were annoyed with one another and dependent on one another, one self-important, the other a little obtuse, how could two such men not remind me of Laurel and Hardy? How could I not see Buster Keaton when Gogo gazed in all directions with hands screening eyes? How could I not see Chaplin when those boots were positioned in that splayed way on center stage? How could I not be reminded of the Marx Brothers' hat routine in *Duck Soup* when Didi and Gogo play with their hats? And, on the more serious side, how could the play's most important activity, or nonactivity, waiting—manifested both physically (as Didi and Gogo nervously paced the boards, listening, anxious to hear if someone were coming) and verbally (in the form of such an exchange as, "Let's go." "We can't." "Why not?" "We're waiting for Godot." "Ah!")—how could waiting, that characteristically frustrating daily experience, not elicit emotional responses that filled in the many silences of the play? How could I not—as part of a post-Holocaust audience—not think of all the homeless tramps, the uprooted wanderers, the dispossessed, when I saw the wretched Lucky carrying a bag and walking so slowly, head down, across a desolate landscape? That image was reinforced, surely, by the loudness and corpulence of Pozzo, a master standing for that master race forever persecuting victims. In that context, how could ill-fitting boots—in fact, the very idea of boots, piles of boots—not recall Nazi concentration camps, where so much waiting was done? (It was much later that I was to learn that Beckett's Estragon was originally called Levy and that Beckett's close friend and fellow fighter in the Resistance, Alfred Péron, died as a result of his treatment by the Germans in the Mauthausen concentration camp.)

With time, with reading the play again and again, with teaching it, with seeing other performances, with reading the critics, the play has become richer for me; but now I'm more troubled with the play's meaning and troubled with what others believe to be the play's meaning and troubled with problems concerning the play's genre. The performance of 1956 seemed so clean, so pure, so accessible. Always I try to go back to those first stage images, those first impressions, in order to take a firm hold on the play lest I leave it too far behind to talk about its philosophy, to discuss absurdism or the stance of art against absurdism, to examine the play's comedy and the tragic implications of its comedy or the play's tragedy and the comic possibilities of its tragedy. These large considerations cannot be avoided because the play's provocativeness seems inexhaustible, which in one respect is not surprising because *Waiting for Godot* is a rich and great work of art, but in another respect is surprising because the stage images are so clear, the words (except for Lucky's speech) so understandable, the actions so elemental, the actors so exposed. The play has become such a puzzlement to critics that they (we) cannot even agree on whether anything is happening onstage. Vivian Mercier's much-quoted assertion that in *Godot* "nothing happens, twice" has a catchy Beckettian ring to it, but it is not altogether accurate. We may wish to argue whether the play has an action or a plot (and those who say no will probably win the argument), but something happens in *Godot*; in fact, many things happen. The play is filled with incidents. We may wish to assert exasperatedly with Guildenstern in Tom Stoppard's Beckettian play, "Incidents! All we get is incidents! Dear God, is it too much to expect a little sustained action?!" But incidents are happenings. It is precisely because some very important things happen that specific emotions are elicited from the audience. I wish to suggest that these are the emotions we associate with the genre of tragedy. *Waiting for Godot*—with Beckett's playfully erudite mind forever at work—derives from many traditions, most of them popular comic traditions, well documented by a number of scholars; but its effect is closer to tragic effect than to any other kind, and the pleasure it affords is what I would call "tragic pleasure."

"Nothing to be done." These are the play's first words, the words that seem to set the tone for the play that follows, and I suspect that these are the words which prod such a statement as "Nothing happens, twice." Gogo says "Nothing to be done" as he tries unsuccessfully to take off his boot. Didi agrees, but he is thinking of his own situation; he can't urinate. But Gogo does pull off his boot a few moments later, immediately after Didi repeats Gogo's opening line, thereby allowing the phrase to become a refrain and allowing us to doubt its truth. And Didi does urinate later, torrentially, with Gogo admiring his offstage performance. In the play's beginning, therefore, we encounter the significant pattern of Beckett's presentation: a statement uttered in a succinct, conclusive way, immediately or later contradicted by deed or word. Here are some obvious examples of the important statement-denial pattern:

VLADIMIR: A ditch! Where?
ESTRAGON: (*without gesture*) Over there.

VLADIMIR: I'm going. (*He does not move.*)

ESTRAGON: I don't know. A willow.

VLADIMIR: He said Saturday. (*Pause.*) I think.

ESTRAGON: What do you say? (*They say nothing.*)

VLADIMIR: I'll give it [the hat] to him. (*He does not move.*)

ESTRAGON: Adieu. Adieu. Adieu. (*No one moves.*)

VLADIMIR: Yes, you know them.
ESTRAGON: No, I don't know them.

VLADIMIR: Don't touch me. Stay with me.

ESTRAGON: Well, shall we go?
VLADIMIR: Yes, let's go. (*They do not move.*)

Gogo validates the pattern in his own inimitable way when he tells Didi: "That's the idea, let's contradict each other." The result of this repetitive pattern of statement-denial is stalemate and uncertainty, which is reinforced, of course, by the play's larger balances and uncertainties: one thief saved, the other damned; one messenger beaten, the other not; the tears of one person transferred to another person; you laugh and it hurts your pubis. And so on. Lucky's speech begins with the words, "On the other hand," and that is where we always seem to be—not least in connection with persons. Beckett is relentless in his strategy of balances, of "on the other hand." Once he sets up his pairs, we are forced to think and feel only in terms of antithesis. Gogo doesn't exist without Didi, Pozzo without Lucky, goat boy without sheep boy, one thief crucified without the other, the waiters without Godot, and conversely Godot without the waiters. Similarly, outside of the play but putting subtextual pressure on it, we feel other pairs that exist only as pairs. Can we think of Laurel without Hardy? Cain without Abel? King Lear without the Fool? One of Chaplin's boots without the other? Again and again, Beckett offers a strategy of balances, of antitheses, of stalemate, a strategy which pushes the audience into an atmosphere of precariousness and uncertainty. There's something unbalancing about balances, disquieting about silences. Beckett makes us alert to contradictions, receptive to a dramatic world based on "perhaps."

We return to "Nothing to be done," the assertion which begins the statement-denial pattern, a statement reinforced later when Gogo says, "Nothing happens, nobody comes, nobody goes, it's awful." Anouilh believed that Gogo's words best summarize *Waiting for Godot*. His attitude is close to Mercier's belief that "Nothing happens, twice." But the play's activity answers the play's assertions. Something—more than one thing—happens; somebody—more than one somebody—comes and goes; and it's awful anyway. Many things happen. The play, in fact, is a busy one. If nothing is an important idea in the play—and it's a word that rings out clear in many and different contexts—then the play's business or "busy-ness" deals with much ado about nothing, so much ado, almost a panic of activity at times, that the frozen ends of each act must be effective, which they are. Whether the ado comes to something is an important consideration in any discussion of the play's genre, but first—in the light of all the critical commentary that suggests that nothing happens in the play—it must be established that there is an ado. This is the ado of comedy, it seems. After all, what have we? Two bums in baggy pants, wearing bowlers, waiting around, scrounging for food, trading insults, being beaten, having trouble with boots, switching hats, losing trousers, pratfalls—traditional clowns coming from the music hall or the circus or the movies. Their routines, producing laughter, are clearly happening onstage. The reason their activity seems to be "nothing" is that Beckett prods us to see it in an antithetical context. He sets us up to see these routines as ways to pass the time while waiting for Godot. If Gogo and Didi were not waiting for Godot, their activity would be a series of vaudeville acts, some broadly farcical, which we would applaud for their intrinsic entertainment value. We wouldn't say, "Nothing happens." We hear that "nothing happens," and we can say with Mercier, "Nothing happens, twice" because Beckett forces us to have a specific something in mind. He posits a frame of reference and never allows us to forget it.

"Nobody comes, nobody goes." Not true. Pozzo and Lucky come and go—and what a coming and going! Beckett punctuates their movement with Pozzo's opening and closing word in act 1: "On!" In that act the "On!" is repeated by Pozzo again and again and mimicked by Gogo and Didi. Of course, Beckett, forever working his balances, is allowing Pozzo's "On!" to accentuate the opposite condition of Didi and Gogo. They are on the road, but they are not going on the road. Pozzo and Lucky have direction; Didi and Gogo are tied to a place. The coming back of Pozzo and Lucky in act 2 reveals the results of their movement, one blind and helpless, the other dumb and helpless. Movement has led to devastation, it seems. Pozzo could utter with Winnie of *Happy Days*, "What a curse, mobility." When Pozzo leaves act 2, that is, when he leaves the play, he exclaims his final "On!", and we know—in the light or dark of what he says about birth and death and the night that comes so quickly—we know that his direction is death. In that respect and in the context of the play, perhaps his mobility may not be as much of a curse as Didi's and Gogo's stationary uncertainty about "the last moment."

Not only do Pozzo and Lucky come and go and come and go, but so, too, does the Boy Messenger of Godot. Whether it's the same boy or two different boys, we still have the coming and going. The Boy doesn't have the emphatic movement of Pozzo and Lucky, a movement emphasized not merely by the driving quality of master and whip and by the word "On!" but also by Pozzo's obvious relish in being able to sit down and in Lucky's desire to stop and sleep on his feet. The Boy is tentative; he enters haltingly, but before each act ends, he too exits running. In short, there are comings and goings, which contrast significantly with the staying of Didi and his friend Gogo (how ironic that name sounds!). Only the Godot we are waiting for does not come, and Gogo and Didi cannot go until he comes.

"Nothing to be done," therefore, must always be interpreted with the idea of waiting for Godot in mind. Whatever Didi and Gogo do cannot bring Godot there, and they cannot stop waiting for Godot. They do a lot, but the waiting must persist. Waiting—even that idea seems to belong to the province of comedy. Whatever comedy we witness, we are waiting for the ending, when intrigues will cease, when harmony will be restored, when Jack will get Jill, when the piano will get to the top of the stairs, when the little tramp will walk into the horizon, jauntily swinging his cane. A lot of things happen on the way to the end, but we know—because we are in a world of comedy—that a specific kind of ending will come. It's a closed world that opens at the end to "happily ever after"—and that is the open secret of comedy. However, the waiting here, in *Waiting for Godot*, is uneasy waiting, hopeless waiting, more tragical than comical. It is

posited in an antithetical, precarious world, where comic routines try
to hide the fact of waiting, but where the dramatist is forever reminding us that we are waiting for Godot. Ah! And because we know that
Godot will not come—and if we didn't know it from the play's texture, we certainly know he will not come during the play because he
is not listed in the dramatis personae—that predictable sense of
closure, that special satisfaction of comedy, is not experienced. Waiting, in Beckett's play, becomes connected with what life is, with the
presentness of the moment, even the preciousness of the moment—
"I'll never forget this carrot!" And this pushes it toward tragedy even
though waiting cannot be thought of as an action in the Aristotelian
sense. *Waiting for Godot* has no beginning, middle, and end. It is all
middle, twice. But end, I wish to argue, is felt throughout, the balance of comedy and tragedy tilting toward tragedy. It is necessary,
in this connection, to confront Beckett's label, tragicomedy, head-on.

It is surprising that Beckett gave a label to his play when he translated it into English. I have found no explanation for this in any of
the accounts of his work that I have consulted, and it needs an explanation because we know that Beckett disliked labels. In his essay
on Joyce, he said: "The danger is in the neatness of identification."
His plays reject a criticism that classifies and defines, that seems
definitive. He believed that critics of *Godot* were imposing specific
explanations on a play that was trying to avoid definition. Then why
did he identify *Waiting for Godot* as a "tragicomedy"? Granted, the
term "tragicomedy" is not a neat identification because it carries the
weight of an unclear tradition and it seems paradoxical. Its oxy-
moronic quality must have pleased Beckett, the lover of complementarity and balance, and perhaps Beckett used it so that we should not
lodge his play in one generic camp or the other. Perhaps he was trying to protect himself against the neatness of identification associated
with either tragedy or comedy. In part, he achieved his purpose, if
that was his purpose, because the critics who discuss the balances in
his work, including the balance between the tragic and the comic,
may have been prodded to do so by the label "tragicomedy." However, because all balances are difficult, because pure complementarity
cannot be achieved, many of our best critics have tilted the play
toward comedy. Ruby Cohn, for example, calls her fine and influential book on Beckett *The Comic Gamut*, and Hugh Kenner, as another example, discusses Beckett in his book *The Stoic Comedians*.

And they may be right because of the rich and various comedy that the play contains and because Beckett's label "tragicomedy," although it does not commit itself to one genre or the other, does tilt its weight toward the noun "comedy," with the adjective "tragi," like most adjectives, having less weight. I assume that Beckett wants us to consider, at least in part, the traditional use of that difficult word. Yeats, for example, said that "Shakespeare is always a writer of tragicomedy," and we would agree with him if we considered a tragicomedy to be any play that contains both tragic and comic elements. *The Merchant of Venice* is tragicomedy, containing tragic moments in a comedy, and so is *Hamlet*, containing comic moments in a tragedy. Sir Philip Sidney, in his *Defense of Poesie* (1595), was contemptuous of any attempt to mingle "kings and clowns," labeling such an attempt "mongrel tragicomedy." (If we consider Beckett's autocratic master Pozzo a king of sorts for some—perhaps for Godot himself—then *Waiting for Godot* comes close to Sidney's description.) Of course, Sidney's classical contempt had no effect on the practice of mingling kings and clowns in the English theater, which grew naturally out of the medieval native tradition, where such mingling took place. A working definition of tragicomedy was provided by John Fletcher, who, in his preface to *The Faithful Shepherdess* (1608), said that tragicomedy lacks deaths and therefore is no tragedy, but brings some near it and therefore is no comedy. Here again Beckett's play conforms to type—no one dies, but some are near it. Fletcher's definition goes on to assert that in tragicomedy "a god is as lawful . . . as in tragedy, and mean people as in comedy." This, too, reflects Beckett's play if we wish to consider Godot a god whose presence (or absence) is felt; certainly Didi and Gogo are "mean people." On the other hand and in the spirit of balance, is it not possible that Beckett's is the modern use of that difficult generic term? Beckett may believe, with Ionesco, that in our time the comic is tragic and, therefore, that there is no difference between the comic and the tragic.[1] After all, Beckett has Nell say in *Endgame*, "Nothing is funnier than unhappiness." Beckett may accept Dürrenmatt's belief that "we can achieve the tragic out of comedy. We can bring it forth as a frightening moment, as an abyss that opens suddenly."[2] Here, too, Beckett's play, so rich, open to so many possibilities, can be a clear example of Dürrenmatt's definition. It is Dürrenmatt's definition, I believe, that comes closest to the tone and effect of

Waiting for Godot because that definition tilts the weight toward the tragic. Beckett places a classification before us, perhaps teasing us (and he is often teasing us) to play with both sides of the oxymoron, perhaps trying to prevent us from committing ourselves to one side or the other. But when a dramatist writes a play that does not provide any screen for his audience to protect itself from a perception of itself, when a dramatist brings us so close to that abyss, when a play elicits the kind of emotions one feels when experiencing traditional tragedies, then Beckett's own balanced classification should be questioned—not an unreasonable thing to do because Beckett seems to want us to question everything. He is always telling us to distrust language, asserting that words "falsify whatever they approach."

I maintain that something happens in *Waiting for Godot*; that the play presents movement of a special kind; and that what happens makes us uneasy, plays with our expectation, elicits questions, prods us to examine what is hidden even as it offers so much that is not hidden, so much that is present, there, in physical stage image. The physical prods the metaphysical, imploring us, it seems, to search for meaning, but at the same time forcing us to distrust meanings because Beckett relentlessly presents balances, antitheses, expectations defeated, certainties questioned, statements contradicted. One such statement, as we have seen, is "Nothing to be done." In one sense, nothing can be done; in another, much is done. Or take the seeming balance of the two acts. Yes, things are happening again, but they are happening more intensely and more speedily—and this is absolutely important when we try to gauge a play's effect on an audience. In *Godot* there is a rush toward the end, one feels, even if the end offers a kind of impasse instead of the conventional closure. The play's movement is more linear than circular. Certainly, Beckett is fond of the circle, and that is what repetition is—a word, a gesture, a movement, an idea, coming back on itself. But his circles are part of the pattern of setting up expectations and modifying them, keeping us ever-alert as an audience, shaping our responses. Take, as an important example, the seemingly circular dog song at the beginning of act 2:

> A dog came in the kitchen
> And stole a crust of bread.
> Then cook up with a ladle
> And beat him till he was dead.

Then all the dogs came running
And dug the dog a tomb—
He stops, broods, resumes:
Then all the dogs came running
And dug the dog a tomb
And wrote upon the tombstone
For the eyes of dogs to come:

A dog came in the kitchen
And stole a crust of bread.
Then cook up with a ladle
And beat him till he was dead.

Then all the dogs came running
And dug the dog a tomb—
He stops, broods, resumes:
Then all the dogs came running
And dug the dog a tomb—
He stops, broods. Softly.
And dug the dog a tomb . . .[3]

We could go on and on with the song, and therefore it is circular and seems never-ending, but Didi's brooding repetition of the word "tomb" "tomb" "tomb" gives that idea a conclusiveness, a finality—the word itself a final destination. The song is circular, but the effect is linear. Interestingly, the dog song—so clear in its syntax, using so simple a vocabulary, so right as a popular round for common folk—the dog song, with its repetition and its emphasis on death, brings to mind Lucky's very different speech of act 1—different because of its incoherence, its obscure allusions, its frenzied delivery, but clear in its repetition of key words, like "on" (Pozzo's word) and "cold" and "dark" and "abode of stones" and clear in its emphasis on death. The dog song ends with "tomb"; Lucky's speech ends with ". . . the labors abandoned left unfinished graver still abode of stones in a word I resume alas abandoned unfinished the skull the skull in Connemara in spite of the tennis the skull alas the stones Cunard . . . tennis . . . the stones . . . so calm . . . Cunard . . . unfinished . . ." That last word, "unfinished," forces us, because of Beckett's presentation of balance and antithesis throughout the play, to think of finished and more specifically the "It is finished" of Jesus (in one of the four Gospels, a less than reasonable percentage) where the stones and the skull and the dark and the cold have led us. The direction is toward the dark. Only Didi and Gogo and Pozzo and Lucky are not there yet. Jesus' agony is over; perhaps he is more lucky because they crucified more quickly in those days. Lucky's speech is unfinished with the word "unfinished," but the speech does go somewhere and where it goes—that cold, dark, stony abode—is situated closer to the locus of tragedy than comedy. And that is where Pozzo's act 1 speech on the sky also goes. So much attention is paid to Lucky's speech—and rightly so because it seems to touch the identity of Godot—that one tends to ignore Pozzo's important words on the sky and the night, words which come before Lucky's speech. Pozzo is concerned that everyone onstage listen to him, as he looks at the sky. Even Lucky must be jerked out of his somnolence. "Will you look at the sky, pig!" Then Pozzo speaks, with Beckett carefully controlling the pauses and the balance between the lyrical and the prosaic, another kind of antithesis in a play filled with antitheses.

> POZZO: What is there so extraordinary about it? Qua sky? It is pale and luminous like any sky at this hour of the day. (*Pause.*) In these latitudes. (*Pause.*) When the weather is fine. (*Lyrical.*) An hour ago (*he looks at his watch, prosaic*) roughly (*lyrical*) after having poured forth even since (*he hesitates, prosaic*) say ten o'clock in the morning (*lyrical*) tirelessly torrents of red and white light it begins to lose its effulgence, to grow pale (*gesture of the two hands lapsing by stages*) pale, ever a little paler, a little paler until (*dramatic pause, ample gesture of the two hands flung wide apart*) pppfff! finished! it comes to rest. But—(*hand raised in admonition*)—but behind this veil of gentleness and peace night is charging (*vibrantly*) and will burst upon us (*snaps his fingers*) pop! like that! (*his inspiration leaves him*) just when we least expect it. (*Silence. Gloomily.*) That's how it is on this bitch of an earth.

This is followed by a long pause. Pozzo's speech does not contain the terror of Lucky's tirade, lacking its intensity and relentlessness. But the dying of the light, growing paler and paler as Pozzo's hands are flung wider apart, thereby allowing the fading to include all of space, brings us to that word "finished," followed by the idea that night bursts on us "pop! like that!" Pozzo is here predicting exactly what we will see onstage at the end of both acts—the failing light, the moon rising quickly, "in a moment it is night."

In short, whether we are journeying "On" toward skulls or waiting for the light to fade into pale nothingness, we are moving toward the night, and that is the movement of tragedy.

Act 2 seems to repeat act 1, but the Pozzo and Lucky of act 2 are in desperate straits. The passing of time has led them to blindness and dumbness. We know that time has passed because of the appearance of a few leaves on that bare tree. Pozzo is now a pitiful creature—"Help!" is the word he utters repeatedly—and Lucky can no longer dance or talk. They are winding down. Pozzo's last "On!" as he leaves the stage, now closely tied to Lucky, is leading them both to death. That "On!" is itself tied to Pozzo's most important last words:

> POZZO: Have you not done tormenting me with your accursed time! It's abominable! When! When! One day, is that not enough for you, one day he went dumb, one day I went blind, one day we'll go deaf, one day we were born, one day we shall die, the same day, the same second, is that not enough for you? (*Calmer.*) They give birth astride of a grave, the light gleams an instant, then it's night once more. . . . On!

For Pozzo, everything is happening in an instant, the same day, the same second. A short day's journey into night.

Didi and Gogo are also more desperate in act 2. They seem to be doing the same things, but they are doing them more quickly, more anxiously. They realize, as Didi says, "that things have changed since yesterday." "Everything oozes," says Gogo. That Gogo's anxiety about Godot is greater in act 2 than in act 1 is manifested in his more insistent questioning of Godot's coming and in his many "Ah"s. (Bert Lahr, instinctively sensing Gogo's desperation, claims that he added many more "Ah"s than Beckett provided.) Didi's anxiety is bound up with a higher awareness than that of his friend. In act 2, in contrast to act 1, he tells the Boy messenger that Godot "won't come this evening," that "he'll come to-morrow." He knows. And he recognizes even more than that when the Boy tells him that Godot "does nothing" and has a white beard. Didi's "Christ have mercy on us!" suggests that Lucky's speech about a personal God with a white beard who condemns or saves us "for reasons unknown" got to him. And Didi's generalizing comments on his condition—

uttered while Gogo is sleeping, just before the messenger comes, and just after Pozzo and Lucky leave—reveal a new awareness and place him on the same tragic ground as King Lear.

> VLADIMIR: Astride of a grave and a difficult birth. Down in the hole, lingeringly, the grave-digger puts on the forceps. We have time to grow old. The air is full of our cries. (*He listens.*) But habit is a great deadener. (*He looks again at Estragon.*) At me too someone is saying, he is sleeping, he knows nothing, let him sleep on. (*Pause.*) I can't go on! (*Pause.*) What have I said?

Death and birth. Gravedigger and obstetrician. Shovel and forceps. Tomb and womb. Cries of tormented man and innocent babe. Watchers and watched. Those awake and those asleep. A series of seeming balances and antitheses, complementarities, but again the emphasis is on death. Didi's journey is slower than Pozzo's; the crucial word is "lingeringly." His is a long day's journey into night—so painful that he says "I can't go on!" Then a pause. A moment's reflection. Followed by "What have I said?" For here, too, "habit is a great deadener"—and waiting will continue. Later, near the play's end, Gogo will say, "I can't go on like this," followed by the wiser Didi's rejoinder, "That's what you think." If we believe that tragedy dramatizes the struggle of a hero with necessity and if we modify— because we are living in our time—the word struggle to include waiting and if we modify the idea of hero to include all representations of humanity, even clowns at a boundary situation, aware that they are situated near that abyss and enduring, then surely the balance of that stalemated phrase "tragicomedy" is tilting toward the tragic. But if my many "ifs" are not acceptable—and in a world of "perhaps" why should they be?—then it is to effect, to subjective response, that our discussion must be directed. That is where I began, trying to recall those moments in that 1956 production, trying to understand how Beckett's dramatic art shaped not only my experience but also my response to that experience, which was—for me, at least—not my response toward comedy, but closer to my response to plays which we call tragedies. Certainly, we should ask ourselves why Jan Kott, Martin Esslin, Peter Brook, and others have seen fit to make Shakespeare's tragedies Beckettian. The most notorious *King Lear* of our time, staged by Peter Brook and starring Paul Scofield, was inspired, the director tells us, by Beckett. I believe that Brook distorted Shakespeare by relentlessly fitting him into a Beckettian mold, but there is no question that the instinct behind that distortion was right. Beckett and Shakespeare, in his tragedies, occupy the same ground. They posit vulnerable men in a world of cries, questioning and puzzled men in a world of mystery, unaccommodated men on a bare landscape. How can anyone who saw Brook's *King Lear* forget that terrible Beckettian moment when the blind Gloucester, alone on a bare stage, is sitting with legs crossed, with bleeding eyes staring directly at the audience, while offstage sounds tell of war and death. But we need not go only to Shakespeare, who is so large that he can include everyone. America's most important dramatist, Eugene O'Neill, is most Beckettian not in his one comedy, *Ah, Wilderness!*, but in his darker play *The Iceman Cometh*, where O'Neill's derelicts, like Didi and Gogo, are frozen in their conditions, awaiting a tomorrow that will never come, where Larry Slade is staring at the skull of death, where Godot comes in the person of a salesman bringing death. I have suggested elsewhere that O'Neill's play could be called *Waiting for Hickey*.[4] (It is no mere coincidence, I believe, that the great revival of interest in O'Neill began with the 1956 production of *The Iceman Cometh*, the year *Godot* came to New York City.) Let me mention one other Beckettian play which elicits a response that is closer to the tragic than the comic, a play whose genre has been disputed by many critics. Chekhov's *The Three Sisters* could be called *Waiting for Moscow*, a title which succinctly describes what's happening or not happening to the three sisters and a title which suggests the play's closeness to Beckett's in its orchestration of effects, its questioning spirit, its balancing of comedy and tragedy, its haunting last image of those three sisters frozen to their condition near a road which others travel but they cannot. Chekhov insisted to Konstantin Stanislavsky that *The Three Sisters* was a happy comedy, and he was disturbed when his own reading of the play to the actors of the Moscow Art Theater produced tears instead of laughter or smiles. However, he labeled the play a "drama," a term that did not commit him to comedy or tragedy, exactly what Beckett's term "tragicomedy" seems to accomplish.[5]

Admittedly, subjective emotional response may not be the most assuring test for genre although Aristotle's idea of catharsis, his tragic pity and fear, continue to find a place in discussions of tragedy. My response to Beckett's play is what my title indicates, tragic pleasure, the pleasure that arises when the terrible truth about life is verified. Beckett, in as pure a fashion as possible, brilliantly using the resources of theater and language, forces us to face the fact of our precarious existence, in which we wait for night to fall, in which we wonder if anyone is watching, in which we resignedly keep a one-sided appointment, in which all the big questions cannot be answered. The feeling of precariousness stems from Beckett's persistent presentation of balances and antitheses, not only in his characterization and in his stage activity, where "nothing happens" leads to much happening, but in his perplexing use of conventional dichotomies, like day and night, awake and sleeping, sight and blindness, saved and damned, speech and dumbness, birth and death, Cain and Abel, and more. These dichotomies often fuse—with death and birth occurring at the same moment, with night coming on suddenly, with a man answering to both Cain and Abel. Beckett is pushing doubt and ambiguity; he is dramatizing the "perhaps" of our lives, the question mark of our existence, an existence that contains much mundane comedy—those comic routines of ordinary daily life—but that also taps deep sources of anguish and frustration.

By showing us man at the boundary situation, confused about place and time, unsure of his relationship with whatever the large force is that controls our lives, if any, and facing darkness with fear and with questions and with some sense of commitment, Beckett in *Waiting for Godot* is evoking the kind of pleasure we derive from *Oedipus Rex* and *Hamlet* and *King Lear* and *Phaedra* and *The Three Sisters* and *The Iceman Cometh*. He forces us to take a closer step to Didi and Gogo because their condition is our condition. That is the step of participation with characters that we find in tragedy as opposed to observation of characters that we find in comedy. On the face of it, it seems difficult to place those clowns, Didi and Gogo, on the same tragic ground as the characters in the plays I mentioned, but that is where they belong, especially Didi, who, at play's end, is awake, has an awareness of what is happening or not happening, who takes up his fate, painful though it is, and goes on. Going on, in the continuously present world of the play, means waiting. Didi and Gogo, as they continue their waiting, watch us as we watch them. The curtain descends on both sets of watchers. The next day the curtain will rise on Gogo's "Nothing to be done," and he and Didi will wait for Godot. We, the watchers of yesterday, will mimic their waiting in our daily lives. It is precisely because Beckett's view of life in *Waiting for Godot* is verified by the lives we live that he takes his place with those other ultimate realists—Shakespeare, Chekhov, O'Neill—whose plays afford tragic pleasure because they allow us to come to terms with what we know, and it is the highest kind of knowledge because it is *felt* knowledge. I believe that is the reason why those stage images of that particular performance back in 1956 remained with me through the years. And surely that must be one of the reasons we celebrate Beckett's potent art today and stand with Cortez's men "Silent, upon a peak in Darien."

NOTES

1. Eugène Ionesco, *Notes and Counter Notes* (New York: Grove Press, 1964), p. 27.
2. Friedrich Dürrenmatt, *The Marriage of Mr. Mississippi and Problems of the Theatre* (New York: Grove Press, 1966), p. 32.
3. Samuel Beckett, *Waiting for Godot* (New York: Grove Press, 1954), p. 37; (London: Faber & Faber, 1956). Subsequent references are to the Grove Press edition.
4. Normand Berlin, *Eugene O'Neill* (New York: Grove Press, 1982), p. 134.
5. I discuss the Beckett-Chekhov connection in *The Secret Cause: A Discussion of Tragedy* (Amherst, Mass.: University of Massachusetts Press, 1981), pp. 109–18.

II
Perspectives

Vitality and Deadness
in Beckett's Plays

MICHAEL GOLDMAN

This essay focuses on Beckett's first great dramatic sequence: *Waiting for Godot, Endgame, Happy Days.** Much of what I say may be applied to the later work, but when I generalize, it will be with these three plays in mind. I shall be looking at them in the context of an important motif in modern drama, which may be described as follows: *the action of most, if not all great modern plays regularly defines itself as a struggle between vitality and deadness.* Characters in modern drama are typically driven to act by a feeling of being cut off from the joy of life or indeed from life itself, a feeling that they are dead. We can recognize the motif in some of the most familiar passages in the modern repertory—in Ibsen's notion of *livsglaede,* in the repeated concern of Chekhov's characters for the woods and orchards of Russia, in Shaw's vitalism, in the announcement of Pirandello's six characters, "We want to live!" The sense of an encroaching deadness and the haunting notion of a possible flowering is the theme which links Brecht's early heroes, Baal and Garga, to Azdak and Shen Te. And it makes itself felt in the great schools of performance style which have grown out of the needs of modern drama and in turn have done so much to shape its development. It is no accident that Stanislavsky began the researches which led to his system because he

* All citations from these works refer to the Grove Press editions. In London the same texts are published by Faber & Faber.

was suffering from a near breakdown, whose chief symptom was an overwhelming conviction of emotional and artistic deadness. The "Stanislavsky method" originated in his attempt to recapture a creative vitality remembered from the past. Similarly, from Nietzsche to the Cambridge anthropologists to Artaud, the attempt, so influential on modern theater practice, to recover the origins of drama, reflects a desire to find signs of a now suppressed primitive vitality embedded in traditional dramatic forms.

Thus, there is an obvious connection between the dynamics of vitality and deadness and the innovative formal or stylistic projects of modern drama. The motif clearly links feeling for life to feeling for theatrical technique; every important modern play attempts to revitalize a stage it thinks of as dead. And if we wish to read with greater accuracy the unique signature of any individual modern dramatist, we can learn much by studying his or her application of the motif. In the case of Beckett, the method will help us to grasp and define the still-elusive texture of his dramatic writing, particularly the difficult matter of the performance style his texts imply and the meaning of that style as it affects our experience of action. Indeed, by seeing Beckett in the light of the relations between vitality and deadness, we can catch him in the act of revising the traditions of modern drama.

Let me give an example of what I mean by this last remark. I need scarcely call attention to the importance of silence in Beckett's plays. *Waiting for Godot* depends on the alternation of dialogue with silence as much as it does on the alternation of movement with immobility. "Silence," Beckett has said, "is pouring into this play like water into a sinking ship." But the silences of Beckett effect a revision in the previous history of modern drama. Silence, of course, is not uncommon on the modern stage, and it can carry many meanings. It can suggest an inability to express, as through excess of feeling or stupefaction; it can refer to what language cannot express; or it can convey the doubt that there is anything to express, that meaning is possible. The realistic practice of accurately imitating ordinary behavior came naturally to place an emphasis on failures of articulation. Beckett's practice, however, allows us to see the dialogue of Ibsen and Chekhov in a different light.

After *Waiting for Godot*, it becomes clear that the old prenaturalistic forms of heightened speech did not fall apart simply because they had been used too often or because the habit of using naturalistic dialogue made them seem pretentious, but because the confident assumptions that lay behind their treatment of language were beginning to crack and erode. If language was no longer an echo of immanent divinity or a transparent medium for describing the world, it had to be deceptive, a treacherous veil between ourselves and our experience. From a post-Beckettian perspective, the use of ordinary speech in modern drama now seems to have been more an attempt to honor this awareness than to repair the difficulty because it introduced silence significantly into dramatic discourse. For the great feature of speech in naturalistic drama is not its colloquial liveliness but its programmatic inadequacy to what is being felt.

Beckett's contribution is to push this sense of inadequacy to its philosophical limit. We now can see that the little pauses, the breaks and failures of utterance that first come into drama in the nineteenth century, grow for a hundred years until they become the silences that threaten to drown Didi and Gogo. Beckett makes them a musical element in his design, but we are meant to feel them as a destructive force. Beckett's silences seem to come from beyond the scene. They are a kind of universal silence, a silence at the root of being, which threatens to crush the little voices of the dialogue. So what once seemed an important technical contribution to the vitality of modern dramatic representation suddenly looms as a deadly threat. The silences, the little cracks from which, in naturalistic drama, buried life appeared to bubble, are now the huge gaps through which destruction pours.

The issue, as we shall see, is capable of further refinement, but it immediately confronts us with the most obvious form that the relation of vitality and deadness seems to take in Beckett's plays. For at first glance, to search for this relation in Beckett is to assure oneself of a disappointingly negative result. The motifs I have been describing appear all too obvious and obviously related, crudely registered, and indeed Pollyannishly beside the point. To look for vitality and deadness in Godot, Endgame, and Happy Days—is it not to speak, as Winnie says, in the old style? Are these terms not simply strategies, as Gogo might put it, to convince ourselves that we exist? To put it another way, if the action of much earlier modern drama is characterized by a campaign on behalf of life or joy or heightened vitality, a campaign which inevitably collapses, in Beckett this pattern of campaign and collapse is surely present only as an after-echo. Beckett's plays begin after the campaign has already plunged into the nullifying absence that asserts itself only at the end of *Ghosts* or *Enrico IV*.

Though it does not do full justice to Beckett, this negative position is, nevertheless, the best place to begin. It is clear that in Beckett vitality is represented in radically dubious form. We might think of Winnie's cheerfulness or, to take the most emblematic example, the leaves on the tree in *Waiting for Godot*. The set of that play alludes to the modern theater's interest in sources of primitive or mythic fertility and renewal—but in a way that is at once perfunctory and ironic. In modern drama, the cyclical is regularly associated with the seasonal. Beckett's cycles, the mound, the mud, the talk of rivers and harvests provide an imagery against which green leaves appearing in an arid landscape might be expected to suggest the flow of vitality from the earth to man. Much of their dramatic force lies in the fact that they do not. The leaves visit the tree in the way the moon rises, in the way smiles and other expressions of feeling visit the faces of characters in several plays—abruptly, arbitrarily, like something tacked on (the sex goes on at the end, as Clov says), and the abruptness undercuts any suggestion of commerce between the emblems of revival and what needs to be revived. Decidedly this tree, as Didi observes, will not have been the slightest use to us.

Like the leaves, anything that appears to combat deadness is presented as detached, outflanked, disauthenticated. To turn toward nature resolutely is a phrase equipped with its own ironizing quotation marks, and Pozzo's speech praising the sunset is presented as a self-puncturing lyric balloon. In *Endgame*, of course, signs of life are greeted with snarls of dismay, which in turn lapse back into indifference because they can lead to nothing.

Memory is another source of defused vitality in the plays. From Ibsen on, memory in modern drama has provided energy in the combat with deadness, a legacy of the romantic tradition in which memory is a source of images of blossoming or intense life which beckons to the present. In Beckett, memories replete with vital images do, in fact, appear, but their effect is reversed. Take the recollection of Gogo's leap into the Rhone:

ESTRAGON: Do you remember the day I threw myself into the Rhone?
VLADIMIR: We were grape harvesting.

ESTRAGON: You fished me out.
VLADIMIR: That's all dead and buried.
ESTRAGON: My clothes dried in the sun.
VLADIMIR: There's no good harking back on that.

This memory seems to parody the revivifying force that recollection has in Chekhov and Proust—most characteristically not by mocking it but by deadening it, not allowing the convention of a shared access of feeling to come into play. Moreover, though the passage is marked by the imagery of vitality—the grape harvest, a great river, immersion, nakedness, the sun—it is a memory of suicide, most probably of suicide as an opportunity missed. And, of course, all memories in these plays are detached, statusless, worthless except as fuel for fictions that serve to pass the time and, occasionally, to discharge a cry of agony.

Vitality thus meets the fate of any encouragement in the plays. Beckett has famously said that the most important word in them is "perhaps," a remark which at first might seem encouraging, even optimistic. And indeed it still provides ammunition for the handful of intellectual Reaganites who want to tell us that maybe Godot *will* come. But if we think of the way *perhaps* or the idea of *perhaps* works in *Godot*, it is, in fact, a cruelly damaging word, another little fissure that does the universe in. For reason is forced to admit that any conclusion is perhaps true. Perhaps it is Saturday, but perhaps it is Sunday or Friday. Perhaps what we call the sunset is the dawn. Perhaps that's the west over there, but how do you know? Perhaps it is the day Godot appointed and perhaps not.

But if this undermining, this withdrawal of ground, affects the notion of vitality, it extends to the domain of deadness, too. This is in no sense a relief (it does not extend to pain or to our intimate awareness of what deadness is), but it makes the point that the motif of vitality-and-deadness must be inspected as a unit in the light of this radical uncertainty. Here we should turn to another paradigmatic instance of the motif in Beckett, which states the opposition between the two terms in the most vivid and direct way. I mean Hamm's speech about his mad friend, the painter and engraver.

> HAMM: I once knew a madman who thought the end of the world had come. He was a painter—and engraver. I had a great fondness for him. I used to go and see him, in the asylum. I'd take him by the hand and drag him to the window.

Look! There! All that rising corn! And there! Look! The
sails of the herring fleet! All that loveliness! (*Pause.*) He'd
snatch away his hand and go back into his corner. Ap-
palled. All he had seen was ashes. (*Pause.*) He alone had
been spared. (*Pause.*) Forgotten. (*Pause.*) It appears the
case is . . . was not so . . . so unusual.

The text figures a very complex theatrical moment. Hamm is playing
a part, the somewhat unlikely one of a younger Hamm imagined as
an exponent of the beauties of nature. He speaks of a world outside
a recollected window, toward which, as the performer of a role, he
gestures. But in the world we see, he is waving toward a wall beyond
which all is "corpsed." Or rather toward a world reported by Clov
and believed by Hamm to be so. Hamm's pauses, his uncertainty, allow multiple possibilities of delusion or insight to be felt. Was the
painter mad, or did he see more deeply than Hamm? Is Hamm's conviction that the world outside now is ashes any more verifiable than
his friend's? And, of course, our possible positions, either as accepting
or denying the existence of a world as Hamm and *Endgame* represent
it, are evenhandedly undermined.

But if Hamm is acting at this moment, he is also being acted. This
is a speech which an actor playing Hamm performs, waving at the
walls of a stage beyond which lies nothing in particular, that is, our
ordinary world. In a single integral gesture, he performs the combat
of vitality and deadness, the ashes and the rising corn. Yet what kind
of performance is it? The speech is marked by the continuous and
convincing rhythms of naturalistic reminiscence, yet how are they related to the rest of the performance, which clearly requires other
styles than the naturalistic and which, even at the moment of the
reminiscence, is enmeshed in a unique mode of presentational acting? Where is the link between the speech just quoted and lines like

Can there be misery (*he yawns*) loftier than mine? No
doubt.

And how, even in the speech itself, are those large inevitably ironic
gestures, Pozzolike in their inflation (the herring fleet! the rising
corn!), to be located? How does the actor achieve the kind of calling
into question that lines like these require and still stay true to the
poignant naturalistic rhythms in which they are embedded? And

what in the part as a whole allows those naturalistic rhythms to arise at all?

What we are getting at here is the question of the performance life of the play. This is a crucial question for any dramatist and more troublesome in Beckett's case than might at first appear. For although his plays are frequently and successfully performed, we have as yet only a very uncertain grasp of the distinctive style of playing that they both require and make possible. In the speech just discussed, for instance, the poising of vitality and deadness depends on an intensity of presentation, a subtextual life that the text is obviously pointing at and controlling, but which, as we have seen, is dauntingly hard to specify. If we are to arrive at any satisfying conclusion about Beckett's dramatic art, we must finally be able to understand such effects, to grasp the unique kind of life he enables his actors to discover in themselves and transmit to their audiences.

It is important to stress the notion of subtext in this connection, because subtext—the felt presence of something added by the actor to and *through* the text—is the immediate source of vitality in any drama. The term "subtext" derives from Stanislavsky, of course, but subtextual life, performance life, has always been a necessary part of theatrical writing. What has been less remarked is that the nature of subtext changes both historically and from author to author, as do the means by which it is evoked in performance and the relation between the subtext and the text. Pirandello's actors, for example, have to negotiate between an Ibsenlike transmission of buried drives, a Shavian presentation of an intellectual position (a kind of supertext), and an improvised playing out of histrionic games with a threatening world which puts pressure on both. Generally, in modern drama (Shaw is the great exception) the relation of text and subtext reflects a gap between the character and some hidden truth about the character, which the actor can convey only by bridging the gap that lies between himself and some buried or alienated source of authentic performance.

In Beckett, as in Pirandello, the subtext is so complex that it is best described as a combination of other, more familiar subtexts from the modern tradition. As we move to Beckett, we find that the subtext can no longer be translated into information which completes the text. We encounter an eclectic variety of subtextual manifestations which cannot be placed. Lucky's speech, for example, uses an

Artaudian athleticism to involve us in an agony which seems to come from the center of the play. He is certainly someone "signalling through the flames," but the emotional connection is broken and distanced in an almost Brechtian way by the parody and slapstick, except that the actor is given no place to stand and comment on the configuration, to render it—in Brecht's term—gestic.

In attempting to describe the Beckettian subtext, one might point to a number of highly varied components, often active simultaneously: a partial Stanislavskian fidelity to the given circumstances; a supertext, more frankly acknowledged in some plays than others, which is quite the opposite of any Shavian one in that it acknowledges a void; an Artaudian expression of anguish associated either with the naturalistic situation or the supertext; and a frequent modification of all these by the presentational processes of popular entertainment—the music hall, the circus, slapstick comedy. Let us look more closely at some of these.

First, the Artaudian expression. No one who saw Alvin Epstein in the role of Lucky in the first New York performance of *Godot* thirty years ago is likely to forget that virtuoso example of Artaudian acting, a physicalization that fully realized the convulsive anguish behind the text. Beckett was well aware of Artaud's work, and there are many stage directions which suggest the kind of physical vocabulary Artaud sought to develop, as for example, "*They remain motionless, arms dangling, heads sunk, sagging at the knees*" or "*They listen, grotesquely rigid.*" Similarly Artaudian are the abrupt outbursts and cries beyond the limits of naturalism. What is most important, of course, is the sense of direct, unmasked expression of inner states of intense psychic pain.

There is at the same time, at least intermittently, something like a Shavian supertext, that is, an overarching intellectual position which must be played *through* the text to give the performance life. We feel it in the sudden outbursts of metaphysical contempt or exasperation, as in the second half of the famous exchange "This is becoming really insignificant." "Not enough!" We can see this supertext at work in the grim epigrams which thrust sharply into the routines of *Waiting for Godot* or *Endgame*. Typically, these epigrams work on a model reminiscent of Oscar Wilde's in *The Importance of Being Earnest*. That is, they take a cliché and transform it. But where Wilde alters the cliché by making it express the pure selfishness of his aristocratic characters, Beckett alters the cliché in the spirit of the supertext. Thus, one sentence begins, "Let us persevere in what we have resolved." Wilde might have continued, "As long as it is not too much trouble." Beckett completes the phrase with, "Before we forget." Even more pungently, he uses the cliché unmodified except by the power of the supertext. A favorite example of mine comes just before the end of act 1 of Godot:

> ESTRAGON: I'm unhappy.
> VLADIMIR: Not really! Since when?
> ESTRAGON: I'd forgotten.
> VLADIMIR: Extraordinary the tricks that memory plays!

For Wilde, Vladimir's riposte might work in the context of, say, remembering an obligation. For Beckett, the cliché becomes a savage transformation of a benign bromide. "Isn't memory wonderful?" becomes "It's really a miracle to forget even for an instant that one is unhappy." The same effect is achieved when Clov hears Hamm say, "It's better than nothing" and replies, "Better than nothing. Is it possible?" In every case, these lines work only if the actor can attach to them the supertext of acknowledging the void, the lack of any ground for meaning or basis for value in existence.

One difference between Waiting for Godot and Endgame is that the supertext seems only intermittently present for Didi and Gogo, but always present for Hamm and Clov. Whenever it is acknowledged, the supertext requires that a convincing feeling of pain be associated with it, that it be not simply entertained or embraced, but suffered. Consider these lines of Hamm:

> HAMM: All those I might have helped. (Pause.) Helped! (Pause.) Saved. (Pause.) Saved!

Here we can see a peculiarly Beckettian mixture of mocking theatricality and intensely registered feeling. Hamm is in one of his familiar theatrico-moral routines; indeed he seems, as the rest of the long speech from which this passage is drawn suggests, to be verging on his narrative mode. But the echoing "Helped!" and "Saved!" reflect his apprehension of the supertext. What does it mean to have helped or saved under circumstances of cosmic hopelessness? The words are treated as contemptible delusions. A moment later, Hamm cries out "violently":

HAMM: Use your head can't you, use your head, you're on earth, there's no cure for that!

The outburst seems at once Artaudian and pretentious.

It is the combination of subtexts, then, that produces the effect, with one important proviso: *that no subtext be treated as privileged.* This is in sharp contrast to the standard convention of modern subtexts before Beckett, in which the subtext is understood to represent the authentic source of the text. The character may not be in touch with the source, but the actor is. In the Stanislaviskian system, the character may not be aware of the drives or inhibitions that run beneath the text of a Hedda or a Lopakhin, but the actor makes them available to the audience as a truth in terms of which the text can be located. In the Brechtian system, this privileged truth lies in the actor's commitment to the social interpretation of the character, which gives the *gestus* its effect. But it would contradict Beckett's vision to offer such a possibility of authentication. Thus, our engagement with the actors, though it can be intense, must not be confidently located. We must not be allowed to feel, "Yes, I can get behind these appearances." It is clear, for example, that Beckett rejects any performance mode that invites the audience in—there can be no cozy sharing of a human essence. The preference is for Keaton's style over Chaplin's. In the same way, there can be no privileging of the music hall routine over the Artaudian anguish or vice versa. This refusal of any privileged structuring of subtexts is the absolute condition of authenticity in Beckettian performance.

Consider the following sequence:

VLADIMIR: When you seek you hear.
ESTRAGON: You do.
VLADIMIR: That prevents you from thinking.
ESTRAGON: You think all the same.
VLADIMIR: No, no, impossible.
ESTRAGON: That's the idea, let's contradict each other.
VLADIMIR: Impossible.
ESTRAGON: You think so?
VLADIMIR: We're in no danger of ever thinking any more.
ESTRAGON: Then what are we complaining about?
VLADIMIR: Thinking is not the worst.
ESTRAGON: Perhaps not. But at least there's that.

VLADIMIR: That what?
ESTRAGON: That's the idea, let's ask each other questions.
VLADIMIR: What do you mean, at least there's that?
ESTRAGON: That much less misery.
VLADIMIR: True.
ESTRAGON: Well? If we gave thanks for our mercies?
VLADIMIR: What is terrible is to have thought.
ESTRAGON: But did that ever happen to us?
VLADIMIR: Where are all these corpses from?
ESTRAGON: These skeletons.
VLADIMIR: Tell me that.
ESTRAGON: True.
VLADIMIR: We must have thought a little.
ESTRAGON: At the very beginning.
VLADIMIR: A charnel-house! A charnel-house!
ESTRAGON: You don't have to look.
VLADIMIR: You can't help looking.

One can hear the cross talk. It's "a little canter" as Gogo calls it. One can also hear the Artaudian subtext of anguished acknowledgment of the void, of what Pozzo calls "talking in a vacuum." But the anguish, for all its intensity, does not achieve priority over the routine and make it merely a vehicle or veil for the anguish. We have no way of saying that the anguish isn't a routine, too. Any actor who wants to insist that he is "more than" a clown at this point will be denying the supertext and ultimately denying the truth of his anguish.

Close inspection of subtext brings us to the question of action. This is because it reminds us of a crucial fact about dramatic action: that it is indissolubly allied to the actions of dramatic performance, that is, to acting.

I want now to continue the investigation of Beckett's unique treatment of vitality and deadness by looking at its implications for dramatic action. Here I must briefly introduce, in rather condensed form, some notions about action that I've developed in the course of some recent work on Shakespeare. It seems clear that what we normally refer to as the "action" of a play is actually a composite of several kinds of action, which in the hands of an expert playwright counterpoint and comment on each other. The kinds of action involved may be divided into three groups: the actions of the *characters* as they move about in the imagined world of the play; the actions of the actors in projecting and sustaining their roles; and the action of our minds as members of the audience in attempting to construe, order, and remember what we are experiencing. Most accounts of dramatic action usually blur the action of the characters and of the audience together and simply ignore the action of the actors. All these types of action usually play off against or engage general notions of human action which are broached in the course of the play.

In talking about subtext, then, I have been talking about the action of the actors in performing their parts. Now let me turn to our own action in attempting to discover the shape and tendency of what we are witnessing, to arrive at an understanding of what we sometimes call the action of the play. The first thing to notice is that in the plays I am dealing with, action in this sense is itself associated with death. In Godot, for example, at the very moment when the large formal design of the play first emerges, Vladimir's song of the dog makes the connection clear. The structure of the song is cyclical, and we hear it at the very beginning of the act, which will show us that the structure of the play's action is cyclical. Is the effect of the song simply repetitive? Is nothing changed by the fact of repetition? Now, in the song, unlike the play, every recurring element is identical; every word is repeated. But even so, the two renderings of the song are very different in function and effect. Repeated once, the song is changed utterly into a form no further repetition can alter. The first time it is a narrative; the second, an epitaph. The fact seems to weigh on Didi, who stops and broods each time he reaches the word "tomb." Similarly, everything in the play is changed by its second act. One act would not be enough; three would be too many. All we need is to establish that waiting is a cycle, and any attempt at action, at progress to a goal, becomes an epitaph for action, the statement of an unalterable condition. In grasping the shape of the second act, we are forced to acknowledge that action is dead.

And, of course, the sense of action as something unavailable, of the play as not construable as action, is regularly insisted on. When Vladimir addresses the Boy at the end of the second act, he makes a desperate attempt to put the two acts together, to convert what he and Gogo have been doing from a pointless passing of the time into an action:

> VLADIMIR: Tell him . . . tell him you saw me and that . . . that you saw me. You're sure you saw me, you won't come and tell me tomorrow that you never saw me!

Or take his earlier attempt to sum up what has happened in the play:

> VLADIMIR: To-morrow, when I wake or think I do, what shall I say of today? That with Estragon my friend, at this place, until the fall of night, I waited for Godot? That Pozzo passed with his carrier, and that he spoke to us? Probably. But in all that what truth will there be?

Tentatively, Didi arranges the play as a neat narrative entity—and the point is that one can present it this way. But though Didi's account vibrates with a poignancy which seems the poignancy of the situation, still it does not give us any meaning we can possess—and this, of course, is part of the poignancy. Indeed, we cannot be sure that it is not all. The best one can say of what happens in these plays is, with Clov, "Something is taking its course," a statement which almost describes an action—except that the subject is not human and the grammar is passive.

To turn, finally, from the audience's construction of the action to the actions of the characters: for them, action is, strictly speaking, impossible. Rigorously considered, the idea of action depends on the existence of meaningful links between self and world, and Beckett's characters cannot establish such links. Indeed they spend their plays unsuccessfully attempting action, trying to extend their unstillable impulse to activity toward a ground for action, keeping an appointment, finishing an endgame. Their projects are illusory or self-thwarting. And the plays are beautifully shaped to allow us to feel these projects not simply failing, but slipping loose of even the basis for possible success. The impulse to construct action in this groundless world is parodied, for example, in Pozzo's repeated efforts to explain why Lucky doesn't put down his bags:

> POZZO: He wants to impress me, so that I'll keep him. . . . Perhaps I haven't got it quite right. He wants to mollify me, so that I'll give up the idea of parting with him. No, that's not exactly it either. . . . He wants to cod me, but he

won't. . . . He imagines that when I see how well he carries I'll be tempted to keep him on in that capacity.

Can we, we are forced to ask, even consider Beckett's characters as selves capable of projects, or is that to grant these theatrical manifestations a unity, a meaning for which Beckett keeps suggesting— *they* keep suggesting—there is no ground? Here's an example of how the problem is driven home to us. When Vladimir, watching Pozzo and Lucky halfway through the first act, explodes, "It's a scandal!" the silence that follows is different from the ones we're already becoming used to. It is unexpectedly filled with ethical possibility. Is this a challenge to our nascent interpretation of the play's action? Is one of the tramps about to do something other than just fill up the time while waiting for Godot? Is he, in fact, about to commit a morally significant act? But then Gogo (*"not to be outdone"* according to the directions) exclaims, "A disgrace!" and *"resumes his gnawing."* The effect is a sharp blow to our newly optimistic construction of the action. Estragon's intervention calls Didi's into question. Isn't this simply another routine, the isn't-it-a-scandal routine? And nothing in this world will ever let us know.

Now, of course, when we watch a Beckett play, we *do* feel the presence of something we're right to want to call a dramatic action. But what is happening to us when we say we feel it, and what does it have to do with our equally powerful impression that, in this play, not only action, but even the possibility of action, is dead? Dramatic action in Beckett is carved out in many ways—by the rhythm of the routines, by the firmly established motifs of passing the time or playing the endgame, by the plays' elegance of shape, by repeated words and phrases, by guides like Didi's song, by the use of silence. As with the silence, the action of the play seems to come from *outside* the characters, from the universal situation that surrounds them. Nevertheless, in what only appears to be a paradox, everything that the characters do, no matter how inconsequential, turns out to have the force of action. The deadness of the landscape and the absence of essence have the effect of promoting all activity to the significance of action because even the smallest piece of business presses instantly against the void, against the idea of action's meaninglessness.

Let me try to make this idea clearer. The first act of *Godot* ends with great force:

ESTRAGON: I sometimes wonder if we wouldn't have been better off alone, each one for himself. (*He crosses the stage and sits down on the mound.*) We weren't made for the same road.

VLADIMIR: (*without anger*). It's not certain.

ESTRAGON: No, nothing is certain.

Vladimir slowly crosses the stage and sits down beside Estragon.

VLADIMIR: We can still part, if you think it would be better.

ESTRAGON: It's not worth while now.

Silence.

VLADIMIR: No, it's not worth while now.

Silence.

ESTRAGON: Well, shall we go?

VLADIMIR: Yes, let's go.

They do not move.

The powerful immobility of the passage is created by the tramps' small initiatives—going to the mound, sitting together, accepting that it isn't worth parting; but it also seems to well up from all around them. At a moment like this, we certainly have the feeling of a completed action, but where does the action in a play come from if not from the actors? It has its genesis in the script and, before that, presumably in the mind of the playwright, but this is merely historical information. In the theater, a play is generated by its actors. There is no other source, and so the action is generated by them. The question, then, is how do Beckett's actors achieve the impression of action required by his plays? How do they generate the sense of a metaphysical pressure from outside that makes their activity at once insignificant and everywhere significant? How do they achieve the feeling—basic to the impression of any action in drama, but particularly difficult given the attitude to action in Beckett's texts—that from them, around them, a play is going forward?

The answer must come from the play of subtexts, the process of acting that Beckett enables and demands. What I have been suggesting in this essay is that it comes from the actors' ability to perform both the project toward action inside them and the disauthentication of action which surrounds them. For Beckett's approach to performance style is unique in this: the disauthenticating gap between text and subtext, which, as I have said, the modern actor typically seeks to leap, in Beckett's plays cannot be leapt and must not appear to be. Yet as we have seen, the actor must negotiate the gap, acknowledging the supertext with an authenticity the supertext calls into question. In Beckett, the actor's willingness to make the situation *really* insignificant, to show it and feel it and confront it as empty of metaphysical comfort, is what makes the performance significant. The vitality comes from the scrupulous removal of all grounds for vitality, all basis for profitably distinguishing life from death, one moment from another. The gesture which vitalizes the performance must be seen as a dead gesture, a false gesture, an empty gesture, a gesture like billions of gestures; but it is no less costly, requires no less commitment for that.

I haven't, of course, talked here about many of the other sources of theatrical vitality in the plays. They are well known, and to enumerate them is not my point. I have been concerned instead with the way notions of vitality and deadness are related and with the theatrical vitality that flows from this relation. What in particular I've been trying to explore is how the theatrical vitality of these plays engages the deadness and hopelessness they portray. It might be more precise to rephrase this as—how Beckett achieves a theatrical vitality which remains true to his material. I am well aware that this is not a subject which can be readily exhausted or summed up. Let me, however, offer two closing observations.

In his book on Proust, Beckett deals at one point with the question of habit. He talks about the moments of transition between one habitual adaptation and another, moments when one responds to what is really there instead of acting habitually, and he describes such moments in a very helpful phrase. He says that there are times "when for a moment the boredom of living is replaced by the suffering of being." The phrase means not simply the suffering that living people endure, the pain that goes along with being alive. It refers to the encounter with being itself, to receiving the impact of the real. Beckett's distinction seems to offer a revealing clue to the design of his work. It is possible to say of *Waiting for Godot* that it is about the boredom of living, that this is what Didi and Gogo undergo, but that the play is organized so that, through it, we in the audience experience the suffering of being. This is accomplished through the intervention of the actors, and it requires of them the discipline it makes possible, that mixture I have been trying to describe of commitment, glee, anguish, and asceticism.

The other point I wish to make can easily be sentimentalized, but it is important. There is a kind of egalitarianism in Beckett, and it gets naturally snobbish appreciators of fine art like me into trouble. Given the lack of any ground for action, given the terrifying silence of the infinite spaces, action, although in one sense impossible in Beckett, is in another sense everywhere and in anything; it simply goes with being human. The most trivial activities—taking off a shoe, letting an alarm clock ring to the end, reading the small print on a toothbrush—are as significant as the greatest undertakings because, for Beckett, every attempt at action is a metaphysical encounter between human restlessness and the fact that there is nothing to be done. Any kind of activity confronts the ground of our being, although habit is a great deadener and ordinarily we do not recognize that the encounter is taking place.

Thus action is everywhere because we are here and can't avoid being here. We are stuck in being, a circumstance that becomes terrifyingly literal in *Happy Days* and several later plays. Because we are stuck in being, we have nothing to do but play against the great negation that encompasses us. And so Winnie, for example, grips us like a heroine, and we are uncomfortable with this sensation and think there must be something more heroic, more significant (or "really insignificant") than filing your nails and claiming it's a wonderful day. But from Beckett's point of view, *that's* the sentimental proposition. Winnie grips us, as the other great Beckett characters grip us. I think that there has been a literature of muddle about these very ordinary heroes, exceptional only in the extremity of their ordinariness, their immobility, self-deception, and restlessness. Like us, they are citizens of the great democracy of the scandal of human existence. For Beckett, the fundamental heroism of life, or shall we just say the fundamental strength of a protagonist, is something we all share—that we are here, stuck in the horrible particularity of being. And to his actors he offers the illumination that comes with suffering being, which in the actor's case means being stuck onstage—playing and being played by the immense unfriendliness of our condition, whose only virtue is that it is real.

Happy Days
and Dramatic Convention

CHARLES R. LYONS

In "An Essay of Dramatic Poesy," John Dryden uses the phrase "the painting of the hero's mind" to describe the representation of character in drama.[1] Dryden's phrase has grown increasingly provocative to me as I have thought about the basic processes of establishing dramatic images. The playwright establishes the image of that fictional mind with the physical presence of the actor in space and the words and movement with which the actor reveals the operation of a consciousness. In very simple terms, the dramatist creates an image of character by writing a text that the actor speaks, a text that reveals the character perceiving his or her environment, including other characters who inhabit it, his or her relationship to that place, and his or her self-conscious awareness of the self as an object within that space and time. The fundamental and sufficient requirement for a dramatic performance is the presence of a character in space and time. Because the operation of consciousness itself is dynamic, the representation of character embodies action. Beckett's dramas have proved that no other system of action is necessary for a full dramatic event.

The spectator's sense of the significance of the scene represented by the dramatic space derives principally from the characters' perception of it. Physical objects may mark the site: the gates of Thebes, the tomb of Agamemnon, a drawing room in a provincial town in

Russia, a mound of sand that holds a woman in place. However, even though an object on the stage may hold some intrinsic literal, iconographic, or symbolic value, it achieves significance in the spectator's mind through characters' physical and mental use of it. The playwright, of course, cannot communicate information directly to the audience during the performance in the same way in which the writer of epic poetry or prose fiction can offer a description of a place, character, object, event, or idea. The medium of the playwright is the representation of the consciousness of characters, and almost all the information the playwright conveys comes through the individual voices of the dramatic figures.

As spectators, we do not always see the scene as the character sees it, but we apply the perception of the individual character to the collection of perceptions stored in our mind during the performance. A major image of place such as the Argive palace in the *Agamemnon* is a composite structure created in the spectator's mind by the mediation of several characters. The image of the *skene* as the house of Atreus, the architectural container and the cursed dynasty it contains, is an accumulation of significations voiced during the performance. The parts of that composite are distributed throughout the text, but the unified concept exists only in the consciousness of the spectator. The text itself, read or performed, never voices that composite in a single encompassing statement or image. The individually mediated perceptions of the characters stimulate the spectator to build the inclusive image of scene we refer to when we speak of the house of Atreus.

Samuel Beckett writes dramas that place figures in barren environments. Beckett's sparse sites do not hold the distinguishing marks that would establish them unequivocally as specific literal or symbolic scenes. The significance of each space derives primarily from the functional value it holds for the characters. Whereas these scenes hold few objects and offer only unconfirmed reference to previous experience, Beckett's characters grapple with their relationship to these peculiarly comfortless sites. The neutrality of Beckett's strange places compounds his characters' attempts to establish a sense of themselves in space. The roadside where Vladimir and Estragon wait seems an alien space because they find in it no familiar object or landmark. They cannot claim with assurance that the tree—and hence the place—of the second act is the same as of the first. Hamm and

Clov perceive their shelter through the difference between its present condition and their sense of its nature in the past. However, Hamm tells the story of the madman in the asylum who saw only ashes from his window where Hamm saw fields of grain, the sea, and the herring fleet. This brief narrative provides a model of perceiver and scene that suggests that the barrenness of the landscape that Clov describes may represent his failing perception, not the nature of the external world. I don't think that we should consider positing a verdant world outside the windows of that room. We should, however, recognize that what Beckett emphasizes in his representation of the space is not the independent significance of the site but rather the presence of that site as an object that stimulates the character's perception of himself in space.

We should recognize that the site itself is not an expressionistic projection of the imagination of the characters. The physical and conceptual difficulties these characters experience as they attempt to perceive the space they inhabit establishes a clear distance between character and scene. The distance between the consciousness of the character and the scene he or she inhabits allows Beckett to depict the character's sense of estrangement from that environment. Beckett's precise stage directions describe spaces that define absences rather than mark connections to a socioeconomic, historically precise moment in time. The absence of referential detail contributes to the epistemological difficulty that Beckett's characters confront as they try to establish images of themselves in the world. Most of the characters (Estragon is an exception) expend energy positioning themselves in an environment that offers them little to use in that effort. Our desire to place a dramatic event within some historically comprehensive "objective reality" has stimulated audiences and critics to perceive the scene of *Endgame* as a shelter in a wasteland devastated by a nuclear war. The significance of that room, however, is that it provides an enclosed space that the characters may perceive as a refuge for the few remaining artifacts of a "then," and its present barrenness allows them to characterize "now" as the manifestation of absence, depletion, attenuation, in concert with their progressive inability to move about and perceive the world. Beckett's dramatic scenes usually mark a discrepancy between the past and the present, and we perceive these sites as the manifestation of loss because the characters speak of them in these terms. They lament the depletion of expendable substances, and they describe themselves as vulnerable to the same kind of progressive deterioration as the places they inhabit. The historical placement of then and now is irrelevant; the focus of the representation is on the character's perception of the present as the manifestation of difference from a past that is inaccessible. The independent, objective significance of the scene, as place, and of the past, as history, is not the important factor of the event dramatized. The drama focuses on the characters' struggle to perceive themselves in relationship to that inaccessible place and time. That struggle must take place in an environment that is simultaneously specific in its coordinates and unspecific in its referentiality.

Samuel Beckett writes complete descriptions of his scenic environments which allow a minimal extrapolation in their realization. This careful definition probably derives from his own visual sense, his mental picture of the environment, but these descriptions must also represent his attempt to ensure the absence of a referentiality that would ground his characters in a specific place and time and undermine the equivocation of their struggle to establish themselves in space and duration.

In *Happy Days*, Beckett presents the image of Winnie, caught in a mound of sand, accompanied by her enigmatically almost silent husband, Willie. The sun blazes in an apparently endless noon. A bell divides the night, the time for sleep, from the day, in which Winnie enacts the routines of a normal, bourgeois life. Winnie perceives her present through its difference from her past.

> WINNIE: Then . . . now . . . what difficulties here, for the mind. (*Pause.*) To have been always what I am—and so changed from what I was. (*Pause.*) I am the one, I say the one, then the other. (*Pause.*) Now the one, then the other.[2]

Winnie attempts to reenact her past within the limitations of the present circumstances. In the first act, buried to the waist, she is free to use her collection of things; in the second, caught to her neck, she needs to invoke the presence of the objects imaginatively. Physically and mentally the process of reenacting the past becomes more difficult. The progressive diminishing of Winnie's ability to mark the difference between past and present accompanies her descent into the mound. As Winnie's consciousness deteriorates, memory itself becomes a kind of fragmented residue like her objects disconnected from the history it may signal.

The physical scene of *Happy Days* presents an arresting, shocking image that seems, on first impact, to hold only oblique or ironic connections to established dramatic conventions. And yet, as Beckett represents the interaction between Winnie and the scene she inhabits, he exercises many of the paradigmatic relationships between character and scene and character and time that we find in the work of earlier playwrights. My objective in this essay is to identify the principal examples of those conventions of character and space in *Happy Days* and also to suggest that the clarity of Beckett's use of these strategies helps us to see the functional value of the same paradigms in the work of earlier playwrights. As I began this process, I remembered Eliot's voice from "Tradition and the Individual Talent." Recall that he says:

what happens when a new work of art is created is something that happens simultaneously to all the works of art which preceded it. The existing monuments form an ideal order among themselves, which is modified by the introduction of the new (the really new) work of art among them.[3]

Eliot claims that it is not "preposterous that the past should be altered by the present as much as the present is directed by the past." Beckett's very simple images of characters in space and time signify a great deal with very little. Although Beckett is radically new ("really new" in Eliot's phrase), he is—in one sense—highly conventional in that he exploits as economically as possible important dramatic conventions. The remainder of this essay attempts the double purpose of showing that conventionality and, at the same, clarifying the ways in which Beckett's idiosyncratic variations reveal more clearly than before the communicative potential of the conventions themselves.

Many heroes, like Winnie, are physically or psychologically removed from the place of their previous existence: Prometheus chained to a rock at the extremity of the world; the exiled Orestes returning as a stranger to Argos in the disguise of a Daulian stranger from Phocis; the younger Oedipus received as a stranger in Thebes and accepted as *tyrannos*, revealed to be a native son and banished as a criminal; the older Oedipus wandering in Attica, an alien in the sacred grove of Colonus; the wounded Philoctetes exiled for nine years on the barren island of Lemnos; Hamlet returning to Denmark estranged from the court; Lear expelled from his daughter's home, suffering the discomfort of the storm; Phèdre, the alien queen, living in Troezen; Ibsen's Oswald returning to his mother's home as a virtual stranger; Pirandello's Enrico IV isolated in the artificial imitation of the eleventh-century German court; the six characters alienated from their author, attempting to realize themselves on the unfamiliar space of the stage; Vladimir and Estragon temporarily inhabiting the unfamiliar roadside, distant from the place of their earlier life.

Tragic sites are frequently marked by an absence and often display a marked discrepancy between the past and the present: the Argos of *The Libation Bearers*, corrupt in the usurping rule of Clytemnestra and Aegisthus, suffers the absence of Agamemnon; the polluted city of Thebes needs to identify and to exile the assassin of the dead king; the "rotten" state of Denmark declines in the absence of the elder Hamlet and the drunken reign of Claudius; Enrico IV lives in a borrowed identity, and the persona of the character himself is absent. Mrs. Alving reveals that the character who dominated the site of *Ghosts*, Captain Alving, was never identical with the strong and moral figure whose identity she sustained; Didi and Gogo continue to wait for the figure of Godot, whose absence becomes the principal characteristic of the site at which they wait.

The examples I cite also suggest that these playwrights, like Beckett, were very interested in the representation of the character's perception of the site. At the conclusion of *The Libation Bearers*, Orestes perceives himself both as the savior of Thebes, celebrated by the Chorus, and as the criminal matricide who is the focus of hatred of the Furies. He has restored the male dynasty to Argos and implemented the will of Apollo, but Clytemnestra's blood has reawakened the chthonic presence of the Furies, whose very being is embedded in Argos. Sophocles dramatizes Oedipus' developing perception of Thebes: his vision of the city as polluted, as the place where he can reenact his role as savior of the city, as a safe place where he is free from the threat of incest and parricide, as a sanctuary in which he is allowed to exercise his will and intelligence with vigor, as the scene of his future; and, of course, as the opposite: as the site of his past, where he has performed the deeds he sought to avoid, as the polluted city his abhorrent behavior has despoiled, as the city that views him as a repellent criminal, as the site from which he is exiled to gain its purification. Shakespeare focuses on Hamlet's perception of Denmark, clearly differentiated from the vision of others. Ibsen emphasizes Mrs. Alving's futile manipulation of her world, her attempt to control the perception of others, and her recognition that her attempt to create an illusion has blinded her to the reality of her son's inherited disease, the manifestation of the corruption she attempted to hide.

In the first act of *Happy Days*, Winnie speaks the following lines:

> WINNIE: Strange feeling. (*Pause. Do.*) Strange feeling that some-
> one is looking at me. I am clear, then dim, then gone,
> then dim again, then clear again, and so on, back and
> forth, in and out of someone's eye.

Whereas *Happy Days* seems to operate as a virtual monologue, the strange location that holds Winnie is clearly a public space in the sense that Beckett's principal character emphatically demands the presence of another—be he Willie or some hypothetical observer.

Whatever the reasons for the tradition of the offstage pathos in fifth-century tragedy, the convention demands that the scene in which the plays took place be an open site in which the hero experiences the narrative report of that event in a public forum. The presence of the citizen chorus demands, of course, that the site is one that plausibly accommodates this political body. Even when the pathos is committed onstage, as with Ajax's suicide, the act exists principally to be witnessed, judged, or evaluated by witnesses. The tragic site is inevitably public in this sense. Of course, in the tragedies of fifth-century Athens, the conceptual antithesis "private and public" does not obtain because Aeschylus, Sophocles, and Euripides do not assume a psyche that has an ego separate from that exercised in political acts. The division between public and private selves that informs tragedy from the Renaissance on is not a division the Greeks tragic poets perceived. However, these poets did construct scenes that represented the hero perceiving or imagining himself or herself as an object in the perception of others. They used the presence of the Chorus in developing a dramatic paradigm in which the hero conceptualizes an image of the self through the recognition of his or her presence as an important object in the sight of witnesses.

Whereas Beckett uses the paradigmatic structure of hero and witnessing public very subtly, he recurrently establishes dramatic moments in which his characters speak of themselves as objects held in the gaze of some external witness. At the beginning of both acts of *Happy Days*, a bell sounds, and Winnie interprets this phenomenon as the announcement of the beginning of her day. After she opens her eyes, she says:

> WINNIE: Someone is looking at me still. (*Pause.*) Caring for me still. (*Pause.*) That is what I find so wonderful. (*Pause.*) Eyes on my eyes.

The eyes that Winnie imagines may be the eyes of the spectator or simply a fictional observer that she creates in order to sustain her consciousness of herself as an object in the world. She recognizes immediately afterward that she needs the presence of Willie, real or assumed, in order to continue speaking:

> WINNIE: I used to think . . . (*pause*) . . . I say I used to think that I would learn to talk alone. (*Pause.*) By that I mean to myself, the wilderness. (*Smile.*) But no. (*Smile broader.*) No no. (*Smile off.*) Ergo you are there. (*Pause.*) Oh no doubt you are dead, like the others, no doubt you have died, or gone away and left me, like the others, it doesn't matter, you are there.

The actual or hypothetical presence of the perceiving other in *Happy Days* transforms the scene, in the protagonist's mind from a private or isolated space into a public site. As long as Winnie can imagine being perceived, she is not in "the wilderness." In the first act, she clarifies that the notion "wilderness" signifies an impossible situation:

> WINNIE: . . . if only I could bear to be alone, I mean prattle away with not a soul to hear. (*Pause.*) Not that I flatter myself that you hear much, no Willie, God forbid. (*Pause.*) Days perhaps when you hear nothing. (*Pause.*) But days too when you answer. (*Pause.*) So that I may say at all times, even when you do not answer and perhaps hear nothing, Something of this is being heard, I am not merely talking to myself, that is in the wilderness, a thing I could never bear to do—for any length of time. (*Pause.*) That is what enables me to go on, go on talking that is.

Here and at several other points in *Happy Days*, Beckett represents Winnie self-consciously establishing a model of self and other.
This model consists of the speaking self as the object of perception
and the other as the perceiver. Winnie focuses on the potential presence of this other in order to provide herself with the opportunity
to conceptualize herself as an object within the other's field of vision
or sound. She wants to be conscious of herself as a discrete, tangible
presence in space. She incorporates the presence of that hypothetical
other into the operation of her own consciousness and performs her
little discourses and mimes for herself.

The publicness of a dramatic space makes the characters aware
that they are subject to observation, not only that they will be seen
as an object in that field but also that they will be observed and
judged. Because the space is public, the actual presence of others is
not always necessary for the hero to invoke the conceptual paradigm
of self and other. The potential for being seen allows the hero to
imagine the presence of a hypothetical other. Beckett, more clearly
than any earlier playwright, uses this paradigm to represent the consciousness of a character incorporating the functions of perceiving
and being the object of his or her own perception, exercising the roles
of perceiving subject and the object of that perception, being the
public witness and the object of that witness. The structural simplicity of Beckett's characterization of the roles of perceiver and
perceived in the same consciousness clarifies the function of self-
consciousness in earlier dramatic characters or, at least, provides a
scheme with which we can discuss them. For example, Phèdre makes
her initial entrance into a scene that, in general terms, is an undesig-
nated area within the palace which, in the spatial flexibility demanded
by the neoclassical unity of place, must be sufficiently neutral to
accommodate, with some degree of plausibility, the diverse characters who must enter it. For Phèdre, the principal quality of the site
is that it is a space where she may be observed by other courtiers.
Her language defines this public area as the opposite of the darkened
private space from which she comes to expose herself to view. The
words she speaks reveal the opposition between her wish to expose
her sinfulness and her desire to hide her lust for Hippolyte. Oenone,
the nurse-confidante, reveals that Phèdre has deliberately costumed
herself in order to present herself to the daylight. Phèdre now finds
that public costume oppressive and desires to flee from the very light

she sought. Phèdre perceives herself as two personae. She sees herself both as the sexual creature who desires Hippolyte and as the ethical person who judges that desire as evil. The ethical persona demands that she present herself and her sin to public view. Phèdre fears that the penetrating vision of the court may pierce her garments and veils and expose the sexual creature they hide; and, as she imagines herself, she substitutes the judgmental gaze of these hypothetical others for her own sight. Identifying with the perception of these hypothetical witnesses, she sees herself as the alien object she imagines they would perceive, and, at the same time, she suffers the pain of being the focus of their condemnation. The specific "character" of Phèdre is divided between those two personae. It would be more accurate to say that the interaction between these two personae—the perceiver who judges her and the object of that judgmental perception—constitutes Phèdre's character.

Both Phèdre and Winnie use the potentially public nature of the scene they occupy to imagine themselves as the object of another's gaze. Winnie, like Phèdre, vacillates between antithetical desires or, more accurately, between antithetical fears; and she uses the paradigm of self and hypothetical other to articulate that division. She wishes to maintain consciousness, or, rather, self-consciousness, to continue to imagine herself as a living presence in space; and she also wishes to lose consciousness, to dissolve that presence. Winnie may use the refrain "happy day" in every minor triumph in her effort to sustain the artifice of a life, but early in the play she defines the meaning of the "happy day": "the happy day to come when flesh melts at so many degrees and the night of the moon has so many hundred hours." The ultimate happy day for which Winnie longs is one in which she would no longer be held in the mound, no longer be exposed to the light and perceived, but one in which she would dissolve in space, free of the consciousness of being observed, free of her own consciousness of self. Winnie fears that dissolution, of course, and expends a great deal of energy in sustaining her consciousness of herself. She is caught, like Phèdre, in antithetical desires; and both Racine and Beckett represent that antithesis in the language in which their heroines speak of perception and self-perception.

Using Beckett's model of the self and the hypothetical eye allows us to see the conventionality of an important moment in Sophocles' *Oedipus Tyrannos*. The hero returns to the public site in which the tragedy takes place after the messenger has reported Oedipus' discovery of the body of Jocasta and his self-blinding. He explains that act with the following statement:

> I do not know with what eyes I could look
> upon my father when I die and go
> under the earth, nor yet my wretched mother—
> those two to whom I have done things deserving
> worse punishment than hanging. Would the sight
> of children, bred as mine are, gladden me?
> No, not these eyes, never.[4]

Oedipus then evokes the image of the polis itself, both the physical space from which he has exiled himself in his condemnation of the criminal who killed Laius, and the city as a body of citizens: "To this guilt I bore witness against myself—with what eyes shall I look upon my people?" He then claims that if it had been possible for him to render himself deaf as well as blind, he would have done so. The strength of his effort to remove himself from the experience of being aware of being perceived demonstrates his desire to be free from that objectification of the self. But he cannot remove the presence of hypothetical others, and his mind turns to the image of standing before his father and receiving that judgmental gaze. Consider the structure of this specific moment in Sophocles' tragedy. As spectators, we see Oedipus as the abhorrent object of the perception of the Chorus and other characters, and, as well, we observe Oedipus' self-conscious awareness of himself as that object. Sophocles presents an Oedipus who, despite his blindness, must live within the limits of the abhorrent identity that he imagines others perceive when they see him. He can remove his physical perception of the presence of these condemning witnesses, but he cannot remove the presence of the hypothetical other, the perceiver within his own consciousness who sees and judges the object that is the self.

We recognize the radical discrepancy between Winnie's situation—her inexplicable capture by the earth that seems gradually to be consuming her—and her attempt to maintain the identity of a highly conventional bourgeoise. This discrepancy between situation and behavior suggests that her consciously enacted identity is a self-sustained fiction, a fiction that offers satisfaction and, simultaneously, as Winnie reveals at critical moments, imprisons her in the relentless performance of being Winnie. The hypothetical other in Sophocles' use of the paradigm is more specifically grounded in the history the tragedy builds, but—like Winnie—Oedipus imagines himself caught and held in the gaze of that other. The abhorrent object that this hypothetical eye sees defines the identity he must continue to enact. Phèdre's use of the hypothetical witness clarifies her self-condemnation, and her suicide attempts to remove that abhorrent persona from Thésée's field of vision. Her final lines reveal her use of the presence of Thésée as the judgmental other and her desire to exist free from his perception of her sinful nature. The operation of the poison has already begun to separate her from the gaze of this other:

> even now a cloud mists my vision of
> Heaven and the husband whom my presence defiles.
> And death, stealing light from my eyes.
> Restores to the day all the purity they soiled.[5]

Phèdre's speech embodies her desire to withdraw from the day in which she is held as an object to be observed. The voice that speaks Phèdre's final speech is the voice of the perceiver persona who wishes to be free of the gaze not only of Thésée but of the imagined other whom she has incorporated into her consciousness. Winnie's day, which echoes Phèdre's *jour*, traps her in the gaze of her hypothetical other.

I want to clarify at this point that when I use a term like "hypothetical other," I am not exercising a psychoanalytic, Lacanian reading of these texts. I am talking about a recurrent paradigmatic structure that playwrights have found useful in representing character in a formal process through which they represent acts of self-consciousness. The paradigm is useful because it allows the character to communicate information about his concept of himself, his perception of the physical and social scene, his perception of the immediate moment in relationship to a history, and—most significantly—his perception of his relationship to that scene and time. The playwright's use of the representational scheme in which the character invokes an image of the self and the hypothetical other may serve as an imitation of a particular psychic process and may be vulnerable to a variety of readings. However, what I am discussing is more technical than interpretative. This essay intends to clarify the usefulness of a recurrent formal pattern, not to demonstrate the continuity of a thematic value or psychological archetype.

Beckett's notion of day informs his representation of both time and space, and the concept of day as a comprehendible temporal unit is obviously important in Beckett's dramaturgy. Didi and Gogo seem unable to think in temporal units beyond a single day and perhaps its immediate successor. Hamm structures his experience on the basis of the beginning and closing of the day, organizing the routines that constitute his life on the basis of their recurrence during the cycle of a day within a series of days that do not seem to accumulate into a week, a month, a year. In *Happy Days*, the principal character is subject to the relentless light of an apparently endless noon, but the bell divides the time into a period of sleep and a period of being awake; and Winnie organizes her routines as daily activities. Beckett divides the night and day as private and public segments. Vladimir and Estragon separate at twilight to rejoin each other during the day. Clov uncovers Hamm to begin their day together. Winnie rises to face herself and her unseen observer and perform self-consciously to realize her day. The day provides the illumination to be seen, and the night provides the potential for privacy and anonymity. Beckett dramatizes his characters' experience in the light: we see Vladimir and Estragon when they rejoin each other, not in their private experience separated during the night; we observe Hamm and Clov when Clov prepares his master for his day; we see Winnie awake, not asleep during the arbitrarily divided night marked off by the bell.

One of the formal differences between dramatic performance and narrative is that drama can represent only the immediate moment or a sequence of immediate moments. Although the text may frame that moment as the representation of a time in the archaic past or the distant future, the actors represent characters who perceive the time of performance as their present. Because the playwright's medium is the representation of consciousness, the playwright can give the past presence on the stage only as the physical residue of an earlier moment or as an image in the mind of a character. The playwright may represent the dramatic figures as they deal with a tangible artifact that signals an earlier moment, receive or voice some type of narrative report of the past, or experience and discuss memory.

Happy Days illustrates this point well because a large portion of the text consists of Winnie's voiced "memories," and she repeatedly discusses her perception of the bag and the objects it contains as the debris of some earlier, more ordinary time. Willie appears to use the yellowed newspaper in a less articulate but similar attempt to sustain a relationship to an earlier moment. Winnie's objects stimulate a series of truncated evocations of the past—the time of Winnie's "then." These familiar segments focus on five key memories: three of the incidents are associated with Willie, one with Charlie Hunter, and one with "Mr. Johnson, or Johnston, or Johnstone." In each case, only a fragment of contextual detail remains embedded in the familiar words that holds the memory, and each of these tropes ends with a variant of the closure: "that day . . . *what* day?" This repeated pattern suggests, of course, that what remains is not the memory but merely the text in which the memory was once sustained.

In the later *Not I*, of course, Beckett presents an illuminated mouth that speaks a text that contains data suggesting that the implied consciousness of the "character" whose mouth speaks hears the repetitive narrative only as sound. The emotional connection the spectator poses between Mouth and the painful narrative it voices applies only to a hypothetical past when this consciousness voiced and perceived the narrative as her story. We assume that the emotional content has been diminished in frequent repetition. We know that "habit is a great deadener." The texts of Winnie's memories have also attenuated in significance, but she has not reached the numbness of the implied consciousness of *Not I*.

Winnie's memories attempt to reconstruct significant moments in which she was recognized, perceived, appreciated by a male figure important to her at that time. Her use of them, at this moment, establishes her present desire for recognition and defines her sense of the difference between present and past. These images of the past in *Happy Days* do not function primarily as narrative clues to assist us in the reconstruction of the history of a typical middle-class woman, but as a scheme through which the character perceives herself within the present. Winnie perceives her "now" only through its difference from her "then," and she uses the patterns of behavior that were normal "then" and imposes them on the strangeness of her "now." These moments from her narrative past document experiences of being perceived erotically, and they define the absence of that recognition in the present and her sense of value lost.

In drama, the past is never an objective structure of facts that the audience receives as independent of character, but, rather, the spectator's sense of the history that precedes the moment of performance is a composite of the series of images of the past voiced by the characters. Our understanding of the past in *Agamemnon*, for example, is built up by the combination of explicit and oblique references made by the old Watchman; the achronologically presented fragments of information concerning the Trojan expedition, voiced by the Chorus, who discuss the events leading up to the sacrifice of Iphigenia; and the report of the messenger-soldier, who describes the ravaging of Troy.

Cassandra's mantic vision, immediately prior to the assassination of Agamemnon, places the present moment in the context of the narrative of Atreus and Thyestes and focuses on the death of Agamemnon and herself as the most immediate in a series of events that answer the sacrifice of Thyestes' children. In this visionary narrative recitation, Cassandra radically alters the existing time scheme of the tragedy by opening it up to encompass these events in the previous generation. She also extends this historical frame into the future as she predicts Orestes' return from exile to avenge his father's murder. As in *Happy Days*, we receive the past in *Agamemnon* only through character, through the highly subjective response to events voiced by the characters and chorus. The past in *Agamemnon* may have more authority than the past in *Happy Days* because the characters perceive it more comprehensively, but its individual units of information are no less mediated or subjective than Winnie's voiced memories. Because Beckett refuses to allow his characters to see the past comprehensively or to give them assurance that their perception of their history is correct, we are able to see that the exposition of the past in his plays has more value as a function of character than as a function of narrative. In other words, the paucity of narrative detail about the past ensures that we focus on the characters' use of metonymic fragments rather than expend effort to reconstruct the implicit history of their prior life. Neither Winnie, Krapp, nor Hamm can envision the past in memory with certainty, and the struggle of each reveals the distance between memory and the hypothetical occurrence that it attempts to invoke. Their struggle to sustain their sense of the past, however, constitutes a major part of their activity in the present. Beckett's particular strategy of representing consciousness clarifies the irredeemable gap between the event and the perception of the event, the wider gap between the event and its reconstitution in language, and the implicit distance between this verbal reconstitution and actual memory. Beckett's drama undermines the authority of the past at the same time that it emphasizes the character's perception of the past as a primary activity in the present.

If we think of Beckett's use of narrative as a model of dramatic structure rather than as an idiosyncratic organizational strategy, it is possible to consider that the images of the past in a text such as *Agamemnon* may not be present primarily to establish an unequivocally certain historical context for Agamemnon's assassination but, rather, as perceptions in the consciousness of the characters that embody their comprehension of the present. As Aeschylus paints the minds of his characters, we see the representation of different forms of historical thinking or rationalization. The Chorus of Elders reports the twin kings' perception that their Trojan expedition has divine authorization. Agamemnon's return voices the same concept. Clytemnestra perceives or rationalizes the assassination of Agamemnon as the consequence of the sacrifice of Iphigenia; Cassandra envisions his death and her own as the fulfillment of a curse, embodied in the presence of the singing Furies, that was initiated in the murder of Thyestes' children, which was itself the consequence of Thyestes' seduction of Atreus' wife. Aeschylus' representation of Agamemnon's assassination takes place not so much within a narrative or historical context as within a context of various perceptions of the history of which that murder is a part.

If we read Aeschylus' text or attend a performance of the trilogy after studying Beckett, we should be more skeptical about our ability to extrapolate a coherent history of the events prior to Agamemnon's return and be more attentive to the processes in which a character's voiced vision of the past informs, determines, or reveals his or her present mental activity. We should recognize that the narrative exposition of the past and the dramatic representation of the present are functions of the complete performance; within the spectator's imagination, the images of the past and the present develop simultaneously. Both Beckett and Aeschylus stimulate the spectator to focus on an image of the past, an image of the present, and the problematic relationship between the two that exists in the character's mind. But it takes the whole text to build this triad.

Exercising these paradigms of space and time in *Happy Days*,

Beckett represents a character who is confined by her perception of what constitutes a day, including her need to be seen by another in the space illuminated by that day; a character who is imprisoned by her relationship to objects; a character who is enclosed by the words of a series of brief texts, the individual tropes that she performs in order to maintain her sense of connection to an inaccessible history. Winnie is as restricted by her words as by the mound. Her dream of freedom is to be free of both.

Happy Days illustrates as well as any text that dramatic character is the product of an interaction between the functions of narration and enactment. The interaction of narrative recitation and dramatic action is a conventional process of organizing the temporal structure of a play. As Oedipus recites his history, he builds an image of himself as the Corinthian stranger who was made the first citizen of Thebes. He experiences the corrective narrations of Jocasta and the two shepherds. Both Oedipus and the spectators experience the establishment of the new identity of Oedipus the Theban. Oedipus' confrontation with these incompatible histories constitutes the action of Sophocles' tragedy. The structure of Happy Days is not dissimilar. Here the woman in the mound voices a series of narrative fragments that, we assume, unfolds a segment of her history, but the image of character the performance establishes derives from the interaction between the present figure and the recitation of narrative passages that, we speculate, reflect her past. The action represents a sequence of highly focused moments in which the consciousness of the principal character confronts her perception of the illusive past and its relationship to the present.

In an analogous sense, Hamlet's experience is his confrontation with the text of the past spoken by the Ghost of the elder Hamlet. In Henrik Ibsen's The Master Builder, Solness's experience is his confrontation and reenactment of the text of Hilde's story of their initial encounter at Lysanger. Pirandello's Enrico IV is imprisoned within the historical text of the character he has elected to perform; and though he can rearrange the chronology, he cannot break away from the coordinates of the relationships that history defines. Pirandello's six characters are confined within the scenario of their novel and the absence of the text that would bring them to life. In later Beckett, the narrative that confines his character's consciousness becomes the whole text of the play, and the performance divides the consciousness of the character and the words that revolve in that character's mind. However, the paradigm of the text of the past that defines the character's experience is as old, at least, as *Oedipus Tyrannos*. Beckett refines and simplifies that structure until he arrives at the fundamental components of the text and the receiving consciousness. In the plays since *Not I*, the relationship between that text and that image of consciousness presented as character becomes a function of the spectator's speculation as he or she witnesses the performance of the actor.

Beckett's process of reducing the theatrical elements to the minimum demonstrates the evocative range of very simple, unelaborated dramatic images of character, space, and time. The objective of my recent book on Beckett was to clarify the communicative potential of Beckett's pared-down dramatic works and to defend, if that needed doing, the vigorous theatricality implicit in these minimalist texts.[6] What I have attempted to do in this essay is to suggest that the economy of Beckett's drama has also clarified some very fundamental dramatic paradigms. The proliferation of detail in texts as rich in reference as *Agamemnon*, *Oedipus Tyrannos*, and *Phèdre* make the basic structure of these paradigms harder to see, but part of the reordering that Beckett's texts demand, to return to Eliot's idea, is rethinking these classics in the fundamental terms that his drama provides.

NOTES

1. John Dryden, "An Essay of Dramatic Poesy," *Selected Works of John Dryden*, ed. with introduction and commentaries by William Frost (New York: Holt, Rinehart and Winston, 1953), p. 351.
2. Samuel Beckett, *Happy Days* (New York: Grove Press, 1961), pp. 50–51; (London: Faber & Faber, 1962). Subsequent quotations from *Happy Days* refer to the Grove Press edition.
3. T. S. Eliot, "Tradition and the Individual Talent," *Selected Essays*, 2d rev. ed. (London: Faber & Faber, 1934), p. 15.
4. Sophocles, *Oedipus Tyrannos*, trans. as *Oedipus the King* in David Grene, *Sophocles I* (Chicago: University of Chicago Press, 1960), p. 70. See Greek text, ll.1371–76, in *Oedipus Tyrannos, Sophocles, I* (Cambridge, Mass.: Harvard University Press, 1912).
5. My translation. See French text (*Phèdre*, 5.6.1639–44) in *Racine: Oeuvres Complètes* (Paris: Editions du Seuil, 1962).
6. Charles R. Lyons, *Samuel Beckett* (New York: Grove Press, 1984; London: Macmillan, 1983).

Krapp's Dialogue of Selves

ANDREW KENNEDY

The haunting invention of *Krapp's Last Tape*, the interplay of live and taped speeches connecting two stages in the life of one man, continues to haunt one with questions. My questions are influenced by two larger contexts, related to each other and, in turn, animated by a critical exchange between Ruby Cohn and myself. The first, larger, context is the hypothesis that dialogue, as the vehicle of interaction between two or several emotionally connected persons, is an essential element of drama.[1] The second context is the transformation of Beckett's dialogue (the rich, multivocal language of the earlier plays—cross talk in *Waiting for Godot*, personal duologues in *Endgame*, a kind of aural tapestry of talkers in *All That Fall*) into a unique type of monologue: the ambivalent, counterpointed voices of one person in *Krapp's Last Tape*, foreshadowing the return to soliloquizers in *Not I* and after.[2] These two larger contexts strengthen one's awareness of a certain oddity of speaking of "dialogue" (as I once did) in *Krapp's Last Tape*. Do we not rather hear something like a failure of dialogue? The grip of solipsism is tightening as the effort of the self to reach out beyond itself ends in soliloquy and silence.

"Semblance of dialogue" was the phrase I coined in a brief discussion of the play over ten years ago.[3] "Semblance" is not a felicitous word ("Seems, madam! nay, it is; I know not 'seems'," protested Hamlet). I feel certainly happier with Ruby Cohn's translation of that phrase into precise sense in *Just Play*,[4] arguing, in particular, that the interplay of voices in *Krapp's Last Tape* is between two different kinds of speech: the taped voice which is normally intended for performance (solo) and the brooding voice of the living Krapp that is self-expressive here and now (soliloquy). It is the live voice of old Krapp which interacts with the taped voice of Krapp, aged thirty-nine, in a "semblance of dialogue."

With that elegant equation the matter might rest. Yet returning to the play compels new questions: what substance can be ascribed to the word "dialogue" used in such a metaphorical sense? What kind of speech act is Krapp engaged in to justify the analogy with dialogue? Starkly, the game invented by Krapp to celebrate—or un-celebrate—his birthday amounts to self listening to self, with commentary. Is listening to one's recorded speech like listening to another person's speech, with readiness for exchange? Or is it like rereading entries in a journal, looking at family photographs, mementos, personal papers? Is Krapp indulging in an annual ritual that has become a habit that kills feeling, or is he performing a creative act of sorts? Has Krapp become so dependent on his tapes that his present solitary listening and commenting amounts to a drugged attempt to simulate company and conversation? Krapp's whole verbal enterprise then has onanistic overtones, mechanically stirring the embers of memory and desire through a fantasy of communion.

Whatever the ultimate effect of a performance of *Krapp's Last Tape* on an audience, the text provides for only one actor, a self-addressing speaker absorbed in contemplating the voice of his former self. The tape recorded by Krapp at thirty-nine includes a somewhat self-indulgently self-critical commentary on an earlier tape, an earlier self; and the tapes cataloged in Krapp's ledger suggest a long series receding in time, like a face endlessly reflected between two mirrors. The whole of Krapp's time is filled by reflections of Krapp. The interplay between the tape and the voice has the "one-sided conversation" effect of the dramatic monologue, "the second voice" as distinct from "the third voice" (that of dramatic dialogue) in Eliot's definition.[5]

Let us look at Krapp's mode of speech from his own existential point of view, as it were. Not only are his voices not connected with any other speaker or listener in an act of communication, but his isolation provides him with a rare monopoly over his tapes and speeches. He is absolute and sole master for all time. He is not, and will never be, heard or overheard, interrupted, distracted, questioned, corrected, corroborated, or otherwise jolted out of pure speech of self. He is his own author, publisher, director, performer, and audience. He is free to shape or reshape these fragments of unpublished autobiography, selecting and adding to whatever he chooses. As mechanical aids to solitude, the tapes can be edited and replayed at random or according to the emotional needs of the moment (the recurrent birthday). It is technically easier to do so than to change the wording of a journal (assuming it was penned and not anachronistically placed on a word-processor disc), and it is easier to listen to a tape than to recall memories at will (as opposed to involuntary and felt memory in Proust). Krapp, in replaying his tape, is both producing his authentic portrait, the Artist as a Young Man, and acting like the common man of the technological age with his push-button distraction. The privileged moments recorded on Krapp's tape are immutable like the images on Keats's Grecian urn, in symbolist verbal music, in the Joycean epiphany. Yet the tapes are disposable; Krapp as typical do-it-yourself home entertainer holds them cheap, at one point violently throwing all but one tape on the floor to join the accumulated debris of discarded bottles and banana skins. The ruthless selection rejects all programs not congenial to the listening self: the significant "vision" ("clear to me at last that the dark I have always struggled to keep under is in reality my most—"),[6] with its dynamic associated scenery of the stormy night, is switched off with impatient curses. In short, Krapp's monopoly over the tapes has the symptoms of monomania: the search for essential moments of living from the past—"separating the grain from the husks"[7]—eliminates everything that does not minister to the needs of the self's present moment.

Krapp's monopoly as author-performer-selector is distinctly marked in the way his "retrospect" is told, in the texture of his taped speech (his "solo," to use Ruby Cohn's term). The dominant mode is that of an I-centered narrative, leaning on intense but simple lyricism in re-creating the "moments" most significant to Krapp as listener and—through pointing, stilled concentration, and replay—to the audience, too. True, the brilliant technique of ostentatious interruptions (old Krapp joining in the laughter of Krapp-at-thirty-nine, opening bottles, singing a hymn, checking the dictionary meaning of "viduity," cursing, switching on and off, and so on) turns the listening session into a performed act. Nevertheless, from the tape it is only that slow, inward-moving voice (speaking in "purity of diction" as it dwells on pure significant moments) that comes through. The death of Krapp's mother and the love episode on the river are presented as if "out of time" and beyond interaction. Encounters are distilled into still points ("moments"); persons are transmuted into presences. The female would-be characters pass through the potential events recorded on the tape as images, "figures," and eyes:

> KRAPP: Not much about her [Bianca in Kedar Street], apart from a tribute to her eyes. Very warm. I suddenly saw them again. (*Pause.*) Incomparable! (*Pause.*) Ah well . . . (pp. 12–13)
>
> What remains of all that misery? A girl in a shabby green coat, on a railway-station platform? No? (p. 13)
>
> One dark young beauty I recollect particularly, all white and starch, incomparable bosom, with a big black hooded perambulator, most funereal thing. (. . .) The face she had! The eyes! Like (*hesitates*) . . . chrysolite! (*Pause.*) Ah well . . . (p. 15)

These evocations draw on the style of the minor symbolist poet, brought up on the power of the image, with inevitable borrowing from greater poets (Othello's "chrysolite")[8] a style gently parodied earlier in the text: "where mother lay a-dying in the late autumn, after her long viduity."[9] We note that the aestheticism of that language shuns the human voice, and the impact of personal speech, if not the person as person. The texture of Krapp's recorded memories is almost devoid of dialogue. Almost, for there are seconds when the voice of another person is distinctly heard. In the opening section of Krapp's replaying of his "perfect moment" (which is also the end of a "hopeless" relationship) the narration is comparatively brisk, erotic:

> KRAPP: —upper lake, with the punt, bathed off the bank, then pushed out into the stream and drifted. She lay stretched out on the floorboards with her hands under her head and

> her eyes closed. Sun blazing down, bit of a breeze, water
> nice and lively. I noticed a scratch on her thigh and asked
> her how she came by it. Picking gooseberries, she said. I
> said again I thought it was hopeless and no good going on
> and she agreed, without opening her eyes. (pp. 16–17)

It is the one point in the solo—as in the play—where Krapp presents
himself in company, in intimate encounter. The narrator succeeds
in re-creating another person he had loved transitorily. And that
young woman has a distinct idiom; she answers in a lightly witty
repartee: "picking gooseberries." For the rest of the narrative, a dialogue is suggested by reported speech (as in a novel): "I said again
I thought it was hopeless and no good going on and she agreed,
without opening her eyes." From that point on, Krapp's evocation
of the moment becomes more and more lyrical and stilled—the image
of the closed eyes and the rhythm of movement-without-motion pre-
cludes all else.

Krapp's predominantly I-voiced narrative is in marked contrast
to Winnie's dramatic speech in Happy Days, with its incessant addressing of Willie as a real or imagined companion, its conjured
dialogue and impersonation (e.g., of the vulgar speech of the Show-
ers). Krapp, as it were, allows just that one-second exposure to
another voice, to dialogue: "picking gooseberries, she said." It seems
significant that, apart from that one quotation, Krapp's spoken text
eliminates all dialogue, just as his existential situation terminates a
relationship. Krapp is then left free to perfect his monopoly of tapes—
in monologue.

The final soliloquy—with its commentary on the taped "retrospect" leading to the replay of the "perfect moment"—can then be
seen as an ingenious version of doubling. Old Krapp is conducting
the performance of his words from an opus of the mature years,
highlighting contrasts between the two phases of the self until two
distinct selves take shape. The present soliloquizer, in turn, is split
and displays at least two voices and rhythms—"like the solitary child
who turns himself into children, two, three"[10] or Richard II in his
prison soliloquy:

> I have been studying how I may compare
> This prison where I live unto the world:
> And for because the world is populous,

> And here is not a creature but myself,
> I cannot do it;—yet I'll hammer it out.
> My brain I'll prove the female to my soul,
> My soul the father: and these two beget
> A generation of still-breeding thoughts.
>   (*King Richard II*, 5.5.1–9)

The vehemence of old Krapp's dialectic of emotions in his soliloquy (ambivalence here, too) could be written out in the form of a traditional poetic Dialogue between the Soul and Body (Andrew Marvell) or A Dialogue of Self and Soul (William Butler Yeats, e.g., "*My Soul:* Why should the imagination of a man / Long past his prime remember things that are / Emblematical of love and war? . . . *My Self.* I am content to live it all again / And yet again . . .")[11] The inner debate, projected as a dialogue of two voices, concerns the "status" of that privileged moment of love:

> A: Just been listening to that stupid bastard I took myself for thirty years ago, hard to believe I ever was as bad as that. Thank God that's all done with anyway. (*Pause.*)
>
> B: The eyes she had! (. . .) Everything there, everything on this old muckball, all the light and dark and famine and feasting of . . . (*hesitates*) the ages! (*In a shout.*) Yes!
>
> A: Let that go. Jesus! Take his mind off his homework! Jesus! (*Pause. Weary.*)
>
> B: Ah well, maybe he was right. (*Pause.*) Maybe he was right. (*Broods.*) (pp. 17–18)

The rest of the soliloquy is largely made up of the rhetoric of self-denigration—time present: "Nothing to say, not a squeak." That sense of imaginative and verbal exhaustion is accompanied by "the sour cud and the iron stool," sudden death-wish, and fantasies ("last fancies," perhaps carrying the Elizabethan connotation of "fancy"—love—as his mind wanders to being "happy" with "Effie," Effi Briest, in a happy fusion of fictional and once-real characters). All these details spoken into the last tape intensify the speaker's isolation. The old man's coarsely avowed lust for a "bony old ghost of a whore" only underlines the deterioration in Krapp's quality of love, another counterpoint to the sublimated eros of the river scene. (It is paralleled by the mockery of the young man's "magnum opus" issuing in the sale of seventeen copies of some unspecified work.) The dominant note of Krapp's last tape can be said to be Richard II's "I wasted time, and now doth time waste me," strengthened in performance by the actor's wheezing and grunting, sweating, cursing, compulsive drinking, and banana eating. But the end of the soliloquy, in preparation for the replay of the "perfect moment" section of the tape, returns to the lyric mode, punctuated by ironic self-apostrophizing:

> KRAPP: Be again, be again. (*Pause.*) All that old misery. (*Pause.*)
> Once wasn't enough for you. (*Pause.*) Lie down across her.

The replay of the privileged tape is then the simple, direct, and sensuous response to that wish "to be again" (like Yeats's *My Self*: "to live it all again"). The whole replay begins, significantly with

> —gooseberries, she said.

That phrase itself is likely to make a stronger impact in the theater than the rather etiolated image of the eyes, whether open or closed. And it finally reinforces the illusion that Krapp is—for once, as once—in company, reaching a shared climax of stillness before reaching the end. Again, the girl's little speech, a quotation that amounts to micro-dialogue, is heard as a good-humored, teasing rejoinder. It does not sound like the idiom and mood of Krapp, young or old; it is a contrary speech, a "not-I." The existential illusion of Krapp's dialogue with the girl at that point reinforces the technical illusion of dialogue through Krapp's recurrent self-interruption as he listens to his voice from the past and his self-doubling as he interrogates himself on the last tape.

It follows from this reading that the end of the play gains added poignancy from our perceiving Krapp as attempting to break out from his isolation through his tapes—but the tape resists, replaying a self-enclosed reality. The seconds of actual dialogue point to a potential and abandoned dialogue just as the transitory moment on the river, replayed for desired resuscitation, points to lost relationship. Whatever Krapp feels at the end of his replay of a moment of essential experience and whatever the impact of that finally serene replay is on the audience, attention is once more drawn to Krapp's inescapable and total solitude. The invocation of shared silence on the tape ("Never knew such silence. The earth might be uninhabited") is juxtaposed within seconds by the austere final tableau: KRAPP *motionless staring before him. The tape runs on in silence.*

NOTES

1. This is a simplified version of the hypothesis that runs through my book *Dramatic Dialogue: The Duologue of Personal Encounter* (Cambridge: Cambridge University Press, 1983), esp. pp. 2–11, 27–33; on Beckett specifically, see pp. 213–20.
2. *Not I* (1973), that is, published and performed fifteen years after the first performance of *Krapp's Last Tape* (1958). The Auditor is a shadowy presence in *Not I* and was eliminated by Beckett himself when he directed the first production of the play in Paris (but restored by the author in the second Paris production). In *Rockaby* (1981), the Woman in the chair prompts the Voice ("more"), but presumably they "belong" to each other. In *Ohio Impromptu* (1981), the monologuist Reader is provided with a silent Listener "as alike in appearance as possible."
3. Andrew Kennedy, *Six Dramatists in Search of a Language* (Cambridge: Cambridge University Press, 1975), pp. 154, 159–60.
4. Ruby Cohn, *Just Play: Beckett's Theater* (Princeton, N.J.: Princeton University Press, 1980), pp. 64–66.
5. T. S. Eliot, "The Three Voices of Poetry" (1953), in *On Poetry and Poets*, 2d ed. (London: Faber & Faber, 1957).
6. Samuel Beckett, *Krapp's Last Tape* (London: Faber & Faber, 1965), p. 16. Subsequent references are from this edition.
7. Ibid., p. 12.
8. *Othello*, 5.2.145.
9. Beckett, *Krapp's Last Tape*, p. 14.
10. Samuel Beckett, *Endgame* (London: Faber & Faber, 1958), p. 45.
11. W. B. Yeats, *Collected Poems*, 2d ed. (London: Macmillan, 1950; first published 1933), pp. 265–67.

Samuel Beckett—Infinity, Eternity

MARTIN ESSLIN

I saw eternity the other night
Like a great *Ring* of pure and endless light,
All calm as it was bright
And round, beneath it, Time in hours, days, years,
Driv'n by the spheres
Like a vast shadow mov'd, In which the world
And all her trains were hurl'd.[1]

1.

That circle of eternity is a haunting presence also in Samuel Beckett's universe. In Mr. Knott's house in *Watt*, that seminal work which contains so much of Beckett's later themes, in the room of the senior servant, Erskine, Watt discovers a picture hanging on a wall:

A circle, obviously described by a compass and broken at its lowest point, occupied the middle foreground of this picture. Was it receding? Watt had that impression. In the eastern background appeared a point, or dot. The circumference was black. The point was blue, but blue! The rest was white. How the effect of perspective was obtained Watt did not know. But it was obtained. By what means the illusion of movement in space, and it almost seemed in time, was given, Watt could not say. But it was given. Watt wondered how long it would be before the point and circle entered together upon the same plane. Or had they not done so already, or almost? And was it not rather the circle that was in the background, and the point that was in the foreground? Watt wondered if they had sighted each other, or were blindly flying thus, harried by some force of merely mechanical mutual attraction, or the playthings of chance. He wondered if they would eventually pause and converse, and perhaps even mingle, or keep steadfast on their ways, like ships in the night, prior to the invention of wireless telegraphy. Who knows, they might even collide. And he wondered what the artist had intended to represent (Watt knew nothing about painting), a circle and its centre in search of each other, or a circle and its centre in search of a centre and a circle respectively, or a circle and its centre in search of its centre and a circle respectively, or a circle and its centre in search of a centre and its circle respectively, or a circle and a centre not its centre in search of its centre and its circle respectively, or a circle and a centre not its centre in search of a centre and a circle respectively, or a circle and a centre not its centre in search of its centre and a circle respectively, or a circle and a centre not its centre in search of a centre and its circle respectively, in boundless space, in endless time (Watt knew nothing of physics), and at the thought that it was perhaps this, a circle and a centre not its centre in search of a centre and its circle respectively, in boundless space, in endless time, then Watt's eyes filled with tears he could not stem, and they flowed down his fluted cheeks unchecked, in a steady flow, refreshing him greatly.[2]

Boundless space. Endless time. The circle of Henry Vaughan's eternity, the three circles of Dante's final vision in paradise,

> Nella profonda e chiara sussistenza
> dell'alto lume parvermi tre giri
> di tre colori e d'una continenza[3]
>
> [In the profound and shining being of the deep light appeared to me three circles, of three colors and one magnitude]

but broken, incomplete, searching for its completion. I apologize for quoting that passage from Watt at such length, but I think it is essential to do so: for the passage not only contains the image of the circle but also an example of the permutations that occur so frequently in Watt and contain so large a portion of that book's ultimate meaning.

Indeed, when Watt begins to wonder whether this picture had always been in the room,

Was the picture a fixed and stable member of the edifice, like Mr Knott's bed, for example, or was it simply a manner of paradigm, here today and gone tomorrow, a term in a series, like the series of Mr Knott's dogs, or the series of Mr Knott's men, or like the centuries that fall, from the pod of eternity?[4]

Watt concludes that, indeed, the picture is one of a series and yet that it is also an eternal fixture, precisely because in Mr. Knott's house the endless change, the endless permutation of its elements was itself an aspect of its unchangingness:

that nothing could be added to Mr Knott's establishment, and from it nothing taken away, but that as it was now so it had been in the beginning, and so it would remain to the end, in all essential respects. . . .[5]

and that

nothing changed in Mr Knott's establishment, because nothing remained, and nothing came or went, because all was a coming and a going.[6]

For if all is change in infinite time and nothing goes or comes—in other words, there is a finite amount of matter in the universe—then all the combinations of a finite number of elements must endlessly recur, and thus unending change ultimately amounts to permanent stasis. For even an infinite number of permutations, ever starting anew, would reveal themselves, to an observer who would have infinite time to watch them, as merely a static, unchanging state of affairs.

All the varied instances of permutation in Watt, "incidents . . . of great formal brilliance and indeterminable purport"—the series of dogs, the croaks of the frogs, the permutations of Mr. Knott's boots and stockings, and the endless permutating changes of Mr. Knott's appearance, to mention but a few of them, "these simple games that time plays with space, now with these toys and now with those,"[7] all tend to suggest or to represent that staggering concept of the infinity of time which is the ground of all being, in the sense in which Heidegger uses the word "Dasein"—being in the world.

This is, however, merely one aspect of Beckett's approach to the concept of infinity. For Beckett is never committed to one concept or one view of a concept: he always allows space for an alternative view; like Watt, he is

obliged, because of his peculiar character, to enquire into what [these phenomena] meant, oh not into what they really meant, his character was not so peculiar as all that, but into what they might be induced to mean, with the help of a little patience, a little ingenuity.[8]

Another view of infinity appears at the beginning of act 2 of *Waiting for Godot*, when Vladimir sings the song of the dog who came into the kitchen.[9] The following is an old German student song. (There are numerous variants of this text; this is the one I learned as a small boy):

> Ein Hund kam in die Kueche
> Und stahl dem Koch ein Ei.
> Der Koch der nahm den Loeffel
> Und schlug den Hund entzwei.
>
> Da kamen die anderen Hunde
> Und gruben ihm ein Grab,
> Und setzten ihm einen Grabstein
> Auf dem zu Lesen war:
>
> Ein Hund kam in die Kueche . . .
> [And so on, ad infinitum . . .]

This is another type of series, not a permutated one, but one that is an endless chain of images containing images of themselves. Another version of the same simulacrum of infinity is that of the magazine cover which represents a person holding a magazine on the cover of which there is the same picture of a person holding a magazine with the same cover—and so on, necessarily, ad infinitum, with ever-diminishing versions of the same magazine cover. It is, in principle, the same as those Russian dolls that contain a smaller identical doll, which, when opened, contains an even smaller version of the same until, at last, there is a final, diminutive one—with the difference that in the picture the end of the series can never come. In our imagination the picture must become smaller and smaller, but it can never wholly disappear. Once that series has been initiated, it can never stop, for each magazine cover contains the picture of itself and engenders the next-smaller version of itself inside itself.

2.

There are, thus, in Beckett's oeuvre attempts to capture the concept of infinite time in several, different, but often overlapping, ways.

First, there is infinity as the circle that runs into itself and thus can have no end. This circular concept of infinity, emptied of the religious content we find in Dante and Vaughan, merges into Nietzsche's idea of the endless cycle of recurrence, based on the assumption that, if there is a finite amount of matter in the universe and infinite time, the same combinations and permutations of the same elements must endlessly recur. This becomes the permutation of a number of elements in all possible combinations, only to start again when all these have been exhausted. And, second, there is infinity as "entropy" as we know it from the second law of thermodynamics, the gradual running down of the universe, which, however, because absolute zero can never be reached, must also go on, diminuendo, forever. The laws of thermodynamics, however, belong to a system of physics on a molecular scale. On the scale of subatomic particles, which involves quite different forces, such a run-down universe would collapse into itself again and produce a new big bang, thus starting the whole process of permutations anew. (Like Watt, I know nothing of physics, but am, as Beckett himself perhaps does, merely inquiring into what these phenomena might be induced to mean, with the help of a little patience or ingenuity.) What matters is that entropy, too, becomes an image of infinity, an infinity that can be compressed into the image within the image on the magazine cover, the story on the tombstone which contained a story which was on another tombstone.

Beckett's whole oeuvre could be characterized as an attempt to explore and to capture the essential nature of being; he is the ontological poet par excellence. Being, being in the world, Dasein in Heidegger's sense, is being in time. Conscious being inevitably entails suffering. Nonbeing is certainly, in Beckett's worldview, preferable to being. But what fills him with the greatest dread is the fact that once a consciousness is in being, it has entered an infinity of being, hence suffering. For once there is a consciousness of being, it can never consciously become aware of having ceased to be. When we are dead, we cannot know that we are dead. The last moment of consciousness, thus, must inevitably linger in the void forever. That, I think, is the meaning of the final scene of *Endgame*. The inhabitants of that circular chamber are, among many other things, images of the divergent elements of a single human consciousness, enclosed in what, in his poem "The Vulture," Beckett calls "my skull, shell of sky and earth."[10] The moment of separation between Hamm and Clov, the final move in that endgame, is thus also, among many other things, an image of the moment of death, which, as the consciousness cannot become aware of its own demise, must remain suspended as an eternal stalemate for all time.

3.

It is this image which is elaborated in *Play*. That the three heads we see emerging from their funerary urns designate human beings who have died and are in limbo is clear enough. That the whole text is to be spoken twice, as indicated in the terse stage direction "repeat play," and that the play closes with a third resumption of the beginning of the opening "choral" passage equally clearly indicate that this repetition will continue forever. There are, however, a number of significant details, emerging from productions involving intervention by Beckett himself, that should perhaps be recorded, for they do not appear in the published versions of the text.

First of all, the repeating of the whole text is not necessarily absolutely identical with the first time the text is spoken, though being absolutely identical nevertheless. Let me explain this seeming paradox: when *Play* was first done at the National Theatre in London in 1964, Beckett supplied a new text for the repetition. Here each character still speaks the identical words in the same sequence as before, but the order in which these three strands of text intertwine is permuted. If, for example, the first time through, the text of the narrative section of the play starts with W_1, the second time through it may be the Man who starts with his first sentence, to be followed by W_2, and then W_1. I don't remember the exact variation, but that is the principle of it. When we did a radio production of *Play* at the BBC, Beckett supplied us with a complete order of the permutations he wanted. We must, thus, assume that not only will these characters repeat the same words forever but also that there will be an astronomical number of different permutations of the manner in which the identical text is intertwined. This is, therefore, a much more economical way to represent an enormously larger number of permutations than the ones that Beckett worked out in detail in the various permutated series in *Watt* or in the shuffling of sucking stones in *Molloy*. For here the series is permuted only twice, with a fade-out at the start of the third series, as if to say, "Now you know the principle of the series; extrapolate all further permutations ad infinitum!" Moreover, the idea of entropy is also made graphically visible in *Play* if Beckett's instructions for the *radio* production of the piece are followed.

The idea to mount a radio production of *Play* came from one of the directors in the BBC's radio drama department, Bennett Maxwell. When we approached Beckett, he was very much against the idea, as he rightly felt that the beam of light that activates the speech of the three characters was essential and could not be transferred to the radio medium. But Bennett Maxwell had an idea as to how that element could be replaced by an acoustic equivalent. He suggested that a recording be made of the three characters saying "I" in unison. Now in the medium of recorded sound, infinity can very easily be created. One merely has to make a "loop" of the tape and put it on the machine. Then the same sound will repeat itself forever as the loop circulates through the machine. Bennett Maxwell suggested that this endless sound of the three characters' "I" would be the background to the play. Each time it was interrupted, one of the characters must be compelled to fill the void by speaking.

We wrote to Beckett suggesting this solution, and he replied that he was interested in it but would have to hear the result of the recording before giving permission for a broadcast. So Bennett Maxwell recorded the piece, and Beckett, at his next visit to London, came to Broadcasting House to listen to the tape. Having listened intently, he said: "No. This is all wrong. You have it all at the same speed and the same level throughout. I'll show you how it should be." He then explained that the text of *Play* was in three sections: (1) Chorus. (2) Narration. (3) Meditation. And he said that, even in the first recitation of the entire text, there should be a change in speed and vocal level from section to section. Thus, if Chorus is at speed 1 and voice level 1, then the first narration should be at speed 1 + 5 percent, and voice level 1 − 5 percent; and the first meditation, at speed (1 + 5 percent) + 5 percent, and at voice level (1 − 5 percent) − 5 percent—and then the repeating of the chorus at a speed again 5 percent faster and 5 percent lower than the preceding section, and so on throughout the entire play. In other words, the last lingering moment of consciousness of these three characters will continue at ever-increasing speed, at an ever-decreasing level, forever. For however much you increase the speed, it will always be a finite value; however much you decrease the level, it will always remain at a finite value, however small, for no percentage reduction can ever reduce a finite number to zero—complete nothingness.

We, of course, undertook to follow these instructions, and Beckett accordingly gave us permission to proceed. Indeed, I think that he was intrigued by one of the opportunities sound recording provides for such a work, namely, that the speeding up and softening down could, on tape, be done mechanically and with the utmost exactitude—something that would be quite outside the capability of live actors during a live performance. Moreover, on tape the three characters needed only to speak their text once—and all in one piece—and the chopping up and permutation could then be done on totally identical renderings of the words on the editing machine. Thus, the deadness of the characters and that irrevocable fixity of their last moment could become wholly apparent.

Bennett Maxwell directed the BBC version of *Play*. It was first broadcast on October 11, 1966. Shortly afterward I was invited to direct a production in German in West Germany. And I remember with pleasure the work of editing the once-recorded short pieces of text, duplicating the recording mechanically, and then cutting it up and splicing the sections together in a permuted sequence.

4.

That the potential of recorded sound for reproducing the fixity of the permutations through infinite time intrigued Beckett became clear from his suggestion that another new piece of his should be broadcast. An initiative of this kind is so rare with Beckett that I strongly suspect that he even wrote this work with a broadcast in mind. The work in question is *Lessness*.

This short prose work, a prose poem unlike anything else he has written, first appeared in its French original version, *Sans* in 1969,[11] and was first published in its English version in the *New Statesman* on May 1, 1970, and subsequently as a small booklet by Beckett's London publisher, Calder & Boyars.[12] *Lessness* reads like the description of an apocalyptic landscape—an endless gray plain, strewn with debris; the last refuge of a little body has burst. That little body is the last thing that stands upright surrounded by the endlessness of the ruins in the timelessness and changelessness. Only very rarely is there a mention of hope that the little body will rise again, that there will be day and night again. There is no narrative line—only the image.

Shortly after I had read *Lessness* in the *New Statesman*, where it occupied a page and a half, John Calder phoned me at the BBC—it must have been in mid-1970—and told me that Beckett had suggested that this should be recorded and broadcast but that he had special instructions about how to record it, namely—surprisingly for so short a piece—with no fewer than six voices. I went to Paris to discuss Beckett's concept with him. The six voices were to make apparent the peculiar structure of *Lessness*. Beckett handed me a written outline of this structure, which was to be made manifest by the recording. This typewritten text opens with the following explanation:

Lessness proceeds from *Ping*.
It is composed of 6 statement groups each containing 10 sentences, i.e. 60 sentences in all.
These 60 are first given in a certain order and paragraph structure, then repeated in a different order and paragraph structure.
The whole consists therefore of 2 × 60 = 120 sentences arranged and re-arranged in 2 × 12 = 24 paragraphs.
Each statement group is formally differentiated and the 10 sentences composing it "signed" by certain elements common to all.
Group A—Collapse of refuge—Sign: "true refuge."
Group B—Outer world—Sign: "earth–sky" juxtaposed or apart.
Group C—body exposed—Sign: "little body."
Group D—Refuge forgotten—Sign: "all gone from mind."
Group E—Past and future denied—Sign: "never"—except in the one sentence "figment dawn etc."
Group F—Past and future affirmed—Sign: future tense.

There follows, in this set of instructions, a list of all the sixty sentences in six groups (or "families," I recall Beckett calling them) of ten each labeled A 1–10, B 1–10, C 1–10, D 1–10, E 1–10, and F 1–10. And then the order in which the sentences are arranged in two sets of sixty, in which the individual sentences all recur but in a different order and different grouping, is indicated in this manner: A3 B9 A2—slash, A9 D3 E9 B8 E2 slash, and so forth, each slash indicating a period or unit of silence. Between each group of from

three to seven sentences there was to be a pause of twice that length
and between the two sections of sixty sentences one twice as long
again.

Each of the two sections contains the sixty sentences in twelve
groups, but the groups themselves are of varying length, containing
a minimum of three and a maximum of seven sentences. In the
first section this arrangement is:

$$4+5+3+5+3+6+7+6+7+4+4+6 = 60$$

In the second it is:

$$3+4+4+6+7+6+5+7+3+6+5+4 = 60.$$

From this it must be assumed that the genesis of *Lessness* was as
follows: first the six groups of ten sentences were written, then they
were cut up into single slips of paper, and then they were pulled out
of a hat at random to be arranged in the precalculated order, which
must contain permutations of the possibilities by which sixty sentences can be arranged in twelve groups containing from three to
seven sentences. The working out of these possibilities must constitute quite a feat of higher mathematics. But be that as it may,
what *Lessness* represents in its form is an image of eternal return:
the finite number of elements are here arranged in a manner which
is both random and yet governed by a rigid formula. Here Beckett
has, indeed, achieved a total merging of form and content. *Lessness*
depicts ultimate desolation. It proceeds, as indicated in his instructions, from *Ping*—which, in turn, is part of a set of fragments that
includes *Imagination Dead Imagine*—descriptions of little bodies
enclosed in narrow interior spaces. In *Lessness* that last space has
broken open, as sentence A6 puts it: "True refuge/long last/issue-
less/scattered/down four walls over backwards/no sound," and there
is only one thing standing upright in that endless gray landscape of
sky and earth, that last little body, "C1:Little body ash grey/locked
rigid/heart beating/face to endlessness," "C3: Heart beating/little
body only upright/grey face/features overrun/two pale blue." Time-
lessness and endlessness are the recurring leitmotivs of this ultimate
landscape. Only one of the groups of sentences is "signed" by a
reference to a future: "F 1: one step more/one alone all alone/in the
sand/no hold/he will make it" and "F10: he will curse God again/as
in the blessed days/face to the open sky/the passing deluge." The

irony of this "hopeful" set of ten sentences, however, lies in the fact
that they, too, endlessly recur. If we are to trust the meaning of the
structure of the poem, the implication is that these hopes are part
of the eternal recurrence of the same everlasting landscape of ultimate entropy—of what? of an individual consciousness or of life and
the world themselves?

The recording of Lessness, which was broadcast in February 1971,
did not satisfy Beckett. He felt that the six individual voices were
too strongly differentiated from each other. He would have preferred
them to sound all like variations of the same voice, which, of course,
would have produced the impression that there was only one voice
speaking and would have gone counter to the intention of making
the structure of the poem, which contains its ultimate meaning,
transparent. There is something like an almost insoluble dilemma
here. What must be stressed, however, is the fact that with the
exception of its publication in a separate slim volume by John
Calder, the piece has not been correctly printed in the few publications in which it is available in the United States. The twenty-four
paragraphs are printed without the break after the twelfth paragraph,
which is essential to indicate the structure of the piece and show
the point at which the permutation of the identical sixty sentences
begins again.

I have no doubt that Lessness, though one of Beckett's least-known
works, is one of his most significant experiments. Just as in Waiting
for Godot the meaning of the play lies to a considerable extent in
its structure, with the second act repeating the pattern of the first
and thus also indicating that these two episodes are part of a recurring pattern, here also, and even more intensely, the structure contains most of the meaning. One might say that Lessness is one of the
few truly "structuralist" literary experiments. Here also Beckett com-
bines his two approaches to the representation of infinity: the image
described by the text is one of entropy, and the structure is one of
an endless permutation of preexistent elements.

5.

Consciousness condemned to an eternal repetition of its last conscious moment—as represented in the final stasis of Endgame, the
entropic recurrence of the same last thoughts in Play, the final landscape of eternal entropy in Lessness, the endlessly recurring streams

of creatures moving through mud in *How It Is* and in many other Beckett works—all these are images of Hell, and we must never forget Beckett's deep preoccupation with Dante. The infinity so frequently represented in Beckett's oeuvre is an *Inferno*.

But there is another aspect of infinity in Beckett that relates the image of the three concentric circles in the Paradiso to the ring that Vaughan saw in his wondrous vision of the world: that infinity is the infinity of eternity. The infinity of endless recurrence, permutation and everlasting entropy, running down, is the infinity of being which inevitably must be being in time. Eternity, on the other hand, is the total cessation, the absolute negation of time and hence the escape from the endless wheel of being. In another of Beckett's Dantesque images, *The Lost Ones*, the endless permutation of time, it is hinted, might perhaps be brought to an end when the last seeker gives up his quest. It is the restless quest, even when reduced to mere hopeful waiting, that keeps Dasein in being, existence being process and change, expectation of the future. For Beckett's characters, that quest, the ultimate quest, is the quest for their own self or rather the pursuit of the unity of that self: attainment of a moment when the split between the thinker of the thought and the observer who hears that thought as the voice that eternally drones on within the consciousness might be transcended. For as long as a human being experiences itself, its own thoughts, its own consciousness as a stream of thought that seems in Beckett's phrase to emanate from elsewhere, "Not I," that split continues and inevitably engenders that quest for the unity of the observer and the observed stream of consciousness, the Beckettian stream of inner voices. Time, the sequential process of serial permutation and recurrence, must continue. If that moment of the total fusion of the observer with the observed could be achieved, the illusion of individuality—Schopenhauer's *principium individuationis* that engenders the illusion of the phenomenal world, time and the eternal wheel of what Indian philosophy calls "Maia"— would dissolve, and the individual would merge into the absolute ground of being itself.

None of the characters in Beckett's plays, none of the narrators of his stories ever succeeds in achieving the ultimate moment of insight, when the observing and the observed self would merge in the ineffable experience of its own ultimate nullity and nonbeing. Then time would come to a stop in that great positive nothingness of which Beckett speaks in *Murphy*, that nothing than which noth-

ing is more real—the ultimate reality of the mystics from ancient
Indian philosophy and Buddhism to the great Christian mystics like
Johannes Eckhart, San Juan de la Cruz, or Jakob Boehme. Unlike
Dante, Beckett has never in his oeuvre described that ultimate mys-
tical moment of insight. Yet all his work is concerned with the pursuit of its possibility, however impossible, however hopeless, however
much of a self-contradiction or paradox it may appear. Beckett suffers
under the thought of eternal recurrence, as Nietzsche's Zarathustra
did at one point of his life.

"Der grosse Ueberdruss am Menschen, der wuergte mich und war mir
in den Schlund gekrochen . . . Ewig kehrt wieder der Mensch, des du
muede bist, der kleine Mensch—so gaehnte meine Traurigkeit und
schleppte den Fuss und konnte nicht einschlafen. . . .

—"ach der Mensch kehrt ewig wieder! Der kleine Mensch kehrt ewig
wieder!

"Nackt hatte ich einst beide gesehen, den groessten Menschen und den
kleinsten Menschen: allzuaehnlich einander—allzumenschlich auch den
Groessten noch!

"Allzuklein der Groesste!—das war mein Ueberdruss am Menschen! Und
ewige Wiederkunft auch des Kleinsten!—das war mein Ueberdruss an
allem Dasein!

"Ach Ekel! Ekel! Ekel!"—Also sprach Zarathustra und seufzte und
schauderte. . . .

["A great surfeit with humanity—it has constricted my throat and has
crept into my gullet. . . . Eternally he returns, Man, of whom you have
grown tired, little Man—thus yawned my sadness and dragged its foot
and could not find sleep. . . .

—"Alas, Man eternally returns! Little Man eternally returns!

"I have seen them both in their nakedness, the greatest Man and the
smallest Man: all too like each other—all too human even the greatest!

"All too small the greatest!—that was my surfeit with Man! And the
eternal return even of the smallest! That was my surfeit with all Being!

"O Disgust! Disgust! Disgust!"—Thus spake Zarathustra and he sighed
and shuddered. . . .][13]

Yet, unlike Zarathustra—and Nietzsche—who overcame that disgust
and at times regarded the idea of eternal recurrence as a joyful one,

Beckett can never overcome the dread of an infinity of time and suffering. His quest, in contrast to Nietzsche's, remains the pursuit of that supreme moment of unity with the eternity that is the end of time, the eternity of Dante's moment of supreme insight, "che la mia mente fu percossa da un fulgore,"[14] when his mind was shaken by supreme splendor by "l'imago al cerchio,"[15] that image in the circle, the image of that eternity which is not infinite time, but nontime, the experience that reveals to the consciousness merging into the absolute ground of being that time itself is nothing but an illusion, a figment engendered by the restless striving and desiring of a human consciousness thrown willy-nilly into the phenomenal world of the fallen state of being, to which we have been condemned we know not by what sin or crime. It is this end of time, that great positive nothingness that Beckett yearns for, the ultimate Time-Lessness which is the diametrical opposite of infinity and eternal recurrence, the mystic's release from the wheel of being—Eternity.

NOTES

1. Henry Vaughan, "The World," in *The Complete Poetry of Henry Vaughan*, ed. French Fogle (New York: Norton, 1964), p. 231.
2. Samuel Beckett, *Watt* (New York: Grove Press, 1959), pp. 128–29.
3. Dante, *Paradiso*, xxxiii, ll.115–17.
4. *Watt*, pp. 130–31.
5. Ibid., p. 131.
6. Ibid.
7. Ibid., p. 75.
8. Ibid.
9. Samuel Beckett, *Waiting for Godot* (New York: Grove Press, 1954), p. 37; (London: Faber & Faber, 1956).
10. Samuel Beckett, *Poems in English* (New York: Grove Press, 1963), p. 21.
11. *Sans* first appeared in *La Quinzaine Littéraire*, 82 (November 1969), 1–15; later it was published in booklet form (Paris: Editions de Minuit, 1969).
12. Samuel Beckett, *Lessness* (London: Calder & Boyars, 1969).
13. Friedrich Nietzsche, *Also Sprach Zarathustra*, Part Three, in Nietzsche, *Werke*, ed. Karl Schlechta (Munich: Hanser, 1954–56), vol. 2, p. 465.
14. Dante, *Paradiso*, xxxiii, ll.140–41.
15. Ibid., l.138.

Not I: Beckett's Mouth
and the Ars(e) Rhetorica

KEIR ELAM

I Not

A familiar, not to say outworn, topos of our literary culture is for authors to resist the interpretative endeavors of their critics, just as it is a rather overworked commonplace for critics to see as their chief professional task precisely the endeavor to interpret. Samuel Beckett, among his rare explicit statements of authorial attitude, has repeatedly expressed suspicion of, or simple indifference to, the spectacle of his commentators going round in self-constructed hermeneutic circles:

I feel that the only line is to refuse to be involved in exegesis of any kind. And to insist on the extreme simplicity of dramatic situation and issue [in Endgame]. If that's not enough for them, and it obviously isn't, it's plenty for us, and we have no elucidations to offer of mysteries that are all of their own making. My work is a matter of fundamental sounds (no joke intended) made as fully as possible, and I accept responsibility for nothing else. If people want to have headaches among the overtones, let them. And provide their own aspirin.[1]

Beckett probably has more reason than most extensively written-about writers to consider himself a victim of others' exegetical enthusiasm. The temptation to attribute, or better still to fix, univocal meanings to his "fundamental sounds" would appear to be irresistible, given the numbers of those who succumb to it among journalistic and academic critics alike. Such anxiety to provide unambiguous semantic definitions seems to be provoked above all—as Beckett's complaint about the label-the-endgame game suggests—by his dramatic, as opposed to narrative, texts: presumably because of the seductive visual definiteness of his stage images themselves.

If, however, the sport of hermeneutic hawking within the happy hunting ground of Beckett's drama has attracted any number of practitioners, it has tended to produce but one species of critical trophy. Most of the interpretative labors expended on texts from *Godot* to *Ohio Impromptu* have a distinctly tropological bias and, in particular, have adopted as their kingpin the queen trope of metaphor or allegory (extended metaphor). More particularly still, they have discovered a single and recurrent metaphorical or allegorical object: Beckett's dramatic situations are all figures for existential and especially psychic predicaments, in a word for the human mind. Thus,

Godot:

ultimately it dramatizes a state of mind, the psychological reality, the "feel" of the emotion of unfulfilled expectancy.[2]

Endgame:

[Critics] have seen the interior space of the room that Beckett describes as the image of the interior of the skull with the two high windows as eyes looking out on the world. In that interpretation of the play Hamm and Clov function as aspects of a single psyche.[3]

Krapp:

the tape on Krapp's machine is an image of the mind, coiling backwards and forwards in time, endlessly repeating itself with the same memories, hopes, anxieties, preoccupations.[4]

Allegories of the mind: this, then, has become the received key to a symbolic decoding of Beckett's stage imagery. Nor can it be said that the plays themselves, despite their author's complaints concerning arbitrary exegesis, offer nothing to encourage this kind of psychotropological reading. The later plays especially present ever sharper and more striking icons—which indeed often look suspiciously like emblematic speaking pictures—of experiential processes of some kind, however one chooses to define them: Winnie up to her neck in it; urned dead-heads trapped in their own dismal pasts; an aged writer narcissistically communicating with his recorded earlier selves, and so on through an iconographic repertoire that has become virtually part of the contemporary collective *imaginaire*. And the search for the "mind," particularly an ailing or failing mind, as source and guarantee of the unitary sense of a given text is further stimulated by the gallery of psychotics and psychopaths that Beckett has affectionately assembled in his narrative and dramatic works alike: from Murphy and his friends in the Magdalen Mental Mercyseat to the homicidal Lemuel, the violent Krap senior of *Eleuthéria*, the sadistic Hamm, the infanticidal Rooney, and the autistic Krapp, we are offered a veritable Bedlam guide to mental unhealth that seems to license any amount of critical "psycho" analysis.

The problem is, however, that the very iconic seductiveness of Beckett's various stage figures for psychic horror has tended to inhibit further analysis, as if the rhetoric of his drama were limited to getting the audience to take part in some spot-the-existential-condition exercise. Moreover, one might see more than a little irony in the critical endeavor to unveil a full and integral, albeit unappealing, semantic substance lying as it were behind the scenes, for the dramatist's own efforts seem to go increasingly in the opposite direction, namely, that of semantic *disintegration*. The first duty of interpretative commentary is evidently to save the *sign* at all costs, presumably because any radical split in the one-to-one sign vehicle/ signified relationship would threaten to put the critic out of business altogether.

That Beckett's poetics moves progressively away from a full semantic and expressive investment in the sign is suggested not only by the increasing fragmentariness and semiotic austerity of his middle-to-late texts (compared to the relative verbal-visual exuberance of the early novels and plays), but also by his escalating series of declaredly negative or privative discourses, signaled as such from their titles downward: *L'Innommable*, *Act Without Words I and II*, *Lessness*, *Nouvelles textes pour rien*, *No's Knife*, *Worstward Ho*, and so forth. The rhetoric of these texts for next-to-nothing is plainly more a matter of how it isn't than of how it is.

Not that there is any radical incompatibility between a "negative" poetics and rhetorical analysis as such. Indeed, one might well define rhetoric in its traditional conception as the art of the what-not: what matters is not so much what is put in as what is strategically left out. This is already true, as Aristotle and Cicero teach us, at the level of argumentation, of *inventio* and *dispositio*, whose efficacy and decorum depend on finding ways of saying by not saying, of persuading by appearing not to persuade, of elaborating by not overdoing. But it is especially true at the level of the figures, of *elocutio*. All the favorite tropes are based on the in absentia principle of the missing or unnamed object, of the *innommable*: metaphor on what is not named but is semantically associated; metonymy on what is not named but is physically or causally contiguous; synecdoche on what is named only through a representative part. Figures of thought likewise entail a conceptual movement from what is to what is not and back: irony—what is deducible from its opposite; hyperbole—what is reducible from an excess; meiosis—what is increasable from a reduction; litotes—what is positively inferable from a negation; and so forth.

In this perspective, Beckett's dramatic figures might, then, be safely accommodated, as his interpreters would wish, within the rhetorical and specifically the tropical tradition of our literary and theatrical culture. Like other great Irish writers from Swift to Joyce, Beckett may be seen as an original and inventive rhetor, one who both knows and does his *ars rhetorica*. Indeed, if rhetoric, especially in its figural branch, is definable as the art of the what-not, then Beckett must be considered in absolute one of its most accomplished and resourceful practitioners, for a strategic leaving out, conceptually, discursively, scenically, is undoubtedly what he knows and does best.

But even if one elects Beckett to the ranks of the masters of rhetoric, one might, nevertheless, ask whether the most promising figure for an effective hermeneutic hold on his dramaturgy is really metaphor or allegory. Two other tropes suggests themselves more readily. The first is synecdoche, figure of reduction, of the lesser *in praesentia* that stands for the greater *in assentia*. All dramatic representation is in some degree synecdochic: what the spectator witnesses is necessarily a "reduced" version of the dramatic world that he takes to be represented; the dramatis personae stand for a larger community; and their dialogue, for a wider network of exchanges; the set represents but the immediately visible slice of dramatic topology; represented stage action figures the much fuller succession of events of plot and fabula, and so on. In Beckett's case, this tropological operation of reduction becomes virtually a surgical operation, regarding not merely the rhetorical but also the human figure and involving not simply the number of representative bodies onstage but the very makeup of the representing and represented body, which progressively loses its physical, ontological, and cultural integrity—and indeed its constituent members—until it becomes, in plays like *Play* and *Happy Days*, a mere talking head. So that in developmental terms, at least, the synecdochic mode does appear appropriate to Beckett's dramaturgic career, whose movement is one of consistent and programmed "lessness" with regard to what went before. The dramatic paradigm here might be Shakespeare's Lavinia, dismembered bit by bit until capable in the end only of desperate vocal but nonlingual sound.

The second and rival rhetorical candidate is litotes, a figure of negative affirmation. There is no doubt that Beckett's characteristic discursive and corporeal negations, his clinical cuts with "no's knife," have at the same time a powerfully persuasive affirmative force precisely in the extraordinary expressive intensity they permit, as if the truncation to the essential, a kind of dramaturgic equivalent of Ockham's razor, lends to what is left an increased semiotic potency. This effect corresponds to the actual theatrical experience of many spectators: where a play like *Endgame* risks at times redundancy in its rather baroque elaboration, especially its long-winded verbal amplification, the irreducible economy of a more directly "negative" drama like *Krapp* allows audiences no letup in the degree of their interest and concentration.

But even these alternative, albeit more "negative," rhetorical categories for his dramatic figurations still presuppose, like metaphor, the semantic integrity of the sign in Beckett's theater: both synecdoche and litotes function only if what is shown is taken to stand for something *other* than itself. This is a question that should, in the case of Beckett, be posed rather than begged.

II   *Not I*

The question in question arises with particular force regarding one of the briefest and most potent of Beckett's middle-to-late plays, *Not I* (1972), a paradigmatic text within the Beckett canon not merely because of the exemplary negativity of its title but also because of the literally irreducible fragmentariness of its main body or of what one might term its principal part. It is the play in which Beckett's rhetorical "leaving out" achieves its most spectacularly iconic form. If the three major plays preceding it chronologically are already and increasingly *textes pour peu*—*Krapp*, which restricts the mechanisms of plot to the mechanics of the recorder and interpersonal relations to intrapersonal revisitation; *Happy Days*, which figures the progressive submergence of the subject beneath the detritus of circumstance, leaving only an inexorably gossiping head; *Play*, whose ghostly adulterers have similarly been left, in an unkind noncut, their eternally narrating heads—here the little is the indispensable minimum for the sheer production of speech or vocal noise onstage: the talking head has become a mere phonating mouth named precisely Mouth. Lavinia has been deprived even of her upper face (though not of her tongue).

Not I offers an exciting, intriguing, and exasperating experience to its spectators. Made up, apart from the illuminated Mouth and her almost invisible Auditor onstage, of a shower of fragmentary spurts of discourse, it seems continuously to promise and at the same time to withhold sense; in the description of one reviewer present at the first performance in New York:

The nearest I can come to describing "Not I" is to say that it is an aural mosaic of words, which come pell-mell but not always helter-skelter, and that once it is over, a life, emotions, and a state of mind have been made manifest, with a literally stunning impact upon the audience.[5]

This is what might be considered an optimal response to the play in performance: a noble spectatorial struggle to construct a unitary meaning out of the mosaic of words (in the standard interpretative terms of a represented "state of mind"); a sense of perplexity at the difficulty of doing so ("I have no idea," adds the reviewer, "what the title means"); and in the end a willing surrender to the "stunning impact" of words and image together.

In fact, it is an extremely arduous task for the audience even to grasp basic bits of narrative information from Mouth's continuously self-interrupted vocal flow, let alone piece the bits together to reconstruct something resembling an underlying fabula. But critics enjoy the posttheatrical and lectorial privilege of putting dramatic puzzles together with text in hand, and willy-nilly a story can indeed be teased, if not eased, out of Mouth's mouthings. Here is the version of a critic present at the first London performance (who confesses to having also read the play):

"Mouth," as Beckett calls her, was born a bastard, deserted by her parents, brought up in a loveless, heavily religious orphanage. She became a lonely, frightened, half-moronic adult, forever trudging round the countryside and avoiding others. . . . Once she appeared in court on some unnamed charge, and couldn't speak; once, and only once, she wept; . . . But otherwise "nothing of note" apparently happened until a mysterious experience at the age of 70. The morning sky went dark, a ray of light played in front of her . . . then, suddenly, her mouth began to pour out words, so many and so fast that her brain couldn't grasp them, though she sensed that some revelation, some discovery, was at hand.[6]

What is particularly notable in this résumé (one of several, which disagree as to details but follow roughly the same main story line) is the critic's brave attempt to restore to Mouth's strikingly incoherent monologue a clearly defined narrative linearity, not to say descriptive dignity, principally on "autobiographical" grounds: Mouth's discursive bits and pieces are reassembled as a direct account of her own experience ("she became . . ."; "her mouth began . . ."). Certainly, the puzzle does seem to fit together well in terms of narrated experience and represented "state of mind." Indeed, one can find in this reading of the rebus many of the familiar components of Beckett's "psychotic" repertory: mental/corporeal dissociation ("feeling so dulled standing or sitting . . . but the brain—"); catatonic muteness ("speechless all her days"), which becomes unstaunchable logorrhea ("and can't stop . . . no stopping it not make a sound"); uncertainty of perception regarding basic facts of life, such as existence ("and all dead still, eyelids . . . presumably . . . on and off . . . shut out the light . . ."); hearing ("all the time the buzzing . . . so-called . . . in the ears . . . though of course actually . . . not in the ears at all"), movement ("no part of her moving . . . that she could feel," sex ("when clearly intended to be having pleasure . . . she was in fact . . . having none . . . not the slightest, and the rest. Thus Mouth becomes a final and chilling reincarnation or, better, disincarnation, of Beckett's earlier monologuing *M's*, from Murphy to Malone. And thus the sign is saved again in the guise of a merely figural disfigurement: the moving mouth onstage may be synecdochically reintegrated with what is missing to the eye (just as Lavinia's dismembered state stands for what has been lost, i.e., physical and moral integrity); her lack of body is at the same time a metaphor for a kind of psychic atrophy or dystrophy ("she seems to show symptoms of what the psychiatrists call 'depersonalization' "[7]); whereas the titular "not I," and the play's emphatic negativity in general may be read as a classic Beckett litotes, a strategic denial of what is tragically the case.

It may be that such a response to the play, the eminently reasonable endeavor to discern a dramatis persona and thus a "life" behind the paucity of visual and verbal clues available, is actually another of the ironies—to remain for a moment in the domain of figural operations—into which Beckett seduces his public, especially his public commentators. The very affirmation, or negation, "not I" seems to invite irresistibly a dialogic response of the "yes, you" kind, with the result that a good deal of analysis of the play is dedicated precisely to denying its titular denial. It is difficult to see any way out of such a rhetorical spiral unless perhaps one decided for the sake of argument to take the text's title and discourse, as it were, at faceless value and so read the play in terms of absence rather than of disguised presence. At least one critic has expressed doubt as to the effective entity of a dramatic Mouth behind the theatrical mouth, thus questioning the standard figural decoding of the text in terms of represented character:

The structure of Not I suggests that this performance consists of one recitation of a text that repeats itself endlessly in the consciousness that belongs to Mouth. Beckett does not, however, provide any dramatic representation of that consciousness. Mouth is neither metaphor nor metonym of the whole personality of a character. As the recitation discusses, the character perceives that text as a sequence of words that her mouth speaks involuntarily. The text lists biographical details and records incidents in the peculiar life of a character, but the only real characterisation of Mouth is the one created in the spectator's imagination by implication.[8]

This seems a promising line of attack, that is, to shift attention from the biographical consistency or otherwise of the dramatic "I" to the effects of the very I/not I dialectic on the audience's perceptions and speculations. It is a shift from a "negative" rhetoric to the rhetoric of negation. The problem is then no longer to solve a teasing enigma but to chart the play's (albeit enigmatic) ways of informing and disinforming, of enticing and distancing, of stimulating and perplexing the spectator. This, indeed, might be the first communicational force of the title: an invitation or warning to the audience to take responsibility for its own projections and constructions as if to say that the one thinking and suffering subject present is inevitably "you."

III Not "I"

Apart from the sheer "pell-mell" rapidity of the performance, the first and most persistent problem for the audience in its straw-clutching efforts to salvage some semblance of diagenetic coherence from Mouth's scraps of discourse is of a strictly referential nature. Her account begins in fabulous ab ovo fashion with a (premature) birth and with an innocent-looking reference:

out . . . into this world . . . this world . . . tiny little thing.

It might be noted that Mouth's repeated "this world" is the only "outward" (exophoric) reference in the entire text just as "this" is her first and last use of deixis. On inspection or reflection—of the kind the auditor is never, of course, permitted—even this modest referential concession is not as straightforward as it seems, however, for there is no represented physical context to which it can possibly be related. Dramatic reference, especially deictic reference, is automatically interpreted by the spectator in relationship to the visual clues he simultaneously receives, if only those provided by the actor's body and its movements. What is he to make of a "this" issued by a no-body in the void? At most one infers that, despite nonappearances, we have to do with narrated bodies and events in a "world" more or less like our own. In any event, the worldly deictic is so uncertain that it simply runs dry on itself: "this world . . . into this . . . out into this. . . ."

Thereafter, this one originating act of reference having more or less taken place, all reference in the play is reference back, no longer exophoric but anaphoric. Mouth's few and paltry predications all presuppose some already-established universe of discourse, constantly *in medias* with respect to her humble *res* ("tiny little thing"). Persons, such as they are, are introduced by pronouns, as if already named and known: "before its time" . . . ; "he having vanished," and so on. Events, with their relative spatial and temporal coordinates, are not so much recounted as reinvoked, again as if in the presence of a listener who already shared the narrator's knowledge: "just at the odd time in her life . . . when clearly intended to be having pleasure"; "or that time she cried"; "that time in court," and so on.

Occasionally Beckett toys—as in his opening "this world"—with ambiguous verbal clues that seem to bring us into some sort of dramatic here and now only to retreat behind the cumuli or nebulas of Mouth's remote narrative universe. Such is the case of the "nows" occasionally dropped into the past-time continuum—"always the same spot . . . now bright . . . now shrouded"; "now can't stop"—which turn out to be indexes not of contemporaneity but of succession, and so merely disguised "thens" (although see the fourth section of this essay).

The play also has a single instance of what is, in effect, a favorite referential conjuring trick of Beckett's (also put to good use by Pinter[9]), namely, the resort to a specific-sounding but peculiarly unhelpful toponymy. Mouth, relating the isolated weeping episode, gives a name to the domestic scene: "where was it? . . . Croker's Acres . . . one evening on the way home . . . home! . . . a little mound in Croker's Acres." The momentary impression of concreteness that the place-naming gives proves once again illusory, for the topographical details that might lend it sense (country, region, neighborhood, description of the scene itself, and so on) is altogether missing. Compare Lucky's grotesque ghost tour of southern England: "for reasons unknown in Feckham Peckham Fulham Clapham"; or Nell's unexpected Italian excursion: "It was on Lake Como . . . one April afternoon"; or again Winnie's characteristically punctilious suburbanism: "in the back garden at Borough green, under the horse-beech." Emptied of any effective orientational force, Beckett's illusory topography fulfills a purely "poetic" function (as in the consonance of "Croker's Acres"), verging on the comic but at the same time hinting at a nostalgia for the irretrievably lost points of reference in "this world."

The purging of reference—especially deictic reference—to any present physical context is a gradual process in Beckett's dramatic career. The language of *Godot* is rich in spatiotemporal indexes, even if of a contradictory and inconclusive kind; indeed, Vladimir and Estragon are obsessively preoccupied with what they uncertainly identify as the *hic et nunc* ("You're sure it was here?" "You're sure it was this evening?"), just as Hamm and Clov are slaves to the here/there, now/ then oppositions. First to go is the spatial *here*, already thin on the ground in *Krapp* and practically absent in *Happy Days* (which enacts, as it were, the disappearance of the stage as scene). *Now* survives until *Play*, where it already takes on the past, successional sense it has in *Not I* ("now in the one dear old place, now in the other"). A similar fate meets the personal pronoun. "I" and "you," indexes of subjectivity and of interrelationship respectively, survive intact even in *Happy Days*, in which Winnie hammers out the first person to affirm her own tenuous and weakening hold on self ("I seem . . . to remember I shall simply brush and comb . . .") and the second person to uphold her dear illusion regarding the accessibility of the other ("So that I may say at all times, even when you do not answer and perhaps hear nothing, something of this is being heard, I am not merely talking to myself"). "You," too, effectively meets its end in *Play*, in which it becomes a ghostly projection, suspended in some timeless and placeless narrative there-and-then ("Some day you will tire of me . . ."). Only the dubious Cartesian "I" seems to suffer on into limbo ("I say, Am I not perhaps a little unhinged already? . . . just a little? . . . I doubt it. . . . I doubt it").

If there is one thing we think we know about dramatic language, it is that "I," the egocentric particular that links the utterance to the dramatis persona and vice versa, is central to it.[10] There can be no properly dramatic "world" without a subject who, in speaking and acting within that world, progressively defines both it and himself. "External" world-creating acts à la Genesis are the privilege of narrative texts. It is, of course, this particular egocentric rule that is the play's main dramaturgic victim. Indeed, its title is in this respect a declaration of the dramatist's characteristic intent to "leave out"; having eliminated context, scene, the body, represented action and all the other Aristotelian paraphernalia of dramatic theater, he now proceeds to operate the final cut, doing away with the minimal deictic

prop of all oral discourse. There is even an element of gauntlet throwing in this last act of lessness: can it be done (without), and how?

The immediate answer is that the not-"I" is simply a "she." If one
does without the speaking-acting first person, one has necessarily to
replace it with an agential third person: either I speak or I am spoken
for just as if one does away with the speaking-acting *body* of the self-
defining (first) dramatic person, one needs at least the mouth and
the voice—the rest is dispensable—of a narrator to put the third person into some sort of being, which is exactly the situation that appears to be embodied onstage. Mouth, by antonomasia an oral teller,
does not act but narrates. And the play is certainly true to its title:
never an I or a me or a my, only a relentless she/it. This apparent
narrativization of the drama is the opposite of what happens, as
Robert Champigny has observed, in Beckett's narrative monologues,
especially *The Unnamable*, with its obsessive and endlessly shifting "I":

> instead of being eliminated, the first person will keep haunting the
> monologue as a kind of question mark. Time and again, the monologue
> will attempt to graft the pronoun on a person, or character . . . On the
> whole, the language of *The Unnamable* belongs to the dramatic sphere
> . . . Could a verbal dissociation of the self from the category of individ-
> uality have been better achieved through another kind of language?[11]

If Beckett's narrative monologue achieves a "dissociation of the self
from the category of individuality" by means of a "dramatic" I, his
dramatic monologue achieves the same effect, and more violently so,
through its abolition because though the audience may be tempted
to take Mouth's remote narrational stance at the letter or, rather, at
the sound, in the search for a ready solution—"could it be, as some
suspect, that the mouth is talking, not of itself, but of someone
else?"[12]—it must at the least entertain an occasional doubt. The
main clue, in performance at least, to the fact that the deictic "she"
may not be so distant from the faltering narrative voice itself is
Mouth's recurrent crisis precisely over the pronominal subject of the
verb: "and she found herself in the— . . . what? . . . who? . . .
no!" . . . she!"—a drama that in turn sets off the play's one piece
of stage business in the form of the Auditor's ritual "sideways raising of arms from sides and their falling back, in a gesture of help-

less compassion." This is the only visual signal, apart from the inexorable Mouthing, that Beckett permits the spectator, and so is presumably designed to foreground the most significant (repeated) moment in the narrator's fifteen-minute oral agony. It is a moment of distinctly *dialogic* conflict: Mouth's "no! . . . she!" takes the form of a reply to some unheard "other" voice. There is no question that what she is responding to is the threatened incursion within the narrative of a confessional "I," the return of a repressed subjectivity and thus of a "personal" voice. Beckett is perfectly candid about this—to the reader, not to the spectator—in his note on the Auditor's movement: "There is just enough pause to contain it as MOUTH recovers from *vehement refusal to relinquish third person*" (my italics).

Not I must be the first drama in history whose central agon has to do with a grammatical category. This is not to say, however, that the tensions it expresses are merely formal. The first person singular pronoun, already firmly at the center of post-Cartesian philosophical reflection, has also come to represent over the past thirty years the main fulcrum of linguistic and semiotic theory in its "pragmatic" branch. Indeed, the deictic evasions of Beckett's Mouth might be a dramatization of, or reflection on, the classic essay on the function of the "I," Benveniste's "On Subjectivity in Language":

It is in and by language that man is constituted as a *subject*; because only language grounds itself in reality, in *its* reality, which is that of being, the concept of "ego." Such subjectivity is the capacity of the speaker to posit himself as "subject." . . . Now we maintain that this "subjectivity" . . . is nothing but the emergence within being of a fundamental property of language. It is "ego" who says "ego." Here one finds the foundation of "subjectivity," which is determined by the linguistic status of the "person."[13]

It is precisely this intimate bond between *saying* and *being* "ego" that would appear to motivate Mouth's desperate shifting away from the shifter: what is at stake is the very determination of the "person," albeit the dramatic person.

The "plot" of the play—as opposed to any underlying story or fabula—is essentially the working-out, without the possibility of any final resolution, of the linguistic-existential agon between the unsaid ego and the oft-stated ea. This less than titanic but, for all that, intense struggle evolves in four phases, each marked by the Auditor's "movement": the first at the climax of the headlong curriculum vitae, which opens the play and culminates in "her" loss of sense: "and she found herself in the— . . . what? . . . who? . . . no! . . . she! . . . (*pause and movement 1*) . . . found herself in the dark"; second, the discovery of "her" own speech: "when suddenly she realized . . . words were— . . . what? . . . who? . . . no! . . . she! (*pause and movement 2*) . . . realized . . . words were coming . . ."; third, the further realization that "she" is doomed to talk forever: "and can't stop . . . no stopping it . . . something she— . . . something she had to— . . . what? . . . who? . . . no! . . . she! . . . (*pause and movement 3*)"; and, last, "her," and Mouth's own, running out of narrative matter before the latter rebegins the telling in even more disorderly fashion: "nothing she could tell . . . nothing she could think . . . nothing she— . . . what? . . . who? . . . no! . . . she! . . . (*pause and movement 4*) . . . tiny little thing. . . ."

That the four phases represent a progression, rather than simply a returning cycle, is suggested by the diminishing force of the Auditor's gestural signal: "It lessens with each recurrence till scarcely perceptible at third." This reduction is proportionate to the *increase* in the intensity of Mouth's agonies, which, in turn, evidently derive from the ever-greater difficulty of maintaining a wedge between the level of the "she," the domain of the narrated, and the level of the "I," the act of narration. This is so acute that in the fourth stage it is the "she" who can no longer narrate. Mouth fights, then, an apparently losing battle—although the struggle has no official denouement—to keep the *énoncé* absolutely separate from her determinedly depersonalized *énonciation*. As Jean Dubois has written:

Let us suppose that the distance [between *énoncé* and *énonciation*] is maximal or, rather, that it tends toward the maximum; this is the instance in which the speaking subject considers his *énoncé* as part of a world distinct from himself. . . . The *I* thus tends to become the formal *he* of the *énoncé*.[14]

Mouth, from her narrative-dramatic purgatory, aspires to the side of the angels, of a controlling *énonciation* quite emptied of subjectivity, but by the same token continually risks becoming "the formal *he* (or *she*) of the *énoncé*," that is, of finding herself in the party of the poor narrated devil of her tale. She admits the danger: "in con-

trol . . . under control . . . to question even this." Ironically, it is
the very absence of a narrating "I," distinct from the narrated *she*,
that renders Mouth's labor of separation not so much Herculean as
Sisyphean. That the separation is illusory in any case—that the "she"
is only a suppressed or repressed "I" and thus the same as the "non
I" of the narrative voice—is left for the spectator to infer, should he
be inclined and should he be cognitively able to do so.

In any event—and whatever the audience's conclusions or incon-
clusions—it is clear that *Not I* is a fully and magisterially *dramatic*
text and that its narrative guise is not a mere expository *disguise*, but
the very condition for the powerful drama of subjectivity it encodes.
Indeed, of all Beckett's plays and perhaps of all late twentieth-century
plays, it is the drama in which the "I," unstable, suffering, depersonalized, is, for all its literal absence, most imposingly felt.

IV   No Tie?

The rhetoric of theater, however, is not limited in its persuasive operations to the body of discourse but is expressed above all through the
body of the actor. Mouth's she-I conflict may prove, on analysis,
eminently dramatic in form and focus, but this does not guarantee
any immediate *theatrical* appeal. It is unlikely that Beckett's "plot,"
namely, Mouth's efforts to translate the threatening here and now of
the dramatic *énonciation* into the remote there and then of a narrative *énoncé*, could exercise even an unconscious hold on the spectator
if there were really no link—as the lack of deictic reference seems to
suggest—with the pragmatic *hic et nunc* of the performance and,
above all, with the immediate doings of the actor (or what is left of
him) onstage.

One apparent point of immediate perceptual and psychological
contact with the representation is the figure of the Auditor, with
whom at least one professional spectator present at the first performance—if only for lack of alternatives in sight—found it "hard not to
identify." The Auditor, with his gestural expression of "helpless compassion," is clearly enough an ideal representative or delegate of the
theatrical audience, so that some degree of identification is indeed
invited: the presence of a stage listener serves as "bridge" between
the *phonē* of Mouth and the all-too-real auditory labors of the theatri-

cal listeners. In this perspective, Not I becomes less a drama of emission than a drama of reception (again, Not I but You).

Still, the Auditor provides cold enough comfort and decidedly
oblique access to the world of Mouth, if Mouth has one. Not only
is he quite uncharacterized (he is even of "sex undeterminable"); he
is all but invisible, being faintly lit, and shrouded as he is in a black
djellaba, and his generally phantasmic appearance is accentuated by
his decentered and "suspended" position (stage left on an invisible
four-foot podium) while his ritual gesture, his one semiotic contribution to the proceedings, his one link with the monologue itself, gradually fades out. Thus, the Auditor turns out to be another no-body,
a dramaturgic chimera or optical illusion who can offer no stable
point of entry into the drama. The play's rhetorical structure remains
dyadic and not triangular, a matter to be fought out without mediation between the agonizing Mouth and the struggling Auditor
proper.

If this is the case, how do Mouth's narrative-dramatic throes relate
to the theatrical occasion in which they are acted out? Are there, in
other words, signs in the monologue itself of the peculiarly *double*,
page-stage textuality that makes possible both the readability and the
performability of the drama?

Certainly, the play is replete with indications of a *literary* textuality
and thus of *some* kind of controlling consciousness although whether
this is attributable to the stage narrator is another matter. At the
most readily perceptible (audible) level of syntax and prosody, for
example, the text is very carefully patterned. Mouth's false starts and
rethinks, interspersed with more or less equal-length pauses, make up
a quasi-musical structure marked not only by verbal leitmotivs or re-
frains—that is, recurring key phrases ("tiny little thing," and so
forth)—but also by a dominant metrical pattern comprising a pentam-
eter with initial and final stress (trochee plus anapaest: $- \smile \smile \smile \diagdown$):

> tiny | little thing
> out be | fore its time
> godfor | saken hole
> speechless | all her days
> even | to herself

once òr | twice à yèar

sùddeñ | urğe ïo tèll

half thĕ | vŏwels wròng

nòthiñg | bŭt thĕ laŕks

It might be noted that these, in some cases repeated, phrases trace out the main lines of development and the main parameters of sense in Mouth's drama. The chief sense unit is, in all cases, the final sylla- able, almost always a monosyllabic word, marked out not only by the stress but also by the pause that follows. The lexical plot is thus: thing . . . time . . . hole . . . days . . . self. . . year . . . tell . . . wrong . . . larks. Here are all the principal paradigms of the text: uncertain temporal reference (time/days/year); the conflict between depersonalization and personification (thing/self); an indeterminate opening or orifice (hole: see the fifth section of this essay); the act of narration (tell); error and guilt (wrong); perceived sound (larks). The semantic coordinates may be perceived only subliminally, if at all, but the prosody itself is imposing.

Such sonic patterns are not simply "poetic" effects, optional dec- orative extras lending the monologue an external textual dignity. They serve, above all, to *materialize* the speech continuum (or, in Mouth's case, discontinuum) and thus to foreground the *phonē* itself as stage "presence" or indeed as theatrical event. In a play like *Not I*, whose efficacy depends in large measure on the voice in its physical as well as narrational qualities, this "embodying" of discourse is indispensable (Beckett's "fundamental sounds" again): there are, after all, no other very substantial bodies about.

There is a further and more explicit mode of textual consciousness in the play. The "inward" (and "backward") looking character of Mouth's references brings her often to refer more or less directly to the act of narration as such, albeit to "her" (the other's) narrating. Mouth's story, the second half of it at least, is largely the telling of a telling or of an urge to tell:

and now this stream . . . steady stream;

no idea what she was saying;

stream of words;

perhaps something she had to . . . tell . . . could that be it? . . . something she had to . . . tell;

something that would tell . . . how it was . . . how she— . . . what? . . . had been? . . . yes . . . something that would tell how it had been . . . how she had lived;

nothing she could tell? . . . all right . . . nothing she could tell; etc.

"She," therefore, is possessed by a sort of text drive that she does not seem able to satisfy for lack of matter ("nothing to tell"). Because Mouth's own dramatic deeds are nothing if not a telling, even if there is nothing to tell, the identification of narrative and metanarrative— the telling with the telling about—is virtually inevitable, not least because at the moment when "she" has run out of things to tell, her life not being exactly rich in incident, Mouth necessarily runs dry as well.

An identification of this kind—irresistibly seductive given the clues —changes, naturally, the whole referential and especially temporal scheme of the play. If "her" hypothetical narration ("something that would tell how it had been") coincides with Mouth's actual narration, then what looks like past reference turns out to be an indication of the current narrative act. The "nows," which in the narrative seem to be adverbs of succession, reacquire their original indexical sense of contemporaneity: "now can't stop . . . imagine! . . . can't stop the stream" becomes a direct description of what is taking place in the dramatic present and is represented to the audience in real (theatrical) time.

But the implications of the telling-about/telling coincidence do not end with this metadiscursive mode of textual self-consciousness. After "her" traumatic discovery of vocal sound, there is an increasing attention in the play to the sheer physical process of speech production. "She," deprived of all other kinesthesia, remains acutely aware of oral sensation and of phonetic mechanics:

when suddenly she felt . . . gradually she felt . . . her lips moving! . . . imagine! . . . her lips moving! . . . what? . . . the tongue? . . . yes . . . the tongue in the mouth . . . all those contortions without touch which . . . no speech possible . . . and yet in the ordinary way . . . not felt at all . . . so intent one is . . . on what one is saying."

Mouth, in effect, offers a clinical account of what she is currently having to go through in order to produce what the audience is currently receiving. She provides, in other words, a vivid impression of what it is to be "the mouth alone," a sort of phenomenology of orality for a public which is instead "intent . . . on what one is saying." And in so doing she also describes—no longer metadiscursively but metatheatrically—what the audience simultaneously sees onstage:

whole body like gone . . . just the mouth.

Here, then, we reach the threshold of an explicit consciousness, within the dramatic text, of the textuality of the performance itself: a consciousness that becomes still more suggestive in the sphere of "her" own, albeit dim, visual perceptions. "She," contemporarily with the discovery of her own voice, perceives uncertainly a strange light of unidentified source:

and all the time this ray or beam . . . like moonbeam . . . but probably not . . . certainly not . . . always the same spot . . . now bright . . . now shrouded . . . but always the same spot . . . as no moon could."

The obvious lexical clue here is "spot," with its inevitable theatrical connotations. If Mouth onstage is the *source* of sound, she is at the same time the *target* of light, whose source, in turn, is precisely a "spot" and "always the same spot" at that. If the telling/telling-about identification holds, then Mouth, for all her visual non-sense (being "mouth alone"), confesses to seeing, from the point of view of its object, the light that enables the spectator to see *her* in turn ("MOUTH . . . faintly lit from close-up and below"). A clear point of comparison is the more overt consciousness of the heads in *Play* with regard to the spot that brings them back to life or at least back to speech:

> Spot from W2 to W1.
> w1: Hellish half-light. . . .
>   spot from W2 to W1
> w1: Get off me! (*Vehement*) Get off me!

Thus, Mouth appears trapped in a kind of cross-channel circuit in which she is condemned to play out forever the paradoxical (and reluctantly self-conscious) theatrical role of illuminated voice. And she is condemned, moreover, to the eternal pains of theatrical audition. Because if Mouth is an eyeless perceiver of faint light (out, damn'd spot), she is still more a perplexed and apparently earless hearer of her own murmurings:

mouth on fire . . . stream of words . . . in her ear . . . practically in her ear . . . not catching the half . . . not the quarter . . . no idea what she's saying . . . imagine! . . . no idea what she's saying! . . . straining to hear . . . piece it together . . .

Here it is Mouth herself—and not the ghostly Auditor—who acts ironically as "internal" dramatic delegate of the suffering public ("straining to hear"), as much as to say that we are all in this together (Not I alone). And what it is that we are all in exactly— Mouth's perception of the playhouse itself—is less than flattering:

sudden urge to . . . tell . . . then rush out stop the first she saw . . . nearest lavatory . . . start pouring it out . . . steady stream . . . mad stuff . . . half the vowels wrong . . . no one could follow . . . till she saw the stare she was getting . . . then die of shame.

Such is Mouth's audience: an assembly of gapers in a place of public convenience.

V Note, Eye

Mouth's not-altogether-distorting mirror held up to the gathering of gapers gaping does, if nothing else, capture the main perceptual attitude of the model spectator who, "straining to hear" and "not catching the half . . . not the quarter" of what he does hear, is nevertheless compelled to stare at what he thinks he sees. Because, quite apart from the catchability or otherwise of its overall "narrative" sense, Mouth's performance exercises an almost literally hypnotic hold on the beholder, who is attracted in any case by the static but mobile point of light held before him. And for most spectators, the staring itself is probably the main experiential business of the occasion: the amoebic form onstage offers its own enigmatic fascinations, inducing the perceiver more or less to abandon conscious cog-

nitive toils and to surrender, instead, to the unconscious or precon-
scious pains, pleasures, speculations, and associations it provokes.

What the spectator actually "sees" onstage is not necessarily restricted a priori to the simple mouth/"mouth" sign relationship.
What he *literally* perceives is a mutable red circle, decentered (upstage audience right) and suspended "about 8' above stage level"—
a position that, together with its disembodied state, weakens the
object's automatic denotation (what is a mouth doing levitated eight
feet up in the air?). In this sense, Mouth's mouth is not only *more*
than it seems, that is, a synecdochic hole standing for a bodily whole
that is not actually shown (and thus a metonynmy for a dramatic
character not fully represented), but in performance is actually *less*
than the text's naming suggests, for even its most immediate definition proves unstable to the perceiving spectatorial eye. And yet it is
precisely this partial bracketing-off of the prefixed cultural unit
("mouth") that allows the stage object to be, as it were, swamped
with sense, opening it up to the free play of the audience's projections.

Octave Mannoni, in his *Clefs pour l'imaginaire*, writes of the "possible alternative," in the audience's experience of the theater, "between identification and projection," adding that "certainly in the
theater projection is a rejected identification."[15] In the case of Beckett's theatrical gapers, the difficulty of identification (of and with
Mouth as "character" or even as object) undoubtedly encourages
projection; the resulting experience is of the "uncanny" kind described by Mannoni—and in a particularly intense form:

in this clear and pleasant perspective, which is that of the theater as it
displays itself, we feel more obscurely the pressure of the unconscious
under the form of a particular uncanniness, at the origin of our interest,
and also a sensation of strange novelty; both are part of the *effet du
théâtre* and accompany, as is known, the unconscious return of the repressed.[16]

This is a quite different psychoanalytic perspective from the attempt
to discern a represented state of mind, for it is limited to the psychic activities of the perceiver (the entity of whose mental facul-
ties is presumably somewhat more verifiable). The range of the spectator's possible projections onto the Mouth is, in theory, unlimited
because the suggestions of his individual unconscious under such con-

ditions are obviously not predictable. But in practice certain power-ful parameters are established both by the items of the collective *imaginaire* and by the promptings of the verbal cotext.

In effect, there are probably no more than three impelling modes of "reading"—whether consciously or not—an oscillating red orifice, and there are strong clues to all three modes in the monologue itself. Mouth's hesitant incipit hints at once at such overdetermination or ambiguity of the object: "godforsaken hole" may be the one *into* which the "tiny little thing" haplessly descends ("this world") or the one *out of* which she is rudely emitted. The first candidate, then, for the spectator's projection-identification is of the orifice as vagina or womb or both. Even without verbal clues, such a viewing of the "hole," given its shape, dimensions, and color, together with the apparent gender of the speaker, is scarcely improbable. Other textual events give body to this vaginal image—"her'" conception; "her" solitary and unpleasurable sexual encounter—events which are, as it were, mimicked at the moment of their telling by the spasmodic activity of the red circle itself.

At the same time or shortly afterward in the progression of the monologue, the orifice reacquires its oral characteristics, but here in the form less of speech-source than of infantile organ deprived of gratification, of contact with the "primal object," the maternal breast:

so no love . . . spared that . . . no love such as normally vented on the . . . speechless infant . . . in the home . . . no . . . nor indeed for that matter any of any kind . . .

In narrative terms, the image of the abandoned infant Mouth search-ing in vain for material sustenance and affection might be interpreted as a cause for the psychosomatic fragmentation to which she is re-duced, as the mater-less matrix for a psychotic experience of the paranoid-schizoid kind theorized by Melanie Klein:

Under the dominion of oral impulses, the breast is instinctively felt to be the source of nourishment and therefore, in a deeper sense, of life itself . . . the ego in varying degrees fragments itself and its objects, and in this way achieves a dispersal of the distinctive impulses and of persecutory anxieties. This process . . . is one of the defences during the paranoid-schizoid position.[17]

But in terms of the audience's *imaginaire* the mouth-(absent)-breast relationship is not so much explanatory as evocative, especially in association with the alternative vaginal image. It is as if the spectator himself were placed in the position of what Klein defines as "early (infantile) confusion, which expresses itself in a blurring of the oral, anal and genital impulses,"[18] whereby the Mouth becomes a kind of floating signifier shifting between, and bringing together, the three Freudian phases of psychosexual development.[19] The third (developmentally the second) of these possible identification-projections, namely, the anal, is the one most directly supported within the monologue. Mouth's lavatorial view of the auditorium transforms her own discursive performance into an altogether different species of emission:

> sudden urge to . . . tell . . . then rush out stop the first she saw . . . nearest lavatory . . . start pouring it out . . . steady stream.

Her earlier anal-verbal retentiveness ("she who but a moment before . . . but a moment! . . . could not make a sound") gives way violently and publicly to a kind of dia-logorrhea ("can't stop").

The putative mouth-anus association is not an isolated instance within the Beckett canon. The dramatist's concentration on "fundamental sounds," despite his own disclaimer—"(no joke intended)"—is, in part, the expression of an abiding fascination with the activities and products of that nether region, with that "throne of the faecal inlet" (*Whoroscope*), which in *All That Fall*, for example, is manifested in Mrs. Rooney's grotesque "lifelong preoccupation with horses' buttocks" (a preoccupation which prompts her to hear a psychoanalytic lecture by Jung in the hope of an explanation), and in *Krapp* in the significantly named protagonist's repeated references to his "old weakness," with his "bowel condition," with "the sour cud and the iron stool" (as in *Not I*, there is a probable pun on "bowel"/ "vowel": compare Mouth's "nearest lavatory . . . steady stream . . . mad stuff . . . half the vowels wrong"). There is more than a suggestion that what Krapp produces, like Mouth, is intricately connected with his name (note the "spooool"/"stool" play).

One can place Beckett's fundamental sounds within the long tradition of exuberantly scatological Anglo-Irish antiverbal satire—what might be termed the *arse rhetorica*—whose motto is the Swiftian "he farted first and then he spoke," quoted in Beckett's most prized reference work, Johnson's *Dictionary*. It is a tradition that expresses a deflating skepticism concerning the pretences of the logos and undermines man's cognitive claims through a colorful version of the *flatus vocis* (voice-flatulence) topos: words are but wind.

But Beckett's "anal" rhetoric is more and less than a satire on linguistic wind or verbal diarrhea. There is actually no phenomenological difference, in Mouth's and Krapp's representations alike, between the bowel movement and the vowel movement, within an autistic corporeal/communicative system in which the speaker-auditor ceases to distinguish between different kinesthetic stimuli and thus between the various forms and sources of bodily emission. The great achievement of *Not I* is to free the spectator's *imaginaire* ("imagine!" says Mouth repeatedly) so as to operate the same kind of "blurring of the oral, anal and genital" aspects of the body in the body's very absence. This has nothing to do with metaphor or allegory, but is the effect of an extraodinarily uncompromising and seductive engagement with the what-not, with that negative *rhetorica*, out of which Beckett has created great ars.

NOTES

1. Letter to Alan Schneider, December 29, 1957; quoted in Deirdre Bair, *Samuel Beckett* (London: Jonathan Cape, 1978), p. 397.
2. Martin Esslin, *An Anatomy of Drama* (London: Temple-Smith, 1976), p. 177.
3. Charles R. Lyons, *Samuel Beckett* (London: Macmillan, 1983), p. 68.
4. Ronald Hayman, *Samuel Beckett* (London: Heinemann, 1968), p. 48.
5. Edith Oliver, review in *The New Yorker*, December 2, 1972, p. 124; reprinted in *Samuel Beckett: The Critical Heritage*, edited by Lawrence Graver and Raymond Federman (London: Routledge and Kegan Paul 1979), pp. 328–29.
6. Benedict Nightingale, review in *The New Statesman*, January 26, 1973, pp. 135–36; reprinted in Graver and Federman, pp. 329–33. Citations from *Not I* and *Play* are from *Collected Shorter Plays of Samuel Beckett* (London: Faber & Faber, 1984).
7. Nightingale, review, pp. 135–36.
8. Lyons, *Beckett*, p. 155.

9. See, for example, Mick's mystifying use of London place-names in *The Caretaker*.

10. See Alessandro Serpieri et al., *Come comunica il teatro: dal testo alla scena* (Milan: Il Formichiere, 1978); Keir Elam, *The Semiotics of Theatre and Drama* (London: Methuen, 1980).

11. Robert Champigny, "Adventures of the First Person," in *Samuel Beckett Now*, edited by Melvin J. Friedman (Chicago and London: University of Chicago Press, 1975), pp. 119–28.

12. Nightingale, review, pp. 135–36.

13. Emile Benveniste, *Problèmes de linguistique générale* (Paris: Gallimard, 1966), pp. 259–60. My translation.

14. Jean Dubois, "Énoncé et énonciation," *Langages*, 13 (1969), 100–110. My translation.

15. Octave Mannoni, *Clefs pour l'imaginaire* (Paris: Editions du Seuil, 1969). My translation.

16. Ibid.

17. Melanie Klein, *Envy and Gratitude: A Study of Unconscious Sources* (London: Tavistock, 1957), p. 3.

18. Ibid., p. 30.

19. See Sigmund Freud, *Three Essays on Sexuality: II. Infantile Sexuality* (1905), in *Standard Edition of The Complete Psychological Works of Sigmund Freud*, translated by James Strachey (London: Hogarth Press, 1953), vol. 2, pp. 173–206.

Beckett and the Act of Listening

BERNARD BECKERMAN

When he was preparing to stage Samuel Beckett's play *Not I*, director Alan Schneider asked Beckett whether the Auditor, a-larger-than-life character rooted firmly and silently onstage throughout the play, was a figure of death or a guardian angel. Beckett, in Enoch Brater's account, "shrugged his shoulders, lifted his arms and then enigmatically let them fall in a gesture of helpless compassion,"[1] thus leaving "the ambiguity [of the figure] wholly intact."[2] This anecdote illustrates Beckett's response to all direct questions about final meanings in his plays. He figuratively shrugs his shoulders, leaving one to make what one can out of an answer that is no more explicit than is the work which provokes the question. So consistent has Beckett been in this regard that critics, directors, and even audiences have at last become reconciled not only to his refusal to offer explanations but also to the likelihood that there are no satisfactory explanations to be offered. "Beckett's plays," Charles Lyons concludes, "do not produce meaning, but rather establish a series of indeterminacies which in turn play on the spectator's imagination and provoke a particular kind of speculation."[3]

But if Beckett's meaning is elusive or, to state the matter more categorically, deliberately incomplete, the theatrical images that provoke the questions are sharply delineated. Over the years Beckett has generated a host of stage pictures so crystallized that they have come

to be accepted as emblems of our distraught age. Two tramps waiting about a bare tree, elderly parents living in ash bins, a well-
preserved blond of fifty sinking into a mound of sand, an old man
hunched over his tape recorder listening to the sounds of his unre-
coverable past—we have lived with these visions for more than a
generation, over which time they have lost none of their disturbing
force. If anything, they have accumulated the associations of our
increasingly fractured period and have become fixed images in our
landscape.

Logic tells us that these images should be unabashedly comic. They
combine antithetical concepts outrageously, so outrageously that the
concepts seem to belong to sophomoric satire or philosophic parody
of the most obvious sort. Old folks in an ash bin! How can a statement on the fortunes of the elderly be more literal? Yet despite the
very baldness of the metaphor, the image is saved from Saturday
Night Live comedy by the concreteness and naturalness with which
it is treated. In the manner of farce, the treatment remains faithful
to its outrageous premise without admitting the existence of that
premise. The image of Winnie, the unrelentingly cheerful heroine of
Happy Days, half-buried in sand, going about her daily chores, invites
but does not sustain allegorical interpretation. Instead, everything she
does, in its absolute ordinariness, accentuates the odd assimilation of
the grotesque to the commonplace. It is by being fantastically literal
that Beckett's images produce so insistent a visual effect.

Among the powerful images that Beckett has impressed on our
minds is one that has gradually come to assume more and more vital
importance in his work. It centers on the motif of speaker and listener. Through the years, that motif has taken on various concrete
expressions until it has led to a type of image so contracted that it
has the quality of "a hard symbolic kernel."[4] Speaking and listening
is, of course, the mode of most drama, but seldom does an author
direct attention to this reciprocal act as an act. Although it is uncertain whether or not Clov does more than pose as auditor of Hamm's
stories in *Endgame*, we are aware of the games between them rather
than of Clov's role as mere listener. It is with *Krapp's Last Tape* in
1958 and then *Happy Days* in 1961 that the prime visual image of
Beckett's drama begins to stress the act of listening. Indeed, it is in
discussing how Beckett directed him in *Krapp's Last Tape* that the
French actor Pierre Chabert speaks of Beckett's insistence on "the

tension present in the act of listening."[5] *Krapp's Last Tape* is the first of Beckett's plays to make that tension explicit. By presenting us with an old man hunched over a tape machine, listening intently to words he recorded thirty years earlier, Beckett fuses speaker and listener, thus providing a closed circuit for nostalgic memories.

In *Happy Days*, by contrast, Beckett begins the process of unhinging the speaker from the listener. The speaker this time is Winnie, gradually sinking into a mound of sand. The listener is her husband, Willie. With the exception of occasional phrases, sometimes his own, more often read from a newspaper, Willie remains unheard and virtually unseen throughout the play. Yet he is present, just on the edge of sight, and the fact that he is there makes living possible for Winnie. "Ah yes," she thinks. "If only I could bear to be alone, I mean prattle away with not a soul to hear. (*Pause.*) Not that I flatter myself you hear much, no Willie, God forbid. (*Pause.*) Days perhaps when you hear nothing. (*Pause.*) But days too when you answer. (*Pause.*) So that I may say at all times, even when you do not answer and perhaps hear nothing, Something of this is being heard. I am not merely talking to myself, that is in the wilderness, a thing I could never bear to do—for any length of time. (*Pause.*) That is what enables me to go on, go on talking that is."[6] In effect, she says: "I live because I can speak, and I speak because I have a listener." This listener, Willie, is her lifeline. Yet it is not the actuality of listening that sustains her, but the image of listening that Willie's presence, however detached, confirms.

The audience clearly perceives the disparity between Winnie as a speaker and Willie as listener, a disparity reflected, moreover, in the contrast between the surreal image of Winnie's plight and the colloquial tone of her conversation. Here Beckett plays one style against another. But as he proceeds to narrow his focus on speaking and listening as abstract functions, he forgoes stylistic contrast and moves toward uniformity of effect. In doing so, he becomes enmeshed in two related problems: first, how to relate the listening a character does to the listening an audience does, and second, how to make images of sound as compelling as images of sight.

In his first disconnections of speaker and listener, the disconnections are situational rather than conceptual. People do listen to themselves on tape recorders; husbands do read newspapers rather than listen to their wives' prattle. In the enactment of such scenes, we, the audience, are located outside the event. We overhear Krapp at sixty-nine years of age commenting on Krapp at thirty-nine; we overhear Winnie talking to Willie and hoping for a reply that will make her day happy. Overhearing is indeed the conventional way we attend to drama. True, since the 1960s plays in which actors address audiences directly have become fashionable. But it is a fashion that Beckett has never adopted. For a few moments Clov seems to focus on the audience in *Endgame*. Turning his telescope on the auditorium, he says, "I see . . . a multitude . . . in transports . . . of joy."[7] This playing at direct communication with the spectator is rare for Beckett either in his early plays or in his late ones. In his early plays, Beckett's characters speak to fictional others, not to the actual us. In his later plays, as we shall see, the nature of the character's relationship to the listener is not always clear.

Particularly significant in this respect is Beckett's short play, *Not I*. Its visual aspect is startling, in some ways more startling than the sight of Winnie half-buried in her mound of sand or even the display of three urns with protruding heads in *Play*. *Not I* presents nothing but the view of a brightly lit mouth moving compulsively in a black void and a shadowy figure, larger than life, facing it. This figure, designated in the stage directions as Auditor ("sex undeterminable"), says nothing, is an absolute listener. Mouth, for that is the name of the never silent, obsessively loquacious organ before us, utters all the lines or rather all the chopped phrases. So literal a juxtaposition of speaker and listener is radically simple, so much so that it challenges the conventionality of Beckett's preservation of fictional space. In *Not I* he appears to open his image to us the audience, enveloping us in the interchange between his stage personae.

Beckett wrote *Not I* in 1972. How long it was in gestation is a matter of dispute.[8] But its emergence, at the time it appeared, may help to explain its chief characteristics. After writing *Play* in 1962–63, Beckett produced some short pieces for radio, film, and television as well as something he called a dramaticule, *Come and Go*, and the even briefer *Breath*. *Come and Go* has barely two pages of dialogue and a page and a half of notes; *Breath*, whose text consists solely of stage directions, hardly fills a single printed page. During the same period, his prose works, namely, *Mercier and Camier*, *No's Knife*, and *The Lost Ones*, are largely pieces of early writing that Beckett had not published hitherto. *Not I*, then, appears almost ten years after his last substantial drama and after a period during which he experimented with radio and video writing. It was in these media, especially in the television play *Eh Joe*, that Beckett carried forward the dissociation of listener from speaker. Seen in this chronological perspective, *Not I* seems to represent a return to theater as a deliberate attempt to explore new ground.

On a visual level, the juxtaposition of Mouth and Auditor could not be simpler. One emits; the other receives. But, in actuality, the Auditor's role as listener is equivocal. The only response the Auditor makes to Mouth's raving is to raise his? her? arms sideways, four times, with decreasing emphasis. But whether the Auditor is monitoring Mouth's utterance, hearing her confession, or standing by helplessly, we cannot be sure. Yet despite our uncertainty, Auditor's presence is vital. Ruby Cohn reports that "in the first Paris production [in 1975] director Samuel Beckett eliminated the auditor."[9] But, as other critics point out, when in 1978 Beckett directed the play a second time, he gave "the role of Auditor . . . greater prominence."[10] The earlier American premiere also made the Auditor prominent. In accord with the printed stage directions, the Auditor stood "downstage and audience left . . . shown by attitude alone to be facing diagonally across [that is, up] stage intent on Mouth."[11] So situated, the Auditor obliquely shares the audience's orientation to the action, and indeed critics and scholars generally consider the Auditor as representative of the audience.

But if the position and stance of the Auditor links him/her to us, the dress and stature alienate us from the figure. Beckett specifies that the Auditor be "enveloped from head to foot in [a] loose black djellaba."[12] One reviewer thought this shadowy apparition might be a symbol of death, another saw the form of a monk, and indeed the vaguely clerical appearance of the long robe encourages a religious reading of the play.[13] For the audience, the figure never entirely connects with Mouth, always seeming somewhat removed. Whether or not we are meant to share in the Auditor's manner of listening is never clearly signaled, nor is it evident what contact, if any, is made between Auditor and Mouth. Neither as a surrogate for the audience then nor as an independent character is the Auditor an effective foil to Mouth. Thus, the speaking-listening relationship is unbalanced, the impetus of the action depending almost entirely on Mouth.

All the reviewers of the initial English-speaking productions remark on the intense and virtually incomprehensible delivery of Mouth's monologue. Apparently, according to Jessica Tandy, who played Mouth in the premiere of Not I, Beckett told her that he was "not unduly concerned with intelligibility. I hope the piece may work on the nerves of the audience, not its intellect."[14] And this is apparently what the actresses sought to do. Both Jessica Tandy in New York and Billie Whitelaw in London spoke with breakneck speed. Miss Tandy's pace, wrote one reviewer, was "dizzyingly rapid." Another described the "aural mosaic of words, which [came out] pell-mell." "The words mean little," noted still another. "An idea darts to the surface, only to sink again in churning fear." Writing of the London production, Benedict Nightingale describes Billie Whitelaw panting and gasping "out the tale of the character to whom it belongs, her broken phrases jostling each other in their desperation to be expressed." All agree that although the gist of Mouth's story comes through, "the breathless pace [of production combined] with the incoherence of the character's thoughts . . . make the piece hard to follow."[15] This, however, Nightingale excuses, for he regards Not I "like good music" that has to be heard more than once to be understood or, better still, read slowly and carefully.

When we turn to the text, as Nightingale recommends, we find that the disjointed phrases, which, when spoken, give the monologue its driving rhythm, when read, describe a struggle and tell a story. The story, like all of Beckett's stories, is not easily penetrated. It has something to do with an elderly woman of seventy who, orphaned from birth and isolated from human contact, has a strange seizure which turns her from an all but mute solitary into a compulsive babbler eager to tell, to tell something, though whether it is her story or some obscure mystery, we never learn. Throughout, Mouth insists on referring to the subject of the story, the elderly woman, as "she." Gradually, the reader perceives that "she" must be Mouth.

Yet although the story may be obscure, the dramatic struggle is quite clear. First of all, it has a dramatic shape; indeed, we might even say a five-act shape. Each miniact, none more than a few minutes long, culminates in identical exchanges between Mouth and Auditor. Mouth insists that the story coming from her is about "she," not herself, to which claim Auditor responds with a "gesture of helpless compassion." The first act is a prologue, introducing the "she" who passed from infancy to seventy years of age without love, without speech until her strange fit one April morning. The second act reports and recreates her sensation ("a buzzing in her ear . . . her brain") after that "insentient" moment, suggesting a confused desperation as she tries to interpret what has happened. The text beautifully indicates the passing thoughts, if they can be properly called thoughts at all, alive with glimmers of insight that finally bring her to the point "when suddenly she realized" words were coming from her. Interwoven with the step-by-step movement toward this realization are recurrent phrases that provide a ground of association for the linear experience. Again and again Mouth qualifies her tale with a recurrent remark: "Oh long after" or "sudden flash" or "Spared that" that meaning "love."

In the third act, she works through her awareness of the compulsive mouthing, recalling her usual inarticulateness and sensing fully the mechanism of speech unbearingly beating at her until she recalls an earlier equal pain when she sat on a little mound in Croker's Acres "staring at her hand . . . there in her lap . . . palm upward . . . suddenly saw it wet . . . the palm . . . tears presumably . . . hers presumably . . . no one else for miles . . . no sound . . . just the tears . . . sat and watched them dry . . . all over in a second."[16] The buzzing in the brain goes on as she mouths recurrent catch phrases: "God is love," "morning sun," "the odd word."[17] The next section introduces the notion that comes to her in a sudden flash: there was

something she had to . . . had to . . . tell . . . could that be it? . . . something she had to . . . tell . . . could that be it: something that would tell . . . how it was . . . how she— . . . what? . . . had been? . . . yes . . . something that would tell how it had been . . . how she had lived . . . lived on and on . . . guilty or not . . . on and on . . . to be sixty . . . something she— . . . what? . . . seventy? . . . good God! . . . on and on to be seventy.[18]

But she seems to retreat from the verge of telling and sinks into babble. The last act recapitulates her compulsion to vomit forth the speech of the past while in the present "all the time the buzzing . . . dull roar like falls . . . in the skull." The buzzing never stops, and she ultimately "not knowing what . . . what she was—," still insists that the person who endures the incessant buzzing is "she! . . . SHE!" not I.

What I have been describing is the potential experience inherent in the script. That potential resides in two pairs of conflicts. First, it resides in the constant tension between past and present, between past speechlessness and present logorrhea. The inability to bridge this gap of time aggravates the conflict within Mouth. After years of silence, broken by rare spasms of uncontrolled garrulity, speech for her must have a purpose, a purpose she faintly perceives but cannot hold to. There is also the second conflict. It is between Mouth's alienation from the subject of the story and her evident familiarity with the most intimate aspects of the character's experience. The rush of speech belies Mouth's function as a mere storyteller. So vivid an evocation of the elderly woman's experience makes Mouth's claim of objectivity incredible. What is compelling in the reading of the play is the immediacy with which Mouth reproduces the woman's sensations, so much so that we cannot attribute such intimacy to anything but personal knowledge. Yet vivid as these sensations are in the writing, little of their individuality comes through in performance. Somehow the terrific force needed to "work on the nerves of the audience" obliterated the details of the experience contained in the words. My own personal response to the New York production of 1972 was the same as that reported by the reviewers: an overwhelming sense of having been through something, but little sense of what that was.

Even after reading the text carefully, one is unlikely to find that the dynamics of the words are recoverable in performance. Beckett has allowed the verbal figures and the narrative ground to intermix in such a way that in the intensity of performance we cannot discern the dramatic shapes. Beckett himself, it appears, was caught in the dilemma of sustaining the driving energy of the play and trying to make it more comprehensible. In the French production with Madeleine Renaud, Beckett sought to speed up her delivery in order to thwart her "penchant for expression."[19] But after seeing the London production, he "took out most of the exclamation points [in the script], slowing the pace of the verbal onslaught."[20] This balancing act also involved the treatment of the Auditor onstage. Beckett never seemed entirely certain about the Auditor's role: was the Auditor a character or a projection of the audience, intended to embody "the tension present in the act of listening"? The Auditor as character seems to have won out at last, for to conclude his French production of 1978, Beckett had the Auditor cover head with hands[21]—a far cry from the figure's austere endurance in the New York premiere of 1972.

But if *Not I* is less than successful in juxtaposing speaking to listening, it is highly suggestive in raising the question whether listening is possible at all. In his next play, *That Time*, also a short piece, Beckett explores once again the relation of disembodied works to passive hearing. *That Time* reverses the visual image, however. Instead of concentrating on a speaking mouth, we now focus on a listening face. From beginning to end, we look on an "old white face, [with] long flaring white hair" suspended in darkness about ten feet above the stage. Beckett calls the character, if character is the proper term, the Listener's Face. Throughout the play the Listener is silent except for the occasional sound of breathing, "audible, slow and regular."[22] When the play begins, the Listener's eyes are open. They close after the first line or two of monologue. Twice this pattern is repeated: eyes open, monologue starts, eyes close. At the end of the play, the Listener once again opens his eyes, smiles for five seconds, and fadeout. Otherwise, the Listener's face is immobile, the closed eyes conveying the impression of deep attention to the three streams of monologue that pour out around him.

From unseen loudspeakers on either side of the stage and from one above the face come the sounds of a single voice, that of the Listener. The sounds are the traces of his memory. Each voice, in a constantly flowing, unpunctuated stream of discourse, relives an incident from old age, middle age, and youth, respectively. Because the incident from middle age involves recollections of childhood, we are witnesses to four past ages of this man. But the listening face represents the man at a still more advanced age, and so we not only hear about his first four ages but gaze on the fifth and presumably last. The three separate streams of discourse are divided into a complex plan of alternation, each stream consisting of twelve separate paragraphs. Voice A tries to fix in memory "that time" when he sought to return to a secret hiding place of his childhood. Voice B revives that youthful time when he lay on "one end of [a] stone she the other,"[23] not touching but loving one another. Voice C speaks of aged wandering from one public building to another, art museum to post office, post office to public library, seeking to escape inclement weather and unexpected reflections of himself. Through it all, the Listener's face betrays nothing of the turbulent flow of memory.

Unlike the Auditor, the Listener's face poses a direct challenge to us in the audience. Even though the words seem to arise from his mind, the fact that the face shows no expression turns it into a kind of projection screen for us. This very blankness, relieved only by the brief opening of the eyes, urges us into a parallel response. Like the Listener, we, too, are listening to interlocking memories. They are not our memories, and yet we listen, as it were, to a recital of a possible past, trying to sort out "that time" when we actually existed. As we concentrate to make sense out of the alternating strands of memory, we face the question Beckett has previously posed but now poses in another way: can listening to ourselves elicit a coherent image of our lives? Are we anything other than listeners to our own memories?

Like Not I, That Time involves a disparity between performance and text. Although it does not have the headlong frenzy of Not I, That Time is hard to follow for different reasons. The continuous, unstopped monologue by a single voice, however distinguished by coming from three different directions, has an incantatory amorphousness. Because repetitive phrases are more numerous and hence more compelling than those in Not I, they promote a hypnotic effect. As one voice segues into another, the audience has great difficulty separating one strand of spoken recollection from another. Everything merges into a rhythmic fog.

Reading the text, on the other hand, reveals the masterly way in which the piece is developed. Again like Not I, the action of That Time is segmented by precise gesture, in this instance by the opening and then closing of the Listener's eyes. Each time his eyes open, a new act begins. There are three acts. The smile closes the play.

Act 1 ends with the puzzled voice of youth telling himself

till hard to believe harder and harder to believe you ever told anyone you loved them or anyone you till just one of those things you kept making up to keep the void out just another of those old tales to keep the void from pouring in on top of you the shroud

Act 2 ends with the thoughts of middle age:

little by little not knowing where you were or when you were or what for place might have been uninhabited for all you knew like that time on the stone the child on the stone where none ever came

Act 3 approaches its end when the aged voice recalls the dust speaking to him in the public library. Then youth evokes the image of "a great shroud billowing in all over" him.[24] Middle age next abandons the pursuit of childhood with not a thought in his head but to get away "to hell out of it and never come back." But, he wonders:

was that another time all that another time was there ever any other time but that time away to hell out of it all and never come back

At the very last the voice of age speaks:

Not a sound only the old breath and the leaves turning and then suddenly this dust whole place suddenly full of dust when you opened your eyes from floor to ceiling nothing only dust and not a sound only what was it it said come and gone was that it something like that come and gone come and gone no one come and gone in no time gone in no time

Three seconds. Eyes open. Five seconds. Smile. Five seconds. Fadeout. And then we might recall that Beckett specifies that the face should be suspended "as if seen from above outspread."[25] "As if seen from above outspread!" As if we, from above, look down on the face, a face buried in dust from floor to ceiling, a face in the grave.

Beckett never seems to have been entirely comfortable with this play. He "occasionally wondered whether the piece was stage drama at all."[26] James Knowlson and John Pilling report a conversation with Beckett from which they surmise that "Beckett was aware *That Time* lay on the very edge of what is possible in theater."[27] They attribute the play's failure as a theater piece to its delicacy.[28] Its "disproportion between the visual and the aural elements is surely too great for a resounding success in the theatre."[29] But its difficulties, in my opinion, lie deeper. They lie at the heart of the theatrical configuration: where to locate the audience psychologically. The blankness of the Listener's face turns the audience into a direct recipient of language rather than an observer of events. Because anything that may be happening within the old man is sequestered behind his impassive mask of listening, the actor's voice must carry the full weight of the drama.

Acting in *That Time* is reduced to a matter of phrasing. None of the thirty-six paragraphs or "versets," in Ruby Cohn's term,[30] are punctuated. Different actors can inflect them differently. Yet Beckett desires a steady, minimally differentiated flow of speech. That precipitates a theatrical problem. The less differentiated one phrase is from another, the harder it is to follow the passage; the more differentiated, then the more obvious and less hypnotic the effect. Clearly, Beckett seeks to "balance audience eye against ear."[31] He strives to fuse a striking visual image in sound, an image that can generate the most intimate access to the audience's psyche. But in *Not I* and in *That Time*, he does not achieve a balance between the dynamic energy needed to sustain stage speech and the comprehension of the pattern embedded in that expulsion of energy. Consequently, he produces a striking visual image and an intriguing literary text, but not an effective theatricalization of the speaker-listener complex. To do that, he would have to do two things: redefine the Listener's relationship to the audience and reexamine the proportion between repetitive and propelling phrases.

Before considering how Beckett managed these two things, I should like to detour into the more general question of actor-audience relationship. By the logic of its form, theatrical presentation presupposes a direct communication by the performer to the audience. After all, the performer comes before the spectator solely to show himself or herself in some interesting and unusual way. That purpose is readily admitted in those types of performance where the performer overtly displays a skill as in acrobatics, magnificence as in pageantry, artfulness as in tricks of illusion, and elegance in many forms of dance. But when the performer seeks to produce an illusion of fictional events, he or she has to create a private space distinct from the space inhabited by the audience. The most common and most effective way the performer does this is by focusing attention on another performer and ignoring the audience. In creating a fiction between themselves, the actors induce and sustain a hypothetical world. For the audience, access to this world is indirect. It no longer hears the actors but overhears them. Inevitably, the audience loses immediate contact, but what it loses in contact, it gains in imaginative involvement. It gains entrance to the hidden life represented by the actor's activity.

Two actors working together are all that are needed to create this hypothetical world. Beckett, either because of his deep immersion in Greek literature or because of a natural dramatic instinct, understands that and rarely strays from the composition of two-person scenes or duets. In his use of duets, he may be said to be the most classic of authors. Although the Greek tragedians relied almost exclusively on the duet for building their action, they did have the chorus to relieve monotony. Beckett is more austere. Even in *Waiting for Godot*, when Pozzo and Lucky join Estragon and Vladimir onstage, Beckett doesn't stray far from a binary pattern. In speaking to Pozzo, Gogo and Didi either alternate speeches with Pozzo so that they function as one, or they reinforce each other in succession so that they seem to maintain a continuous conversation. In his later plays, Beckett emphasizes the dualism even more rigorously, *Endgame* having only two brief transitional sections where Nagg and Nell intrude on the byplay of Hamm and Clov. *Krapp's Last Tape* and *Happy Days* carry the contraction still further, the onstage figure often addressing an unseen secondary person on tape or behind a hill.

In the standard duet, one character is usually engaged in a transforming encounter with another. That is, one character tries to transform the terms of understanding with the other. Put another way, we might say that one *self* seeks to neutralize the alien *other* and absorb or obliterate it. Depending on the theatrical culture and the individual artist, the assault of one self on the other may be extremely direct (as in Greek tragedy) or quite tangential (as in Chekhov). The most direct confrontations in Beckett occur in *Waiting for Godot* and *Endgame*. There the masters Pozzo and Hamm impose themselves on their subordinates so massively that we tend to find parodies of dramatic encounters rather than the encounters themselves. But it is not long before Beckett abandons the simple duality of such open confrontation and adopts more elusive patterns of exchange.

In *Play*, for example, he explores a middle ground between direct and indirect address. Once again the visual image is striking. At front and center of the stage, Beckett places "three identical grey urns . . . about one yard high. From each a head protrudes . . . [Each head faces] undeviatingly front throughout the play,"[32] unaware of the others besides it. A spotlight relentlessly cues each head to speak and so acts as an impersonal master of ceremonies. Although the three heads tell overlapping stories, they speak neither to each other nor to the audience, but at some remembrance of the past. As a result, the tripartite image of bodiless voices is unitary rather than binary. It engages in none of the dialectic exchange that characterizes action in a duet. Only the mechanical force of the light cue suggests interaction of any sort.

But ten years later, with the writing of *Not I*, Beckett returns to the duet, though a substantially altered one. The grotesque juxtaposition of Mouth and Auditor schematizes the idea of duality. By abstracting each element, Beckett disembodies the performer in a novel way and deals with the pure energies of dramatic exchange. At the same time he appears to relocate the audience in respect to the duet. He seems to associate the Auditor with the audience, but in so inconclusive a manner that the contact between the two is not made. *That Time*, in its turn, relocates the audience more radically. It undermines any sense of detachment without completing identity. Beckett's insistence on a single, continually flowing expression is an attempt to concentrate full dramatic energy in one half of a duet so that the other half becomes a neutral reflector of audience imagining.

In two of his subsequent plays, *Footfalls* in 1975 and *Rockaby* in 1981, Beckett continues to dissociate speaker and listener. Following the model of *That Time*, he keeps the dominant voice offstage. Only with the writing of *Ohio Impromptu*, in 1981, does he bring both the speaker and listener onstage again. For the third time in his plays, Beckett introduces a silent figure openly designated as Listener. This time the Listener is paired with a Reader. More richly than he has done hitherto, Beckett plays with patterns of duality, particularly in setting visual image against auditory image. On the surface at least, he does this by returning to the more conventional relationship between audience and action. Listener and Reader are represented by fully human beings who inhabit a fictional, albeit abstracted, space. Unquestionably engaged with each other in a "mimetic" event, they present us with a situation that we can follow even if we have difficulty interpreting it.

Visually, *Ohio Impromptu* is stark and virtually static. As the lights fade in, we see two figures seated at a plain white table. Measuring four feet by eight feet, with the long side facing the audience, the table has a "black wide-brimmed hat" at the center. Behind the table, somewhat toward the audience right, sits the Listener. Still further to the audience's right, at the end of the table and in profile, sits the Reader. (Actually, in the New York performance, the table was set diagonally onstage and slightly raked toward the audience so that Listener and Reader faced each other obliquely.) Both figures appear to be reflections of each other. Both are garbed in long black coats and crowned by long white hair. Both sit with heads bowed and propped on their right hands. Their left hands rest on the table. The only difference between them is that Reader has a book before him, opened to its last pages whereas Listener has nothing before him. White light gives the scene a sharp edge.

Immediately we are made aware of the interplay between sameness and diversity, unity and duality. The figures replicate each other, and yet the book separates them. Moreover, when Reader turns a page and starts to read aloud from the text before him, the contrast of speaking and listening asserts itself once again. Throughout, only the Reader speaks, and virtually all he speaks comes from the book he is reading. Listener, like the Auditor of *Not I*, is limited to gesture. This time, however, gesture is more authoritative. Periodically, Listener raps sharply on the table with his left hand, seemingly to correct and then prod the Reader. Interaction between them is more evident than it was between Auditor and Mouth, although the meaning of the interaction is not necessarily any more decipherable. Nor do Listener's gestures identify the phases of the action as precisely as in the earlier plays. Rather, they reinforce the action, causing it to proceed less schematically and, as a consequence, more powerfully.

That action consists of Reader going through the last pages of his book. Here Beckett returns to formal storytelling, an activity that he used to such effect in *Endgame*. As in *Endgame*, the story that unfolds may or may not be autobiographical. But whereas our uncertainty about this fact in *Endgame* was due to the lack of corroboration between the events of the story and observable events of the play, the uncertainty in *Ohio Impromptu* arises from contradictory hints between the oral recital we hear and the visual image we see. As a result, we experience tension in various forms: between clues that suggest Reader and Listener are identical and clues that indicate their distinction from each other; between clues that point to the scene as an illustration of the story being read and clues that make the story a product of the scene being observed; and, finally, between clues that treat Listener as our alter ego and clues that distance him from us.

The outline of the story being read is simple enough. The Reader's first words, "Little is left to tell," inform us that the tale is near its close. An unnamed "he," apparently after a love affair that has ended in death of the dear one, attempts to obtain relief from . . . what? his sense of loss? by moving to a single room where "he could see the downstream extremity of the Isle of Swans." He spends his days pac-

ing the islet in his black coat and his "old world Latin Quarter hat,"
like the coats and hat we see before us. In his dreams his dear one
had warned him against moving away, had urged him to "stay where
we were so long alone together, [for there] my shade will comfort
you." He wonders whether he can return but concludes that "No.
What he had done alone could not be undone. Nothing he had ever
done alone could ever be undone. By him alone." This realization
terrifies him. Once again, as before, "white nights [are] his portion.
As when his heart was young. No sleep no braving sleep till . . .
dawn of day."

   "Little is left to tell," Reader continues. During one of his sleep-
less nights, a man appears, sent he said by the dear one to comfort
the fearful man. From his black coat the stranger draws a volume out
of which he reads until dawn. Then he disappears. From time to time
"unheralded" the man would appear, "read the sad tale through again
and the long night away," and then disappear. In the course of time
"with never a word exchanged they grew to be as one [until] the
night came at last when having closed the book and dawn at hand
[the stranger] did not disappear but sat on without a word." Finally,
he says that he shall not come again. "I saw the dear face and heard
the unspoken words, No need to go to him again, even were it in
your power." They sit on together "as though turned to stone . . .
buried in who knows what profounds of mind. Of mindlessness.
Whither no light can reach. No sound. The sad tale a last time told."
There is a pause. Reader concludes, apparently still reading from the
book: "Nothing is left to tell." He starts to close the book. A knock
from Listener stops him. He repeats, "Nothing is left to tell." He
closes the book. Listener knocks again. Reader and Listener remain
silent for five seconds, then "Simultaneously, they lower their right
hands to the table, raise their heads and look at each other. Unblinking. Expressionless."

   The tale has elements of a ghost story. It floods the play with a
spirit that comes closest to those affinities with the No drama that
Yasunari Takahashi has pointed out. The men before us share a story,
but the story haunts them. In their partnership of teller and told,
they mirror the *waki* and *shite* of the No, the former earthbound, the
second the tormented soul of one dead, often unable to free himself
or herself from a long-lost love. Suffused with this unearthly spirit,
the play evokes "profounds of mind"—Takahashi associates these
"profounds" of mind with the "unknown country" of the No—with-

out defining the relationship of the two men onstage to the story. On the face of it, they are the two men of the tale. But which is which? Charles Lyons as well as Takahashi claims that the Reader is the man who has brought comfort and the Listener the bereft lover.[33] But this explanation does not accord with the way the reading unfolds. From time to time, as we heard, Listener interrupts Reader with a knock. The result is to force Reader to go back and repeat a line or two. After he does so, Listener knocks a second time, seemingly as a signal for Reader to proceed. At one point Reader is about to turn the pages back to an earlier description of the lover's "fearful symptoms" in the night. Listener, however, checks him with a gesture. In such ways, Listener seems to exercise control over Reader, the reverse of what the tale describes in which it is the man who reads the tale who is in command.

Furthermore, the story seems to report what has already happened. It tells how the stranger has closed the book which he is reading although it is plain to us that the Reader has yet to close the book. Is the story thus foretelling as well as telling? In its last description of the two men sitting "as though turned to stone," the story seems to be foreshadowing what we see a few moments later, the two men looking at each other. But are there two men? The single hat on the table before us indicates that there may be only one, that they are shades of each other. The image flickers: they are and are not one with the figures in the tale.

My last point in this essay repeats my first: we cannot be sure of final meaning in *Ohio Impromptu*. But we can be sure of our experience. In *Ohio Impromptu* we oscillate between singleness and duality. It is significant that it is the Listener who is placed upstage, facing the audience, as though he might have something to say to us or the other character. Initially, we are led to assume that he shares a common action with the Reader. As the play proceeds, however, we find ourselves sharing the role of listening with him, and because we are listening to a story that we can follow, we don't expect much of a response from the Listener but await the outcome of events. We fall under the spell of the story. Then we discern in the scene elements that exist in the story. We are drawn about the whitened table and that haunted recitation. When Reader merges into Listener as they exchange glances, we experience that sensation, so chillingly described by Beckett, of being "alone together."

Ohio Impromptu is an extraordinary play. In it Beckett achieves that fusion of visual image and poetic voice that escaped him in the two earlier plays I discussed. And he does this by finding a way to position us, the audience, both inside and outside the experience at one and the same time. Every theatrical artist has the task of knowing where to place his audience imaginatively. It is *not* what he tells us that strikes deeply *nor* what he shows us, *but* where and how he places us so that we feel the distinctive pulse of fantasy life. It is evident that for some years Beckett wished to bring us to confront individually and isolatedly the experience of life expiring. But how to place so singular and singly an event in a medium that thrives on doubleness: doubleness of performer and spectator, of perceptible and imperceptible action, of illusion and reality? His direct assaults of *Not I* and *That Time* failed to bring impact and idea together. With his use of Listener in *Ohio Impromptu*, however, he enables us to hover on the mysterious border of living and dying. He does this by giving us a literal image of the duality that is the root of drama and then questioning the separateness not only of the two figures but of each of us who is a listener. More adroitly than anywhere else, he makes us aware of the "tension present in the act of listening," either to others or to ourselves.

NOTES

1. Enoch Brater, "Dada, Surrealism, and the Genesis of *Not I*," *Modern Drama* 23 (March 1975), 57.
2. James Knowlson and John Pilling, *Frescoes of the Skull: The Later Prose and Drama of Samuel Beckett* (London: John Calder, 1979), p. 197.
3. Charles R. Lyons, *Samuel Beckett* (London: Macmillan, 1983), p. 70.
4. Jacqueline Piater, "Review: *Mercier and Camier*," *Le Monde*, June 13, 1970; reprinted in *Samuel Beckett: The Critical Heritage*, edited by Lawrence Graver and Raymond Federman (London: Routledge and Kegan Paul, 1979), pp. 307–8.
5. Pierre Chabert, "Becket as Director," in *Gambit* 28 (1976), 50.
6. Samuel Beckett, *Happy Days* (New York: Grove Press, 1961), pp. 20–21; (London: Faber & Faber, 1962). Subsequent page references to this play are from the Grove Press edition.
7. Samuel Beckett, *Endgame* (New York: Grove Press, 1958), p. 29; (London: Faber & Faber, 1958). Subsequent page references to this play are from the Grove Press edition.

8. Knowlson and Pilling, Frescoes, p. 196.
9. Ruby Cohn, Just Play: Beckett's Theater (Princeton: Princeton University Press, 1980), p. 69.
10. Knowlson and Pilling, Frescoes, p. 198.
11. Samuel Beckett, Collected Shorter Plays (New York: Grove Press, 1984), p. 216; (London: Faber & Faber, 1984). All quotations from Not I, That Time, Rockaby, Ohio Impromptu, and Play are from the Grove Press edition.
12. Beckett, Collected Shorter Plays, p. 216.
13. See Walter Kerr, "Beckett, Yes, but Also a Tandy-Cronyn Festival," The New York Times, December 3, 1972; and Edith Oliver, "Review: Not I," The New Yorker, December 3, 1972, pp. 124–25.
14. Enoch Brater, "The 'I' in Beckett's Not I," Twentieth Century Literature 20 (July 1974), 200.
15. See Harold Clurman, "Review: Not I," The Nation, December 11, 1972; Oliver, review, p. 124; Clive Barnes, "Review: Not I," The New York Times, November 23, 1972, p. 49; and Benedict Nightingale, "Review: Not I," The New Statesman, January 26, 1973, reprinted in Graver and Federman, The Critical Heritage, pp. 329–33.
16. Beckett, Collected Shorter Plays, pp. 220–21.
17. Ibid., p. 221.
18. Ibid.
19. Cohn, Just Play, p. 266.
20. Brater, "Dada, Surrealism and the Genesis of Not I," p. 53.
21. Knowlson and Pilling, Frescoes, p. 198.
22. Beckett, Collected Shorter Plays, p. 228.
23. Ibid.
24. Ibid., p. 234.
25. Ibid., p. 238.
26. Cohn, Just Play, p. 269.
27. Knowlson and Pilling, Frescoes, p. 219.
28. Ibid.
29. Ibid., pp. 219, 220.
30. Cohn, Just Play, p. 72.
31. Ibid.
32. Beckett, Collected Shorter Plays, p. 147.
33. Lyons, Beckett, p. 184; Yasunari Takahashi, "The Theatre of Mind: Samuel Beckett and the Noh," Encounter 58 (April 1982), 72.

Beckett's Auditors:
Not I to Ohio Impromptu

KATHARINE WORTH

In the phase of his art from *Not I* to *Ohio Impromptu*, Beckett's long-standing preoccupation with "auditors" and the process of listening has been expressed in startlingly new dramatic forms and opened up new domains of feeling. The favorite situation of earlier plays, a struggle between listener and voices crowding in on him from the void (as in *Embers* or *Eh Joe*), has given way to an altogether more benign, if still somber and mysterious, process, in which listeners cooperate more easily with the voices and sounds that come to them, often without effort on their part. Sometimes, as in *Rockaby*, the listener identifies a recorded voice as his or her own by joining in with it; sometimes the relation between teller and listener is more ambiguous (as in *Footfalls* and *Ohio Impromptu*) but equally without tension and struggle. Listeners may still perform rituals to bring sounds into being, as do the figures in *Ghost Trio* and . . . *but the clouds* . . . , but even then there is a dreamlike sense of being carried along on an irresistible wave, possibly to a longed-for climax.

Whatever it may be, the thing they are listening to—or for—is of supreme value, seeming to hold the meaning of a life. Though elusive—in *Not I* painfully so—it can be grasped, as it is in *That Time*, with unusual certitude and calm.

"Calm" would seem a very odd word for the first play I wish to consider. *Not I* (1972) is a play of agony which has strong links with the television play almost immediately preceding it, *Eh Joe*. In both, a woman's voice unrolls a tale of misery which the listener, male in *Eh Joe*, sex unknown in *Not I*, is obliged to endure helplessly. The listeners in both plays are mute throughout. *Not I* might well seem to belong with *Eh Joe* and those earlier radio plays in which disembodied voices or unstoppable sounds build up narratives involving the listener figure in pain and anxiety. These listeners would avoid if they could the woeful sounds they cannot help but hear. Henry in *Embers* talks busily and incessantly to try and extinguish the sound of the sea which invades all his pauses; the Opener in *Cascando* is drawn against his will into the agitation of the Voice he claims only to "open" and "close," and Joe, as his voice knows, will struggle to still her, doing so at last in a violent act of will, "mental thuggee," as she dryly puts it.

In these plays, Beckett gives us an alarming glimpse into the artist's vulnerability to "voices" only he can hear, voices which seemingly threaten to take him over—unless he can find a channel to release them for an audience outside himself. Reluctant, perplexed, terrorized, the listeners of that phase are in a dangerous and uneasy relationship with their voices.

With *Not I*, however, we have a change. The listener—called Auditor—is kept at a distance from the ordeal undergone by the Voice, in this play reduced to the physical organism from which the voice emerges, Mouth. Both are located in the same unearthly void: the Auditor stands on an invisible podium four feet above stage level, diagonally opposite the luridly lit Mouth, eight feet up in the stage dark. But though off the ground, Auditor is closer to the ordinary expectations of reality, being all there, for one thing, and standing upright, at a safe (though perhaps really fatal) distance from the raging Mouth as she pours out the story of a wretched, "speechless" life in an intense babble of seemingly uncontrollable broken phrases.

The silent, still figure, wrapped in the loose, black, hooded djellaba which conceals the sex, is suggestive of some force or faculty bound up with the fate of Mouth. From start to last, the Auditor is "intent on Mouth." Attention never relaxes, and, despite the "safe" distance between them, there is an emotional connection, for each time Mouth refuses to tell her story of the orphan waif in the first rather than the third person—". . . what? . . . who? . . . no! . . . she! . . ."— Auditor makes the significant movement of raising and dropping the arms, which Beckett tell us is "a gesture of helpless compassion."

What then is the function of the Auditor? Is this primarily a counseling figure, as it might be a doctor, nurse, psychiatrist, or priest, someone whose professional business is to listen, diagnose—and perhaps cure? Some such suggestion is undoubtedly made by the still, watchful presence in conjunction with the symptoms described by Mouth, which are often overwhelmingly and terrifyingly physical; the sense of being cut off, plunged into the dark ("all went out . . ."), the buzzing in the head, the sudden flashes, the dissociation ("whole body like gone"), the loss of feeling ("no part of her moving . . . that she could feel . . . just the eyelids . . ."). Central in this shockingly vivid account of the physical organism is the sense of speech getting out of control, flowing out like an illness, beyond the power of the brain to shape, and all the stranger because in her life the woman Mouth tells of was almost speechless:

. . . now can't stop . . . imagine! . . . can't stop the stream . . . and the whole brain begging . . . something begging in the brain . . . begging the mouth to stop . . .

For most people, as criticism has indicated, thoughts of doctors, hospitals, strokes, brain damage will inevitably be called up by these graphic descriptions of the void in which the woman nearing seventy finds herself.

Clearly, too, we can recognize the possibility of psychological causes for the trouble Mouth is in. The story she tells is the story of a life deprived of love and full of bitterness. Born illegitimate ("parents unknown") and premature, the "tiny little thing" goes through life as a waif and orphan, hardly able to express herself, even in the most mundane situation, like shopping at the supermart: ". . . then stand there waiting . . . any length of time . . . middle of the throng . . . motionless . . . staring into space . . . mouth half open as usual . . . ." She has had a listener only when there was official necessity, as when in court for some offense—"Speak up woman . . ."— or when, overcome by private need, she has pounced on a stranger: ". . . then rush out stop the first she saw . . . nearest lavatory . . . start pouring it out . . . steady stream . . . mad stuff . . . half the vowels wrong . . . no-one could follow . . . ."

In that light, the Auditor's absorbed attention may well seem the professional listening of a psychiatrist, someone who may have deliberately induced or encouraged a long repressed accumulation of emotion. Or, from another angle, a priest is attending to the spiritual desperation of a woman whose life experience has turned her against God, who mocks both her own need for love ("spared that") and the concept of divine mercy:

. . . brought up as she had been to believe . . . with the other waifs . . . in a merciful . . . [Brief laugh] . . . God . . . [Good laugh].

In line with her experiences, God is more likely to mean punishment: this is the first thought she has—for she acknowledges the brain can still function ("still . . . still . . . in a way")—after "all went out" and she found herself "in the dark." She was to be made to suffer for her sins—but she was not suffering—so what is the purpose of her ordeal? That there is a purpose she seems intent on believing.

In this sphere of judgment, she and the Auditor are in complicity. She establishes the idea of a purgatorial dimension, speculating on the possibility that she is meant to be suffering and wondering why she does not suffer more. The naming of the silent listener as an Auditor looks like Beckett's confirmation of her anxious thought. An auditor scrutinizes accounts, and as the OED puts it, "listens judicially and tries cases, as in the Audience Court." In the theater the Auditor does indeed exercise the function of listening "in an Audience Court." Judgment is involved, on the part of audience as well as characters. We cannot escape an awareness that Mouth, for all her seeming openness—she claims that she is "incapable of deceit"—is making one gigantic evasion. She cannot bring herself to acknowledge the waif's story as her own: the fourfold shrieks of "vehement refusal to relinquish third person" are moments of failure, as is made clear by the placing of the Auditor's gestures "of helpless compassion" at just these points.

In the television version of the play (BBC, 1977), that aid to judgment disappeared. The Auditor was gone: we were left with a very extraordinary experience, but surely a less complex and subtle play. We know that Beckett was fascinated by the strange spectacle of the human mouth seen in televisual close-up as a kind of writhing marine organism, and that he greatly admired Billie Whitelaw's virtuoso performance. For this he was obliged to lose the Auditor.

Just how much was lost it is possible to see, with both stage and television experiences in mind. In the theater Mouth is not babbling into a void, as on the screen. There is someone listening; there is someone judging—not in the punitive sense, but in the sense of reckoning what needs to be done to put right what has gone wrong. Is there any comfort in this, we may ask. What use is it to have a "helpless" Auditor, however compassionate? Better than having none, perhaps; better to have a witness, the suffering to be registered, recorded, as artists register and record. In one aspect the Auditor indeed looks like a surrogate for the artist; Beckett drew inspiration from Caravaggio's painting *The Beheading of St. John the Baptist*, where, as has been said,[1] "a shadowy group in the background observes the beheading." The observers are helpless: yet one observer has made the picture, given us a unique understanding of the experience. In a later play, *Catastrophe* (1982), Beckett has expressed his sensitivity to the moral ambivalence of the artist's role: perhaps something of that feeling colors the presentation of the Auditor, whose gestures of compassion lessen with each recurrence "till scarcely perceptible at third."

Yet the Auditor cannot be seen only as a figure separate and utterly distinct from Mouth. There is also an impression that this may be a case of violent dislocation, as in Caravaggio's picture, and that the Auditor has to be located within the psyche which has split up: though it feels itself to be no longer receiving messages, that may not be the case.

From where else, after all, do the thoughts and questions come which pull her up from time to time, force her to confront truths she is desperate to avoid? In the very thick of presenting herself as helplessly detached from her own words and deeds—("no idea what she was saying")—she will suddenly admit to having been in the grip of delusion: ". . . till she began trying to . . . delude herself . . . it was not hers at all . . . not her voice at all." She can see, really, that she is her words: "the whole being . . . hanging on its words." She has the recurring conviction that she hasn't got the story right yet: there is "something she had to . . . tell." The one admission she cannot make is the one for which the Auditor is waiting: that it was she herself who did and suffered the things experienced in the story she is compelled to tell.

If she were able to say, "I," we may imagine that the separation between Mouth and Auditor would end and a new, unified being emerge, one capable of seeing beyond the pain of her life to the freer dimension just envisaged in the lyrical image of the April morning and the field where the woman nearing seventy gathered cowslips. In an early draft of the play, Beckett had Mouth seeking a distant "bell," glossing this in the margin with Ariel's line "In a cowslip bell I lie."[2] This is an echo which suggests that the possibility of freedom is always there, even if in the confines of the play Mouth cannot win an Ariel-like release.

The presence of the Auditor is what allows the audience to believe in that possibility. Whatever we make of the ambiguous figure—human healer, angelic judge, Jungian archetype—we cannot but feel that it is benign, and it is a point of rest. "Listening," source of such unrest and unease in earlier plays, has here become an island of calm in a tormented sea.

In the next play, *That Time* (1974–75), a calmness extends to take in both listener and narrating voice. They are, in a way, one. The old man whose face alone is visible high in the stage dark is listening to his own voice—or voices—and is listening without sign of strain or resistance. No question here of the listener, now called unambiguously Listener, refusing to acknowledge the life experience narrated as his own. Yet ambiguity remains: the recorded voices are not just an ingenious way of dressing up a long monologue so as to make it less theatrically monotonous. The relationship between Listener and voices is enigmatic, raising questions not dissimilar from those of *Not I* about the way the self sees and reflects its life experience.

That Time, too, eschews the use of the first person. The old man whom we see only as an "Old white face, long flaring white hair as if seen from above outspread," is addressed by his voices as if from space outside rather than inside him. The three voices, A, B, C, come from different areas of the stage, a physical effect which reinforces the impression that they have a life of their own distinct from the passive listener whom they call on to remember the times of his life. There is even at one point a suggestion that, despite the enormous difference in style between the calm and melodious voices and Mouth's raging, this play, too, might be concerned with evasion of

the self: ". . . for God's sake did you ever say I to yourself in your
life come on now," says Voice C, repeating for emphasis, "could you
ever say I to yourself in your life."

There is a great difference here, however. The question is voiced;
it can be received by the Listener and so assimilated into the web
that is being spun from the life experience, not avoided. Perhaps he
would prefer to avoid it: we might wonder whether it is significant
that his eyes close at just the point where it is asked. But the closing
of the eyes, which occurs three times, actually heralds each long
sequence of reflection and is an acceptance of inward probing rather
than an evasion of it.

The physicality of the event in the theater makes very clear to us
the paradox Beckett has built into the "listening" structure. The
voices are outside the old man, but yet somehow inside. They are
separate strands, yet all one. The separateness was important; the
switch from one voice to another was to be "clearly faintly perceptible." In the first production at the Royal Court Theatre in 1976, the
effect was strengthened by tonal variations; Beckett had suggested
some mechanical assistance such as threefold pitch might be needed.

Separation is maintained, too, through a context in which each
voice has its own special sphere. Yet, even as we realize this, we realize too how closely they are joined. Voice A is preoccupied with
childhood:

or talking to yourself who else out loud imaginary conversations there
was childhood for you ten or eleven on a stone among the giant nettles
making it up now one voice now another till you were hoarse and they
all sounded the same . . .

Voice B recalls the time of lovers:

muttering that time altogether on the stone in the sun or that time together on the towpath or that time together in the sand that time that
time making it up from there as best you could always together somewhere . . .

Voice C dwells on old age:

was your mother ah for God's sake all gone long ago all dust the lot you
the last huddled up on the slab in the old green greatcoat with your arms

round you whose else hugging you for a bit of warmth to dry off and on to hell out of there and on to the next . . .

In these passages, as throughout, the reflections overlap: recurring phases and images such as the "stone" link the scenes of childhood to those of maturity, and in all the different phases the same spirit is heard at work, "making it up," making "one voice now another," continually turning over the times of his life, registering what is bleak or grim as well as what is beautiful—the dead rat in the lovers' landscape, the ruined tower that calls into consciousness what has been lost—"all gone long ago"—along with the vividness that once was.

We are continually aware of both the separateness and the oneness of the life revealed in the tripartite narrative. The voices are the Listener's own: Beckett wanted there to be no mistake about their essential unity. They are "moments of one and the same voice"; they "relay one another without solution of continuity." There was certainly no question of doubting that unity when in the first production Patrick Magee's rich tones encircled the Listener and the audience.

So this Listener, we may say, has achieved a unity of being denied to Mouth and her Auditor. But is this more than passive acceptance of what life has given and taken away? Certainly, the Listener is in a passive situation, on a death bed, some have thought, judging from the curious view of the hair, flaring out "as if seen from above outspread." We hear his breathing, slow and regular; we see his eyes open, at the beginning and the end and twice in between; otherwise they are closed. All this might be consonant with the kind of drifting reverie of an ill or dying man.

However, such a view does not begin to account for the power of the play: the Listener's physical reactions are minimal, but what has come out from him—the meditation woven by the voices—is a work of extreme energy, enough to exhaust its maker, though perhaps only for the time being.

Although in *That Time* the images are aural rather than visual, the nature of the Listener's verbal tapestry calls to mind Jung's account of the process of meditation:

In old age one begins to let memories unroll before the mind's eye and, musing, to recognise oneself in the inner and outer images of the past.

This is like a preparation for an existence in the hereafter. . . . The inner images keep one from getting lost in personal retrospection. . . .[3]

The final comment seems highly appropriate to *That Time*. The Listener's voices recall his own life to him, but in such a way that he is not "lost in personal retrospection." The recognition of truths is involved: the self sees itself, as in the wonderful passage in the Portrait Gallery when the Listener peers into the "vast oil black with age and dirt," picturing "some famous man or woman or even child such as a young prince or princess some young prince or princess of the blood black with age behind the glass." And a face appears which "had you swivel on the slab to see who it was there at your elbow." The self of the Listener is placed against the images of antiquity. And always, in the sound pattern he has drawn from his life, there is the sense of renewing as well as of decline and loss.

There are times of spiritual panic: "just another of those tales to keep the void from pouring in on top of you the shroud." And there is the sadness of losing feelings that were once intense: ". . . hard to believe harder and harder to believe you ever told anyone you loved them or anyone you. . . ." But there is no claim such as Mouth makes that this is a peculiarly hard lot. It is unusual only in that there is this searching imagination at work, going back, recalling, examining, and, above all, weaving the separate strands into one distinctive voice, with stoicism and humor, till even the void can be faced: "a great shroud billowing in all over you on top of you and little or nothing the worse." And finally, the magnificent image that draws everything together, the little details of ordinary life and the visionary awareness of life sub specie aeternetatis; the public library where the old ones draw their "old breath," and suddenly all becomes dust:

the whole place suddenly full of dust . . . and not a sound only what was it said come and gone was that it something like that come and gone come and gone no one come and gone in no time gone in no time

The Listener listens so well that he hears the still small voice where at first there was "no sound." With the aid of his voices he has drawn out of the personal life a vision that floats free of him, is both his and not his. Perhaps he is recognizing his achievement when at the close his eyes open and he gives us something unexpected and delicious, "a smile; toothless for preference." Perhaps, as some have thought, he is signaling his pleasure at being still safely tethered to the earth despite the transcendent experience. Or perhaps it is a Nunc Dimittis. Interpretation, as always, remains open. One theme is sure: what the Listener hears is something that has been completed, brought to a satisfying close. He has no more work to do on it.

In the play that falls naturally into place beside *That Time*, *Rockaby* (1981), the process of listening to a recorded voice is almost, but not quite, complete. The act of completion is both desired and pushed away with the recurring lines: "Time she stopped" and "More." It is the old woman in the rocking chair in person who cries, "More"; that cry—on a rivetingly high, thin note in Billie Whitelaw's performance—opens the action and seems to force it to resume each time the other cry, "Time she stopped," comes together with the slowing down of the rocking chair and the faint fade of the light upon it.

"More" is the only word spoken by the Woman independently of the recorded voice. Otherwise, she is listening to that voice, joining in with it at intervals on the key line, "Time she stopped." And yet "hearing" might be a more accurate word than "listening" for the distinctive effect created in *Rockaby*, a very different one from that of *That Time*. Partly this is because we are so conscious of the other activity in which the Woman is involved—the hypnotic rocking in the chair with inward curving arms which holds her as if in an embrace, moving her without her volition. The recorded voice streams on along with the rocking motion: it is all bearing her along; she is somehow *in* the voice as she is in the chair, knowing it so well that she never fails to join in the echo of the ritualistic "Time she stopped" until the last fade-out, when her head slowly inclines to the sound of the voice saying:

> no
> done with that
> the rocker
> those arms at last
> saying to the rocker
> rock her off
> stop her eyes
> fuck life
> stop her eyes

> rock her off
> rock her off

Remarkably in this play the use of the third person—in *Not I* a symptom of dissociation—helps to build up an impression of strange unity. The Woman's voice is telling of a woman in a rocking chair, doing what she is doing, feeling what she is feeling, talking to herself—"whom else"—trying to get out of herself, coming "back in," looking out of her window "for another / another like herself / one other living soul." The voice is hers, and yet because it is recorded, outside her, something she only joins in with at intervals, it becomes for us, like the rocking chair, extrapersonal. So, too, with the figure before us, with its prematurely old face, unkempt gray hair, black lacy evening gown and incongruously frivolous headdress. The recorded voice begins to describe this figure, but it is "mother" it speaks of:

> right down
> into the old rocker
> mother rocker
> where mother rocked
> all the years
> all in black
> best black

Aided by the mesmeric force of the rocking rhythm, a composite image develops: the figure in the chair is the woman we see, and her mother and her mother before her, all the women who have sat in the "mother rocker," talking to themselves, "but harmless," till in the end they go down, "right down / into the old rocker."

By the time Woman and chair come to their last rest, the Voice she was listening to has become far more than the voice of one individual telling of her own life experience. Like the rocking chair, it is a force that is moving her—and that knows the time it must stop, as it did for her mother before her. The disconcerting and paradoxical "fuck life" which breaks into the old lady's reverie carries with it, like the incongruity of the frivolous headdress, a refusal of the purely passive and elegiac acceptance of death. Life will continue, whether we like it or not, as the rhythm of the rocking chair and the echoes of the voice continue long after we have left the theater.

In *Rockaby* and *That Time*, what the listeners hear no longer involves conscious effort: they have done their audit, come to terms with their experience. Two plays written before *Rockaby* might seem to return us to the more stressful, hardworking listening activity of plays like *Eh Joe*. *Ghost Trio* (1975) and . . . *but the clouds* . . . (1976) are also television plays, and in them again Beckett takes advantage of the medium to explore ways of separating visual and aural images, making mute figures listen to offset voices. In *Eh Joe*, however, the result was an unwelcome invasion of a man's mind by a woman's voice. In *Ghost Trio* and . . . *but the clouds* . . . , it is the other way around. The protagonist in each play is longing to hear the sound of a beloved woman. Neither longing is achieved, or not fully. Yet each play gives us a sense of partial revelation: the listener has a transcendent experience, is enabled, even if for only a moment, to extend the dimension in which he is confined.

In *Ghost Trio* the confinement is, as Beckett dryly points out, the "familiar" kind; a room in shades of gray with closed door and window, a room that seems to become even grayer as the Female Voice (V) describes in "faint" but authoritative tones the wall, floor, and so forth as the camera shows them. In this almost empty, depressing room, there is a "pallet" and a mirror on the wall—the Male Figure (F) is utterly alone. He shows no sign of hearing the voice, and there is nothing else to hear (in early notes, Beckett stressed that even F's footsteps as he moves about the room should not be heard). Silence, that is, until we come to the end of the first sequence, when faint music is heard, becoming louder as the camera moves in on the figure crouched on his pallet. It is only then we realize the object he is holding is a cassette. Whether the music proceeds from the cassette we cannot be sure, nor even whether he hears it. We know we hear it and that it grows in volume as the camera brings nearer to F its staring gaze. Beckett has said that this "stare" is "mainly in vain" and that the "starving vision" of the camera is essential to the play. What is going on in the mind of F is beyond the camera's power to see. Similarly, the understanding of the female narrator is limited, though she expounds and apparently directs the proceedings in her dictatorial way, telling us to "Look again," calling for repeats of F's movements to door, pallet, and so forth. She sometimes offers us what seems like inside information, as when she explains, on F's raising his head sharply, "He will now think he hears her." Only once she appears taken aback: it is with a surprised "Ah!" that she reacts to the moment when F looks into the mirror and the viewers see him in full face for the first time.

But none of this takes us deep into F's experience. It is only when the female voice ceases and there is utter silence except for the music that the rituals of listening lead to the opening up of the sealed-in room. The tense pose of the man, thinking he hears "her," gives way to movement, no longer "irresolute." Real sounds flood in, described in terms that make them seem like an extension of the music: there is a "crescendo" and "decrescendo" creak when F opens door and window. The attainment of these sounds and of the sound of rain outside the window involves him in some effort, for he is obliged to hold door and window open. When he relaxes his hold, they close of their own accord. We do, therefore, have a sense of F as an active, not a purely passive, agent in the process which leads to a strange epiphany. It is announced by a sound loaded with theatrical shock in the silent, claustrophobic domain, a knocking on the door. We experience with our ears and then with our sight the mysterious visitation for which the title, Ghost Trio, has already prepared us, as has the music. Its haunting quality must make its effect, whether or not we have recognized it as the "Ghost Trio" of Beethoven, which lent its name to Beckett's play.

Music has brought us to the magical and poignant moment when the Boy appears outside the door, a "glistening" figure in black oil-skin streaming with rain, his white face lifted to F's. The sudden brilliance of tone contrasting sharply on the screen with the ubiquitous grays of the "familiar chamber" contributes to the sense that this is an inspiring revelation despite the fact that the Boy shakes his head twice, a gesture of negation. We cannot tell what is being denied—release from the gray room perhaps or perhaps the gesture means only "not yet." The camera's vision continues to be starved; the Female Voice long since fell silent, the Figure, as always, is mute. Yet we have experienced, with him, a revelation—ambiguous as such things are, but unmistakably a moment of release from the self, a glimpse into another order of being. The ritual of listening practiced in the room leaves us hearing in a different way—with the inner ear—the sound of the largo from the "Ghost Trio," which swells out as the camera closes in for the last time on the crouching figure. The cassette, cradled in his arms, is invisible now as it was at the start; a suggestion here perhaps that the source of the music is as much a mystery as the source of the footsteps slowly approaching and then receding from the room as the Boy vanishes into the dark at the end of the gray corridor. Finally, the man with the cassette raises his head, and we see his face, no longer reflected in a mirror. Something in what has occurred, some release, some new force, allows him to show himself entire.

In the play which follows *Ghost Trio*, another television play, . . . *but the clouds* . . . , the auditor similarly experiences a transcendent moment. Beckett again chose to separate visual image from narrative voice in a way that creates a rather similar effect of detachment and distance. This time, however, the voice, V, is not that of an unidentified narrator. It belongs to one of the figures we see on the screen, M. And unusually among the plays of this phase, it speaks in the first person:

When I thought of her it was always night. I came in—

The line, which opens the play, is spoken by the man sitting in a position very like that of F in *Ghost Trio*. M sits on an invisible stool, bowed over an invisible table, clearly in the posture of a writer. It is himself he projects into the imagined scene as the silent figure, M1, who, like F, in *Ghost Trio*, at the promptings of a voice, goes through a series of ritualistic movements designed to bring about a revelation. This is probably the clearest statement Beckett has ever made about the autobiographical aspects of his art.

Again like F, M1 is engaged in listening: "Came in, having walked the roads since break of day, brought night home, stood listening." Unlike F, however, M1 moves in and out of a confined space—a circle of light in this play—emerging from the outlying shadows of the west, changing clothes and presumably personae or functions, in the shadows of the east and vanishing into his "little sanctum" in the north, crouching "where none could see me in the dark." At that point there is a dissolve to M, still in the writer's posture: his voice takes up the tale exactly where M1 left it off: "then crouching there in my little sanctum, in the dark, where none can see me, I began to beg, of her, to appear, to me." The composite identity is established.

Through this elaborate projection into rituals of light and shadow, the writer, M, achieves the desired evocation—not only for himself but for us. We see what the detached voice dryly describes: the materialization of a woman's face, in the BBC production of 1977 confined to Billie Whitelaw's expressive eyes and mouth, as Beckett had required (the face was to be "reduced" as far as possible in that way). Yet the revelation is incomplete, frustratingly so, for M is so near achieving what he above all desires, the sound of the woman's voice. We see her lips move but cannot quite make out what they are saying—an effect much diminished if we receive the play only from the text, where the words are plainly laid out. It is when we are straining with the physical ear (and perhaps with the memory) that we enter more fully into M's tantalizing experience and can recognize the strength of passion in the line of direct address to the presence that finally—and once only—breaks through the elaborate structure of distancing devices:

Speak to me.

She does not, the face goes, the camera returns to M crouched over the invisible table, brooding on the most common outcome of his travails, "case nought," when there is no response to his evocations and he has to turn to more rewarding matters, "cube roots, for example"—a wry little joke that gives us a hint about the link between Beckett and his surrogates in the play. All are engaged in the same business—materializing the immaterial, hearing what disembodied voices have to tell—and projecting that unearthly sound.

It might be said that the materialization fails in this instance. The lips of the evoked presence never send out a voice fully audible to us. M himself has to tell us what she was saying, filling out the broken phrases, "clouds . . . . but the clouds . . . . of the sky" into the full beauty of Yeats's closing lines from *The Tower*, lines which are both a lament over old age and the death of friends and an acceptance of human sadness. "Now shall I make my soul," Yeats's last stanza begins: it is in that context that the death "Of every brilliant eye that made a catch in the breath—" may come to seem, along with other ills, ". . . but the clouds of the sky / when the horizon fades; / Or a bird's sleepy cry / Among the deepening shades."

M's achievement, however, is to have expressed this complex feeling for us with the aid of the images he called into being. It is only when the woman's face has appeared and her lips moved that the scrap of poetry on the borders of memory can emerge into full consciousness—in terms of the play, into full hearing. And there is no doubt that, on at last hearing the lines after the frustrated hearings, we experience a sense of completion and satisfaction: the ritual has been concluded on the high note of tribute to poetry—poetry seen as a mode of communion, however partial, with the longed-for presences that are drawn from the shadows surrounding the circle of light on which M1 has his existence.

I conclude with a view of two plays in which "listening" is a more oblique and equivocal experience than in those I have been discussing, *Footfalls* (1975) and *Ohio Impromptu* (1981).

Footfalls is a structure of echoes, so artful that we are never able to know for certain who is listening to whom and in what dimension of reality. "Hearing" is presented as a conscious need for which special preparation has to be made. The woman, May, who paces in darkness a lighted strip allowing her nine steps and a wheel at each end, obsessively requires to hear the sound of her own footfalls. So we are told by the voice that comes out of the dark and tells how as a young girl the daughter (for it is mother's voice that speaks), already committed to the endless pacing, demanded a bare floor, clear of carpet:

the motion alone is not enough, I must hear the feet, however faint they fall.

There is some likeness here with the elaborate rituals undertaken in . . . *but the clouds* . . . in order to hear certain words. Like M in that play, May has another persona, surprisingly turning herself late in the piece into the narrator of a story in a different vein from anything that has gone before about a daughter, Amy (obvious anagram of May), and her mother, a Mrs. Winter, whom "the reader will remember." This remarkable tour de force allows her to communicate what she presumably could not do in her own person, the strange sense the fictional character experiences, that although present to her mother's eyes, she is somehow "not there."

I observed nothing of any kind, strange or otherwise. I saw nothing, heard nothing of any kind. I was not there. Mrs W: Not there? Amy: Not there. Mrs W: But I heard you respond. [Pause.] I heard you say Amen [Pause.] How could you have responded if you were not there?

That same question was raised in another form at the start of the play when May calls out to the mother who is "not there," yet whose voice comes out of the dark: "I heard you in my deep sleep. [Pause.] There is no sleep so deep I would not hear you there."

The daughter is visually there, though dimly so—the light is strongest at floor level—and the mother is not there. Yet both are auditors: they hear and respond to each other, reenacting a scene, perhaps of memory, in which each expresses concern for the other, the daughter for the physical needs of the ninety-year-old, sick, and bedridden mother, the mother for the agony of the daughter "revolving it all" in her "poor mind." The dialogue is extraordinarily vivid, bringing the mother fully alive for us: yet at this point it must seem that the figure we can see is somehow creating and projecting the voice of the unseen one. Seeing is believing, as it is said. The play suggests that we should not be too sure of that.

Perhaps the strangest volte-face in the whole strange experience is the moment when light first fades out on the strip, the chime heard at the opening is heard more faintly, as are, therefore, its slowly fading echoes, and then in the returning light we see May, standing still now, apparently unaware of the voice—"Woman's Voice" is Beckett's sole description—coming out of the dark, unaided by dialogue. What the Voice says creates a perfect ambiguity; it speaks in the first person as though in May's place ("Rather I come and stand") before dissociating and describing May as a separate being:

I walk here now. [Pause.] Rather I come and stand. [Pause.] At nightfall. [Pause.] She fancies she is still alone. [Pause.] See how still she stands, how stark, with her face to the wall.

The Voice then tells the story of May—"the child's given name"—constructing a dialogue between them, as May later constructs a dialogue between Amy and her mother. Each "does" the voice of the other; each, in turn, directs the attention of the audience to significant features of the story; each can seemingly "hear" the other whether or not the other is present in the sense usually understood by the word.

Whether the standing figure "hears" as the Voice tells how May in her lonely vigils "tries to tell how it was," we cannot know. By this time it is not possible to distinguish what is being heard in the head at any moment and what is coming through the mysterious structure of echoes in which the figures of mother and daughter move in and out of the roles of listener and narrator. Every moment is equivocal. When the Voice out of the dark tells the story of May, complete with snatches of dialogue, Beckett directed that M should be muttering to herself. Is she unhearing, oblivious of the Voice, or is she rehearsing or in some strange way projecting it, as she later successfully projects the voice of Mrs. Winter talking to the daughter, who is May in another form?

We cannot tell any more than we can be sure who the "she" is whom M describes, in her ghostly sequel, the "tangle of tatters" that walks at nightfall, haunting the church, pitying the suffering Christ, before "vanishing the way she came," making no sound. "None at least to be heard," M adds, a remark that draws our attention yet again to the mysterious nature of sound in the play: voices continually echo each other as the chime sends out its diminishing echoes.

The visual image is tenuous in this play. By the end an impression has been created that the figure pacing and wheeling on the exiguous strip, like the mysterious "semblance" she conjures up for us, is herself conjured up and kept in being by the voices and sounds that convey her story. Beckett gives us a strong hint to this effect in his direction that the dim light on the figure should be strongest at floor level, the level at which comes the "clearly audible rhythmic tread" of the footfalls. It is sound—the tread of footfalls or the voices—through which the experience is most sharply registered.

We, the audience, become, above all, auditors; we wait for the echoes of a chime to die away; we speculate on the source of this voice or that; we extend our perspective to take in the new possibilities opened up by a change of voice, May's unexpected humor in the "Mrs. Winter" story, for instance. There is pain in the drama created by the voices; the recognizable "ordinary" human pain in the first sequence, when we hear the middle-aged daughter waiting on the sick or dying mother, and the more obscure inner pain related to the "poor arm" of Christ and the universal suffering of living.

But in the listening process itself there is no suggestion of strain, effort, or reluctance. One voice picks up another or turns into another with dreamlike ease; they spread out irresistibly as the echoes from the chime spread out; only when the chime dies away for the last time does the faint light on the strip reveal "No trace of May." A ghostly unity has been achieved, a communion such as Mrs. Winter speaks of in M's story of Amy: "the fellowship of the Holy Ghost."

In *Ohio Impromptu* (1981), there is again an obscure, ambiguous relationship between listener and narrator, and again the process of listening to the story of human pain they convey breeds a deeply moving sense of mysterious communion. The connection glimpsed in earlier plays between the listening process and the creative life of a writer takes on both more explicit and more deeply mysterious form in *Ohio Impromptu*. "Profounds of mind," that phrase proffered by the Reader at the close of the play, describes perfectly the location the audience members feel themselves in from the moment when the strange pair, Reader and Listener, begin to mesmerize us with the "sad tale" of the bereaved man to whom night after night a reader tells a story—as Listener is read to before our eyes.

The one who listens and the one who speaks are hard to separate— and yet utterly separate. Visually, they are inseparable look-alikes; Listener a mirror image of Reader or Reader of Listener (we cannot tell which). Each wears the same long black coat and white hair; each sits in the same posture with head bowed on right hand, left hand on table. Beckett hoped for actors as physically alike as possible to keep the twin effect intact through the few seconds at the end of the play when they raise heads and look at each other, showing full face to the audience for the first time.

Yet there is encouragement from the visual pattern, with its emphatic contrasts of black and white, to think in terms of opposites as well as likeness: Reader and Listener in their black coats sit at a white table on white chairs, a wide-brimmed hat making a black mark at the center of the table. And likewise their functions are opposite, if complementary. Beckett emphasizes this; Reader is completely taken up with the "old volume" from which he reads to Listener, and Listener is so quintessentially a listener that he remains mute throughout. He interferes in the reading by knocking on the table, but appears to have no power of speech. Reader, on the other hand, has the power of speech in high degree.

In the theater he must use it to cast a spell; something that certainly happened when David Warrilow played the part,[4] hypnotizing us through his gravelly, unemphatic voice, with its subtle intonations and rhythms, as he traced the story of the bereaved man driven by the sense of loss to seek relief in a room free of memories, only to find himself haunted, taken back in dream to the room "where we were once so long alone together." The dreamlike effect Warrilow achieved with his voice was accentuated by the uncanny sound of the knocking by which Listener entered the narrative, forcing a return to key lines or a continuation after a held pause. The mysterious relationship between the two was vividly embodied in the commanding knocks. Warrilow has commented[5] on the difficult task it was to achieve this rhythm, which must be precise within split seconds and yet seem totally spontaneous. The achievement of the rhythm between teller and listener powerfully hints at obscure correspondences between their relation to each other and what is being told in the story.

Listener's editing role is totally accepted by Reader, even when it is clear that the latter would rather go off on his own. He tries to do this at one point, following a pedantic impulse to go over the details of the panic experienced by the fictional character when his "old terror of night" afflicted him with "fearful symptoms described at length page forty paragraph four"—a humorous moment, which Beckett points up by having Listener intervene (silently, as usual) with his left hand, to prevent Reader from turning back to page forty. Listener knows, we may deduce, that this would be a literary mistake. Though these two have such separate and distinct functions, they are seen— and heard—to make up a single process like the "two arms" of the stream observed by the man in the story: "in joyous eddies its two arms conflowed and flowed united on."

Listener is also in some strange way the subject of the story he is listening to. It is essentially about a man listening to a voice from another world; it warns him in dreams not to move from the shared room: "stay where we were so long alone together, my shade will comfort you." He disregards the voice, changes his room, and is plunged into the misery and terror which the Reader would have liked to dwell on. Then there appears in the story a reader, announcing himself as a messenger from the dream region where the voice was experienced and the "dear face" glimpsed. The "shade" is, after all, bringing the promised comfort—comfort which takes the form of a nightly reading from the "worn volume" carried by the Reader in a pocket of his long black coat. And now the audience does not know whether it is within the story or outside it. The scene described in the story is the scene on the stage, not just on the visual surface but in its dreamlike mood and, especially, in the sense engendered above all by the aural rhythm that Reader and Listener are in deep correspondence, despite the fact that they never speak to each other nor, until the very end, look at each other. This is a true reflection of the story where the reader comes and goes without a word and "With never a word exchanged they grew to be as one."

Or is the story a reflection of what we see? The audience is drawn into a mystery: it is *in* the process by which the figures on the stage came into being. It is a process which involves listening to "unspoken" words from a source far beyond the sounds of the ordinary daylight world. In the story reader and listener are oblivious to those sounds, signal of "reawakening." The story done, they sit—like Reader and Listener on the stage—"as though turned to stone," in some "profounds of mind," as Reader speculates before he and his Listener come to the end of their reading. The silence that falls then in the theater (so I experienced it) is deep, absorbed: the audience seemed to have been brought into the state Reader describes, freed from the restless agitation of mind which disturbs the fictional listener at the start of his story. Perhaps, like Listener, we could not quite believe we had come to the end. He knocks when Reader makes to close the book, on the line "Nothing is left to tell." But Reader can only repeat what went before, and on the second "Nothing is left to tell," the book is closed.

Yet there is something to follow. The two who share one hat and are mirror images of each other place their right hands on the table, raise their heads, and exchange a look, "Unblinking. Expressionless." It is as if the writer, after finishing his story, were resting his writing hand and taking final stock. A moment of clear self-understanding, it seems; psychic unity has been achieved, though only through the absorption into the imaginative process of a desperate sense of loss and separation.

In this compelling, intense play, as in the other plays of the sequence I have been tracing, the listener is an auditor in the dual sense of the word so clearly indicated in the nomenclature of *Not I*. The Listener of *Ohio Impromptu* is a critical as well as a receptive listener; Reader must heed his interventions if he is to get the story right. It makes the interventions more, not less, valuable that they come from a wordless source. Like the mute figures in Yeats's plays on themes of supernatural inspiration, the Listener is in touch with an impalpable world, receives messages in "unspoken words." His relationship with the other self, the Reader, shadowy and ambiguous though it is, is what the creative act depends on.

In these plays the role of the auditor is often equivocal, but it is always profoundly accepting, always offers a way to some kind of precious release or communion from which creative achievement might flow. By simply being there and making his silent gestures of compassion, the Auditor in *Not I* subtly changes our view of Mouth's despair. Those intent listeners, the "old ones" of *That Time* and *Rockaby*, create a soundscape which reveals the true value of their lives. Another order of experience, freed from the limitations of an imprisoning world, is opened up by the listening rituals practiced in *Ghost Trio* and . . . *but the clouds* . . . while, in *Footfalls* and *Ohio Impromptu*, listeners and narrators reflect each other in a way which takes us far out into a ghostly world of communion between the living and the presences of the imagination.

As I remarked at the start of this discussion, Beckett's plays in the past have been full of voices demanding to be projected, often forcing themselves on an uneasy or resisting listener. In this later phase, listeners respond to the voices which come to them with a calm which allows the emphasis to fall on what is achieved by the mysterious communion rather than on the struggle to achieve it. This is not to say that the more violent and demonic aspects of this dangerous listening have gone from the scene. They are still there or hinted at in the obvious horror of Mouth's raging, for instance, or the uncanniness of the mimicked voices in *Footfalls*. The world brought to us by the voices of those who are "not there" remains a world shadowed by the "old terror of night." If it were not so, the listeners' achievement of more tranquil regions would be less impressive and moving than it is.

His ability to convey the awesome, at times bizarre, grotesque, or even comic aspects of the listening which brings forth voices keeps Beckett still closely linked to Yeats, whose presence has haunted his theater since *Godot*. *Footfalls* indeed, with its strange moves in and out of the voices of others, calls up irresistibly Yeats's play about a medium who "produces" the voice of Swift, *The Words upon the Window-Pane*.

In that play, an acute sense of danger warns one of the regular attenders at Mrs. Henderson's séances that something is going to happen that night. She tells a new, skeptical visitor that his skepticism makes her feel safer: "I feel like Job—you know the quotation—the hair of my head stands up. A spirit passes before my face." Just such a sense of awe and fear is transmitted by the ghostly scenes and semblances Beckett conjures up in the late plays, despite the fact that a daylight as well as a dead-of-night angle is offered on these phenomena. Yeats's skeptic, a Swift scholar, is deeply impressed by the medium's remarkable evocation of Swift—entirely done through the voice—but attributes it to her scholarship and acting ability rather than to supernatural power. But who could confidently say how far the medium is consciously acting, how far possessed, moved by uncontrollable forces outside herself? Yeats ends the play on a stunning theatrical note which leaves the question provocatively open. Alone in her room after the séance, Mrs. Henderson, muttering to herself like May in Footfalls, suddenly produces the voice of Swift, lamenting his decline into old age and decay. If this is acting, then it is indistinguishable from a state of possession. So, in Beckett's ghost plays, we can never rule out the possibility that some alien, unknowable force is the real controller of events, even when it is clear that the artist/medium is working hard to move the action in a desired direction. "We do not call up the spirits," says Yeats's medium, "we make the right conditions and they come." The listeners of Ghost Trio and . . . but the clouds . . . go through elaborate rituals, make "the right conditions," but may still end up with "case nought" when attention to cube roots would be more rewarding. The region from which the shades and the voices come can never be possessed, only glimpsed, as the hierophant of . . . but the clouds . . . glimpses the face that almost succeeds in voicing Yeats's lines about the deepening shades.

Also in the background, as always, is Shakespeare, above all the Shakespeare of The Tempest. Prospero has great mastery over the spirits who perform for him, conjuring up voices and creating illusions. But Ariel reminds us constantly that the magician's power is limited: he cannot enter the domain to which the released spirit goes at the end of the play; and it is only with the aid of that spirit that he is able to come to terms with his bitter life experience. From the Ariel-like yearning of Mouth for the freedom represented by the cowslip field to the yearning of Listener for the "dear face" that has left him, the sense of another freer and more complete dimension is powerful in Beckett's late plays. The voices speak of it and the listeners understand it. They are moving toward it in their willingness to listen—and thereby to assist in the weaving of the stuff of life into patterns of art that both express and transcend the life.

And through all the brilliant changes of tone, rhythm, and idiom, which give us the voices of the "others," can be heard from time to time the unmistakable, reassuring voice of Beckett's humor, reminding us of the ordinary oddities and pleasant jokes of life. It is good to have in these awesome plays that go so far into the unknown the pleased smile of the Listener in *That Time*, "toothless for preference," or the sudden access of pedantry in the other Listener of *Ohio Impromptu*. We can never mistake Beckett's voice, however diverse and remote the voices he draws into the hearing range of his listeners.

NOTES

1. Beryl Fletcher et al., *A Student's Guide to the Plays of Samuel Beckett* (London: Faber & Faber, 1978), p. 198. It might be worth noting that this is said to be Caravaggio's only surviving signed work, a fact that has raised speculation about a special degree of personal involvement on his part with the picture. Caravaggio is a strong presence in the background of *Not I:* his serpent-crowned Medusa, with wide open, silently screaming mouth, has an obvious and surely sinister relationship with the Mouth who shrieks ". . . she! . . . SHE! . . ." It is also worth noting that the Auditor was cut from the performance in Paris (with Madeleine Renaud as Mouth), following the London production, where severe lighting problems were experienced. However, Beckett did not remove the character from the text, nor has he done so in any subsequent edition.
2. For this and other instances of Beckett's comments in unpublished drafts or notes, I am indebted to the Beckett Archive of the University of Reading and to its curator, Dr. J. A. Edwards.
3. C. G. Jung, *Memories, Dreams, Reflections*, translated by Richard and Clara Winston (London: Collins, 1967), p. 352.
4. My references are to the production of *Ohio Impromptu* at the Edinburgh Festival in August 1984.
5. David Warrilow's comments on the demanding rhythm of *Ohio Impromptu* were made to the present writer during rehearsal of a piece with equally complex rhythm, *Cascando*. The new production of

Cascando, mounted in September 1984 by David Clark and myself at the University of London Audio-Visual Centre, involved a tripartite relationship among two actors, David Warrilow and Sean Barrett, and the composer Humphrey Searle, whose music was written and recorded for the production before his death.

Ghost Trio / Geister Trio

JAMES KNOWLSON

There have been two different recorded versions of Samuel Beckett's television play *Ghost Trio*, on which the author himself worked: one was produced by the BBC in London, when Beckett acted as adviser to the director, Donald McWhinnie;[1] and the other, by Süddeutscher Rundfunk in Stuttgart, when he directed the play himself,[2] working with a cameraman, Jim Lewis, whom he knows well and with whom he has worked on a number of occasions before and since.[3] These two versions introduce a number of changes into Beckett's original script and seem to go beyond it in satisfying aims that can already be detected in the manuscript and typescript drafts that have been preserved. Beckett's own German version also differs from the BBC one in several significant ways. In discussing Beckett's play, I want, then, to take as my two main points of reference some unpublished notes that were written by Beckett as part of the first available manuscript draft and the two completed television films. My essay lies, therefore, somewhere between the work that has been done on manuscript and typescript versions of the play[4] and the work of interpretation that has been produced by a number of critics.[5]

Let me begin by referring to the first holograph manuscript preserved in Reading University's Beckett Archive (Ms. 1519/1).[6] Here Beckett has made lengthy notes on the Figure (F), the camera, the door and the window, the boy's steps and F's steps. None of these notes has been included in published editions of the play, although a version of them (revised in the light of production changes) would seem to be necessary for any future productions. Unlike Voice in the first part of the play, who comments on the presence of the Figure last, only after describing every other element of the stark set, let us start by looking at how Beckett first envisaged the protagonist and then consider how this figure emerges in the two productions with which he has been involved. F is described in the following way in the manuscript note (which I quote with Beckett's permission):

> F: White face, absent look, untidy grey hair.
> ? Plain dark suit, coat buttoned up to neck, no buttons showing. Bowed throughout, sitting, standing, moving, except when having to raise head to look (out of door, out of window, into mirror. Face seen clearly only once, in mirror). Slow drifting walk.
> ? Makes no sound. Only sounds those of music, rain, steps in corridor, knock, things (cassette against stool, door, window).[7]

The two marginal question marks apply to "Plain dark suit" and "Makes no sound," both of which are ringed in Beckett's text. The first of these queries is then reconsidered in the first typescript, when Beckett adds in a handwritten note: "Long dark dressing-gown. Affinity with boy's garment. Feet out of shot when moving. Sim. [similarly] boy's feet."[8] In the two television productions, the Figure does indeed wear a long garment, although, in both cases, this is more of a heavy, floor-length overcoat ("for warmth," as a later note suggested [Reading University Library Ms. 1519/3]), than a dressing-gown. The garment is gray, however, rather than dark, echoing the "shades of grey" that are referred to by Voice rather than the dark color of the black oilskin worn by the boy. It may well be true, as S. E. Gontarski suggests, that "in revision Beckett simply exchanged one parallel, one balanced pair for another,"[9] that is, substituting the grayness of the garment and the grayness of the room for the F/boy parallel. Yet it seems to me that the parallel between F and the boy is still partly established through the length of the garment, particularly, as we shall see later, in the German version. Indeed, in my own view, the analogy is far more likely to be registered by the change from a "plain dark suit" to a long gown than simply by relying on the similarity in color.

The second query concerning F's silent steps focuses on the same parallel. This is taken up again in another note entitled "F's steps" on the penultimate page of the manuscript.[10] Here Beckett once more contemplates a change in his initial idea for the sake of the parallelism between F and the boy visitor/messenger. And so he wrote, " 'F makes no sound': reconsider for sake of F-boy analogy. Feet in any case not to be seen. He moves bowed through space with no visible propulsion."[11] In neither of the two finished versions with which the author was involved, however, are F's steps made audible. It seems likely that Beckett decided to override this consideration because the silent "slow, drifting" walk of F seemed far more in keeping with the mysterious tone of the *Ghost Trio* and was likely to be more powerful dramatically, precisely because, in this way, it both echoed and contrasted with the boy's audible steps.

The full point of these considerations on the parallelism between the boy and F emerges, of course, only when one sees the finished television films. For the entire play is built on such elaborate structures of intriguing parallels and contrasts. In Part I and most of Part II, as Beckett's manuscript synopses reveal,[12] voice and action follow each other in carefully balanced pairs. Pattern and change constitute the whole nature of the action within the play. Part I (what Beckett calls the "Pre-Action") has a mobile, staring camera but a totally immobile male figure whereas, in Part II (what Beckett calls the "Action"), this figure moves around the room, going to the door, the window, and the pallet, then once again back to the door as he thinks he hears the woman for whom he is waiting. In Part III (what Beckett calls the "Re-action") these same movements are all repeated, but this time with small but striking differences: from opening quietly, the door and the window now creak audibly, as he pushes them open, and they creak once again as they close by themselves. In Part II, we hear no one, and, when F opens the door, we see an empty corridor. In Part III, there is a sound of footsteps from outside, and this time, when F opens the door, someone (the boy) is standing there. The music similarly is organized around a careful patterning of what is heard and what is unheard.[13] All of F's gestures and movements, too, are governed by repetition and contrast. They are always slow and deliberate, except when he "thinks he hears her," at which point F's response is immediate, and the gesture of his hand resembles that of a marionette. In Beckett's German production, this raising of the hand is even more abrupt and puppetlike than in the BBC version. At other times, the movements of Klaus Herm playing F are slower, more deliberate, even more ghostly than those of Ronald Pickup in the British recording.[14]

Beckett's manuscript notes also focus attention on the male figure's "slow drifting" walk and it is worth considering for a moment the characteristics of this figure in the two television productions. The beginning of Beckett's own German version differs somewhat from that made for the BBC. With the fade-up of the gray light at the opening of the BBC version, the human figure, though totally immobile, is still recognizable as a human being. In the German recording, I suggest that this is much less clearly the case and that the figure is perceived more as an abstract shape than as a human being.[15] Voice's "sole sign of life a seated figure" seems, therefore, to confirm something which, until then, had been by no means certain.

Because of its "man alone in a room" situation, *Ghost Trio* has sometimes been compared with Beckett's earlier television play *Eh Joe* (1966). But Joe was a far more earthy, substantial creation than is F in the later work. The words in *Eh Joe* probably emanated from one of the "dead voices" in Joe's head. But his face registered a living torture as he strove to "throttle" the voice and his feet shuffled audibly around the room. In *Ghost Trio*, as we have seen, Beckett finally decided that F's steps should make no sound, and, in fact, great effort was made to ensure that no marks should be made on the gray floor of the constructed set, Beckett himself wearing soft, cloth, pull-on overshoes whenever he went on to the set in Stuttgart.[16] As I suggested earlier, F's steps were made inaudible partly so as to accord with the mysterious tone of the play. But the decision has other consequences. For by being made to drift soundlessly in his "slow transit through space without visible propulsion," the figure himself (the one apparently "real" figure in this strangely bare, rectangular room) is partially dematerialized so that he appears as something of an ethereal presence, matching the ambiguous female voice with its flat, unearthly tone and preparing for the "tryst," not with the woman that he is expecting to meet but with the strange boy visitor who shakes his head with a negative message at the end. In this respect, the play has far more in common with the almost contemporaneous *Footfalls* than it has with the television play of ten years earlier. For *Footfalls*, too, is a ghost story of an unusual kind. It seems at first as if we are listening there to the main protagonist, May, as she recounts the story of a ghost. It is perhaps only after the play has ended that we realize that what we may have been watching was a ghost telling the tale of a ghost (herself), who fails to be observed by someone else (her own fictional alter ego) because she, in turn, was not really there.

The ghostly figure of May in *Footfalls* could at least be heard pacing. Beckett's final decision to make F's steps inaudible (which agreed, of course, with his initial note), meant that the protagonist in *Ghost Trio* established no such contact with reality. From discussions with the actor Ronald Pickup, Donald McWhinnie, and myself at rehearsals at the BBC Film Studios at Ealing, it became clear that, by analogy with the marionette described in Heinrich von Kleist's essay "On the Marionette Theater," F's movements were deliberately divorced from the effects of gravity and that his hand movement when he thinks he hears her was executed exactly like that of a puppet. Since I have written more fully elsewhere concerning this parallel,[17] I want to touch here only on what is relevant for my argument. In Kleist's "Über das Marionettentheater," Beckett read that the movements of marionettes are superior to those of the human dancer because "[t]hey are not hindered with the inertness of matter, the quality most resistant to dancing, because the lifting power is greater than that which keeps them down. . . . The puppets need the floor only to touch and enliven the swing of their limbs by momentarily retarding their action."[18] According to the speaker in Kleist's essay, puppets possess, therefore, a mobility, symmetry, harmony, and grace greater than any human dancer (or, one might add, actor) can possibly achieve. One of the reasons given for this is that they are, inevitably, totally lacking in self-awareness, which destroys natural grace and charm in humans. Kleist's essay goes on to explore how self-consciousness affects people, putting them permanently off balance. Consequently, humans lack the unity, harmony, grace, and economy of movement that characterized the marionette or the remarkable fencing bear that Kleist also refers to in the same essay. For this bear, too, is a creature without awareness of self, who is able to respond naturally and unselfconsciously to the thrusts of a human fencer and not be deceived by his false passes. As the male figure in *Ghost Trio* moves around the room, opens the door or the window, looks up from the pallet to the mirror, his moves appear so slow, deliberate, economical, and graceful that they seem to belong to someone who is not truly of this world, a marionette—or, of course, a spirit. In this way, we are led to question the substantiality of the male figure himself, physically there, it would seem, as a figure on the television screen, but silent in his movements and obsessive in his patterns of behavior.

Ghost Trio assumes, too, like Footfalls, the form of a complex set of variations on appearance and dramatic reality. The strange, disembodied commentary spoken by the female voice that opens the play imparts information that is disarmingly simple, apparently straightforward, and yet oddly inappropriate to the series of nonnaturalistic images that we watch on the television screen. "The familiar chamber," comments the voice. Yet it is this only in the most schematic way. The door may be "indispensable," yet it is perceived by the viewer only as a geometrical shape, cut out in the larger rectangle of the wall, and is, as Beckett comments in his notes, "knobless." One of the changes Beckett made in revising the play was to do away with such a naturalistic feature as "Feverish hand fumbling to find key, to get it into lock."[19] Earlier, floor and wall have been distinguished only by the position of the rectangular specimen of each that is displayed on the television screen. "Knowing this, the kind of wall," says the voice; and yet, of course, we know absolutely nothing that we would normally consider essential to distinguish one wall from another. There is, in other words, a deliberate play on the disparity between "looking" and "knowing" that leaves the spectator aware of the strangeness and the ambiguity of what he is observing, intrigued and disturbed rather than reassured by the speaker's words.

The whole status of the speaker in the play is highly ambiguous. She appears able to instruct the camera as to what it should reveal. Yet it seems to move independently of her too, as if free to change the closeness or the remoteness of its "stare"[20] at the end of Part I, and it functions either without commands from her in Part III or follows only the general instruction issued by her at the end of Part II: "Repeat." In Part II, the voice either knows the male figure's habitual patterns of behavior or can act herself either to anticipate or prompt his actions. Yet here either she makes mistakes and gets the order wrong or she exercises uncertain control over him. For, on one occasion, when she states "Now to door," F fails to do this and returns instead to his stool to take up the cassette recorder. Is this, moreover, the voice of the woman for whom he is waiting, the ghost with whom he has a secret "tryst"? Is she a reluctant muse unable or unwilling to come to him, only able to state the obvious, observing and commenting on his repeated peregrinations around the "familiar chamber"? Or is she a loved one, who may already be a "shade," as the later *Ohio Impromptu* (1981) suggests may be the case? Or is she death herself or nothingness who will not come to release him from a life to which he barely clings? The answers are certainly not written into the play itself and its many ambiguities seem to me to have produced a particularly haunting, compelling piece for television.

Another intriguing ambiguity in the play may be explored by considering how the visit by the boy messenger is described in Beckett's manuscript notes and how he actually appears and behaves in the two television productions. In the notes Beckett had written, "Long slow fade up of sound, as many as 20 footfalls if possible, & culminating not loud. Exact reverse in other direction. Keep boy's feet out of shot. Or hidden by oilskin too big for him."[21] These recommendations were only partially followed in the British and German versions. There was a slow fade-up of the sound of footsteps, and this indeed never became loud. But, in the BBC version, there were only ten approaching steps, but twenty retreating ones. These sounded like the taps of a stick or a crutch rather than steps, something which became clear on the boy's departure as he was seen to walk like a cripple. In the German version, there were thirteen approaching footsteps and just over twenty receding steps before the sound faded. These were, moreover, normal footsteps. But Beckett introduced a striking innovation into the German production. In retreating slowly backward, the boy leaves clear footprints on the white floor of the corridor, marking the dust or the sand on its surface with tangible signs of his presence. In fact, the whole ending of the play with the appearance and disappearance of the boy is strikingly different in Beckett's German version. First, the boy is dressed in black, as he was in the BBC production, but the garb is less naturalistic, the "black sou'wester" and oilskin being replaced by a much less recognizable garment that frames the boy's head and body in a more mysterious way. Second, the narrowness of the corridor extending behind the boy and the way in which he is filmed on it make it seem as if he is emerging from a coffin. It is a most startling image. In London, Beckett had some difficulty in getting the too angelic-looking boy to shake his head as

enigmatically as he wanted him to do. In Stuttgart, the head movement is slow, enigmatic, just discernible, and more in keeping with
the movements of the main protagonist and the strange tone of the
play as a whole. In the published script, Beckett wrote of the boy's
look, "White face raised to invisible F. 5 seconds. Boy shakes head
faintly. Face still, raised. 5 seconds. Boy shakes head again. Face still,
raised. 5 seconds. Boy turns and goes."[22] The parallel with F himself
is made clearer if we recall that, in the original manuscript note
quoted earlier, F is described as having "white face, absent look."[23]
In general, in Beckett's own production of the play, the boy is a
much stranger figure than in the earlier version and presents a much
closer parallel to F, the male figure himself.

The music plays a crucial part in each of the three parts of the
play. It comes from the largo of Beethoven's Piano Trio No. 5 in D,
Opus 70, No. 1, commonly known as "The Ghost." In the first typescript, Beckett writes in hand "Macbeth" on the two occasions when
faint music is heard as a close-up of the door is shown (I, 11 and I, 21
in the manuscript, which become I, 13 and I, 23 in the published
script). He repeats this same note at the beginning of Part III (III, 1
and 2 and again 4 and 5 both in the manuscript and the published
script). When I asked Beckett why he referred to the music in this
way, he explained that, on the sleeve notes accompanying his own recording, he had read that Beethoven had written out this music with
sketches for an opera based on *Macbeth*. It was clear that for Beckett, "The Ghost" had clearly retained something of *Macbeth*'s doom-
laden atmosphere and involvement in the spirit world. Now I do not
know which particular record of the Fifth Piano Trio Beckett owns,
but the notes accompanying my own recording relate interestingly to
Beckett's *Ghost Trio:*

The most original movement of the trio turns out to be the Largo assai
espressivo which plunges into the spirit world of the night. The fact
that sketches for this D minor movement are on the same sheet as those
for an opera planned on the basis of Shakespeare's *Macbeth* (including
a witches' chorus in D minor) is certainly more than mere chance. The
nickname "Ghost Trio" sometimes applied to this work is in no way
inappropriate, if only because of this D minor movement. Outlines become blurred, softly flickering expanses of sound, piano tremulos, and
descending chromatic scales conjure up an uncanny, oppressively deathly
mood.[24]

The particular bars of the largo that are chosen by Beckett—and the manuscript drafts show with what meticulous care he selected his extracts—do indeed reflect this "uncanny, oppressively deathly mood," but they also seem to me to capture a sense of tense expectation which may be regarded as one of the main links between Beethoven's dark motifs and the play which, until very late in its preparation, Beckett had entitled *Tryst*. Before the end of the movement there is even a slight lightening of mood and a hint of hopefulness (before the fall into the pizzicato) which may well encourage the waiting figure to persist with his vigil and perhaps partially explain the strange, haunted, half-smile that flickered on the face of the actor, Klaus Herm, at the end of Beckett's production.

One of the several changes that Beckett made in the German production concerns the music. In the first part of the play, he cut out the "faint music" which accompanies the Voice's allusions to the door (I, 13 and I, 23). The first musical phrase from the largo is, therefore, heard only toward the end of Part I, that is, from I, 31 to 34. The effect of this is to dissociate the music from the external world and to make it seem instead much more internalized.

There were other changes in the German version that were not related to the music. Two shots in Part III are entirely omitted by Beckett. The first is the separate shot of the cassette recorder, seen in close-up from above, "small grey rectangle on larger rectangle of seat" (III, 12). The second, which represents a visual parallel to the cassette recorder, is that of the mirror. Beckett cut shot III, 24 "close-up of mirror reflecting nothing. Small grey rectangle (same dimensions as cassette) against larger rectangle of wall." Presumably, after seeing the earlier BBC version, Beckett came to the conclusion that these two related shots added nothing that had not already been established in Part I by the rectangular shapes of floor, wall, door, window, and pallet and detracted from the pattern of actions and camera shots repeated in Parts II and III. It is worth stressing also that, in the German production, everything had much more precise lines and angles than in the earlier version, the corridor in particular being narrower and more sharply geometrical.

Hardly surprisingly, *Ghost Trio* provoked considerable disagreement among newspaper reviewers when it was first shown. Michael Billington wrote in *The Guardian* of "the concentrated beauty of the images: no naturalistic clutter, no fact cutting, no colour but simply a mesmeric piece of painting for TV."[25] He commented in addition that the three plays which made up the program of "Shades" made one wonder why naturalism remained "television drama's dominant mode." Several reviewers, on the other hand, found the three plays extremely tedious, and Denis Potter wrote more sharply of their "affirmation of pointlessness."[26]

Critics with rather more time to ponder have scarcely been less divided in their views as to what they think Ghost Trio is actually about. What has happened, I believe, is that a number of them have fallen into the traps of allegory and autobiography, the same traps into which some of the early critics of Waiting for Godot also fell.

The authors of A Student's Guide to the Plays of Samuel Beckett, for instance, consider that Ghost Trio is making an important statement on the arts and the position of the artist. They argue that in this play Beckett is "calling on the resources of all the arts and presenting a critique of what they can and cannot achieve . . . no artist is the saviour, no artist presents the truth for we no longer grant him this degree of presumption."[27] So images with pictorial resonance (windows and doors suggesting seventeenth-century Dutch interiors) lead nowhere or open on to nothing. But they also contend that Ghost Trio takes up the metaphor of the artist as musician, with Beckett demonstrating that "music exists outside of human control . . . and by its very structuring it has that order (of beginning, build-up, middle, end etc.) that no other art can be trusted now to aspire to."[28] Hence, Beckett is seen as using the music of Beethoven's "Ghost Trio" "both to counter-point the dramatic action and to crystallize his assumptions about the artist and especially the differing status of the individual arts."[29] Although I find this essay illuminating in some of its detail, its main thesis seems to me to be brilliantly ingenious but probably wrong. Beckett's plays are surely far less allegorical and message-ridden than this particular interpretation suggests. On the other hand, the British publisher of Beckett's novels, John Calder, argues for an autobiographical reading of Ghost Trio, viewing it as reflecting Beckett's situation as "the most studied, harried and pursued writer of our time . . . doomed to be observed and never able to hide"[30] and seeing in the play numerous deliberate references to Beckett's own earlier work. This autobiographical approach seems even less convincing to me than the allegorical one. Beckett has never expressed personal stresses like this in his work and is by temperament most unlikely to have begun making such personal statements so late in his life. Even an explicitly autobiographical work like *Company* is not confessional at all in this way. However, the autobiographical aspect represents only part of John Calder's reading, and he seems to be on much firmer ground when he writes of the play being composed of units of three. It is, he points out, conceived "within three frames, each containing another frame and another world like a chinese box"[31]: first, the outer frame of the television screen; second, the frame of the visual narrative, partly commented on by the voice of the woman "announcer"; third, the interior of the mind of the protagonist with the music emanating from the tape recorder that he holds. According to Calder, the three named objects in the room (the door, the window, and the pallet) represent in the author's mind—after T. S. Eliot's "Sweeney Agonistes"—birth, copulation, and death (in that order). These elements of the room strike me as functional rather than symbolic. They are there as "givens," undoubtedly prompting unanswered questions in the viewer's mind but directly related only to the "tryst." For F opens the door and the window to look for the woman for whom he is waiting, hoping that she will eventually appear to him. And if the slight hand gesture toward the pallet which Beckett introduced into his own production is to be trusted, it too reminds him of her. It is worth noting that Beckett wrote in his manuscript note on the camera that the pallet should be the object of a "special gaze,"[32] something which was achieved in production by having the camera linger on the pillow as it zooms in on it from above.

Yet we must remember that the identity of the woman is not known, that this may be no ordinary "tryst," and that F may be waiting for no ordinary woman. There are several pointers within the play that death may be lurking furtively behind some of its most striking visual and auditory images: the recurring rectangular shape of wall, floor, door, window, pallet, stool, cassette recorder, and mirror inevitably recall the shape of a coffin; the *Macbeth* associations of the main Beethoven "Ghost Trio" motif referred to explicitly by Beckett in the manuscript note quoted earlier invoke death and a spirit world; in Beckett's own production, the boy messenger is made into much more of an "angel of death" than he is in the published script; and, finally, the overall title of "Shades" reminds one that the play which followed *Ghost Trio*, . . . *but the clouds* . . . , quotes from W. B.

Yeats's lines from "The Tower," in which the memory of friendship and love

> Seem but the clouds of the sky
> When the horizon fades,
> Or a bird's sleepy cry
> Among the deepening shades.[33]

And so, just as men waited in vain for Godot over a quarter of a century earlier, so man waits here alone, haunted by Beethoven's ghostly theme, for a woman visitor who never comes, who may be death or may equally well be nothingness. For it needs to be said very clearly that, in spite of these pointers, she is known only as the one for whom he waits and who does not come.

The play's dominant structure is of three parts or movements. And, within the work, another trio is formed, consisting of the male figure, F; the female voice; and the boy messenger. Yet, as I have suggested, the status of these figures or voices is totally uncertain; and their relationships, incomplete. Everything in and about the play suggests a crucial absence: F's own "absent look" and concern for what is not there; the problematic status of the voice; the boy's strange appearance and retreat after the negative shaking of his head; the Beethoven theme, which evokes a spectral world; and the tripartite structure of the play leading to a climactic meeting which never takes place. Indeed it may not be too alien to Beckett's ways of thinking to suggest that the visible shapes and the sharp lines of its rectangles may be formally contrasted with the uncertain, insecure nature of its suggested triangles.

For ambiguity and mystery not only hold the attention of the viewer, but they also lie at the very heart of this meticulously constructed little play. All the unsolved questions relating to the unusual room, with its "familiar" yet strangely abstracted features, the unidentified Voice, the insubstantial figure with his "slow drifting walk," the boy messenger, and the haunting music all point to an absent center and are crucial to the play's deeper meaning. It may be much neater to foist allegorical or autobiographical meanings onto the work than to accept that no specific meaning can be abstracted by merely supplying one's own answers to the unanswered questions within the play. The truth seems to be that *Ghost Trio* can be seized only in and through its formal shape, where everything is shaped around that absent center, longed for but never attained. So the theme that "being is being perceived," which arises in this play as it did in *Film* and *Eh Joe*, emerges in such a way that it reflects a crucial absence. Instead of the meeting for which he waits so patiently, F encounters in the room only a reflected image of himself seen in the mirror. The final images, as he stares back at the camera for the first time since camera shot and mirror image combined, suggest that the eye of the camera may be the only way of keeping him vicariously in being.

I hope that my analysis of Beckett's manuscript notes and certain aspects of the productions on which the author worked may have helped to reveal how carefully he worked on the formal patterning of the play so as to attain an ambiguity and a sense of mystery that is crucial to the play's impact. It is not surprising if, when asked about the play's "meaning," the critic should fall back on the haunting beauty of its images or its intricate parallels and repetitions. For, if I have understood it correctly, that "meaning" is itself the indefinable, the absent center.

NOTES

1. *Ghost Trio* was the first of three short plays in a program entitled "Shades" on BBC 2; the other plays were . . . *but the clouds* . . . and *Not I*. *Ghost Trio* was directed by Donald McWhinnie, with Beckett's help, and was produced by Tristram Powell. The Male figure F was played by Ronald Pickup; the Female Voice, by Billie Whitelaw; and the Boy, by Rupert Horder. Rehearsals were from September 30 to October 5, 1976, and the play was filmed (with . . . *but the clouds* . . .) from October 6 to October 8. It was first broadcast on April 17, 1977.
2. *Geister Trio* was produced for Süddeutscher Rundfunk in Stuttgart by Dr. Müller-Freienfels and was directed by Samuel Beckett. Again it figured as the first of the films in the program called "Schatten," with the BBC *Not I* as the third film. Klaus Herm played the male figure; Irmgard Forst, the Female Voice; and Matthias Feil, the Boy. The plays were first broadcast on November 1, 1977.
3. Beckett had worked most recently with Jim Lewis when he directed *He Joe* for Süddeutscher Rundfunk in 1979. He later worked with him again on *Quadrat I + II*, first broadcast on October 8, 1981, and on *Nacht und Träume*, first broadcast on May 19, 1983.
4. See S. E. Gontarski, *The Intent of Undoing in Samuel Beckett's*

Dramatic Texts (Bloomington, Ind.: Indiana University Press, 1985), pp. 121–25.

5. See, for example, John Calder, " 'The Lively Arts': Three Plays by Samuel Beckett," *Journal of Beckett Studies* 2 (Summer 1977), 117–21; Beryl Fletcher et al., *A Student's Guide to the Plays of Samuel Beckett* (London: Faber & Faber, 1978), pp. 210–16; and Linda Ben-Zvi, "Samuel Beckett's Media Plays," *Modern Drama* 28 (March 1985), 22–37.

6. Reading University Library (hereafter abbreviated as R.U.L.) Ms. 1519/1 is the first of a series of documents relating to *Ghost Trio*. The manuscript was first entitled *Tryst*, which was amended only at a late stage. Even the BBC script (Project no. 4154/9166) was prepared with the title *Tryst*.

7. R.U.L. Ms. 1519/1.

8. R.U.L. Ms. 1519/2 (a corrected typescript of twelve leaves). The note quoted precedes Beckett's typed notes at the top of leaf 12.

9. Gontarski, *Intent*, p. 123.

10. R.U.L. Ms. 1519/1.

11. This note appears on a leaf numbered by Beckett as page 23 in R.U.L. Ms. 1519/1.

12. In R.U.L. Ms. 1519/1, Beckett writes out four pages of synopses of what happens in each of the three sections of the play, where he lists every camera shot, all the interjections by Voice, and the movements of F, and gives the number of seconds that each separate "unit" takes up and the total time of each section. In Part I, he corrects several of the times, probably in the interest of balance, making the camera close-ups of the floor, wall, door, window, and pallet each last a total of five seconds.

13. There are six leaves of the original manuscript devoted to the music, where "Beckett fragmented the melodic line the way he would fragment narrative line, all with stopwatch precision" (Gontarski, *Intent*, p. 124).

14. The total running time of the two versions are as follows: BBC version, 21½ minutes; Süddeutscher Rundfunk version, 29 minutes.

15. The initial camera position is farther away from the seated male figure in Beckett's production and also appears to film the "general view" from a lower camera angle.

16. As may be seen in a photograph by Hugo Jehle reproduced in the *Journal of Beckett Studies* 3 (Summer 1978), 90c.

17. See "Beckett and Kleist's essay 'On the Marionette Theatre,' " in James Knowlson and John Pilling, *Frescoes of the Skull: The Later*

    Prose and Drama of Samuel Beckett (London: John Calder, 1979),
    pp. 277–85.
18. Heinrich von Kleist, "About the Marionette Theatre," translated by
    Cherna Murray, *Life and Letters Today* 16 (Summer 1937), 103.
19. R.U.L. Ms. 1519/1, leaf 11.
20. The word is Beckett's. In R.U.L. Ms. 1519/1, leaf 3, under "Gen-
    eral Notes," he writes: "Camera. Once set for shot it should not
    explore, simply look. It stops and stares. Its mobility is confined to
    stealthy or lightning (cut shots) advance or withdrawal to positions
    established in view of the most telling stills."
21. R.U.L. Ms. 1519/1, leaf 23, "Boy's steps."
22. Samuel Beckett, *Ghost Trio* in *Ends and Odds: Plays and Sketches*
    (London: Faber & Faber, 1977), p. 47. References to the numbers in
    the three parts of the play are to this edition, which is more accurate
    than the Grove Press edition.
23. R.U.L. Ms. 1519/1.
24. Liner notes by Hans Christoph Worbs to the Phillips recording by
    the Beaux Arts Trio of Beethoven's piano trios.
25. Michael Billington, *The Guardian*, April 19, 1977; reprinted in
    Fletcher et al., *Student's Guide*, p. 210.
26. Dennis Potter, *The Sunday Times*, April 24, 1977; reprinted in
    Fletcher et al., *Student's Guide*, p. 210.
27. Fletcher et al., *Student's Guide*, p. 213.
28. Ibid., p. 214.
29. Ibid., p. 215.
30. Calder, "Lively Arts," p. 118.
31. Ibid., p. 117.
32. R.U.L. Ms. 1519/1, leaf 3.
33. W. B. Yeats, "The Tower," quoted in *Ends and Odds: Plays and
    Sketches*, p. 56.

"Wham, Bam, Thank You Sam":
The Presence of Beckett

THOMAS R. WHITAKER

I

When playwrights respond to an enigmatic predecessor, they direct useful crosslights on the texture and meaning of his work. Even a selective look at Beckett's presence in the contemporary English-speaking theater may, therefore, suggest a few hypotheses that would be worth testing more fully, on some other occasion, against his texts-in-performance. I suspect, however, that we have no chance of thinking clearly about Beckett's "presence" anywhere unless we first acknowledge the "absence" that has often seemed the burden of his work. "Every word," he has said to an interviewer, "is like an unnecessary stain of silence and nothingness."[1] And critics often remind us that he has declared a preference for an art that is "the expression that there is nothing to express, nothing with which to express, nothing from which to express, no power to express, no desire to express, together with the obligation to express."[2] Though the origin of that obligation may remain a mystery, it's clear that art so construed could never do more than express an "absence" to an "absence."

The most memorable situations, images, and sentences in Beckett's plays incline us toward that same desperate conclusion. "Nothing to be done," says Estragon at the outset of *Waiting for Godot*, where any nontrivial question about human existence seems impossible to resolve. And though Vladimir and Estragon finally say, "Let's go," they don't move. "Finished, it's finished, nearly finished, it must be nearly finished," says Clov at the outset of Endgame, which reduces the world to a bare room where an unspecifiable something is "taking its course." "Absent always," says Hamm near its end. "It all happened without me."[3] Later plays find yet more extreme images of uncertainty, immobility, impotence, and isolation. In Happy Days Winnie is being sucked into the earth by a force that seems to have reduced her life to a babble of memories on the verge of annihilation. In Play the heads of two women and a man rehearse from funeral urns a repeatable script at the behest of an arbitrary or cruel spotlight. And in Not I, the speaker has become a Mouth in a black void, physically and syntactically divorced from any personal identity, whose stammerings of a past life can be heard only by a silent Auditor of whose responses it can't be aware.

Quite understandably, critics have often concluded that Beckett is, or wants to be, the serious reductio ad absurdum of an age in which the mind has lost its illusions of any divine source, order of values, or sustaining world and finds itself trapped in the arbitrary, the incoherent, and the meaningless. One has summed up Beckett in the phrase "zero identity." The modern "declining vitality of the self," he has said, here "reaches its low point," and human existence is "suspended over a void made palpable."[4] Another for whom Beckett's subject is "the imminent collapse of being itself" has found in his plays "a theatrical metaphor for man suffering an existence which is in the process of continuous devaluation."[5] Yet another has argued that Beckett's entire canon consists of efforts to find a shape for "the proposition that perhaps no relationships exist between or among the artist, his art, and an external reality."[6] And yet another has told us that Beckett's plays sum up the audience's preexisting intuition that no form can exist outside of consciousness. The stage, therefore, becomes "a model of consciousness, which, if it creates order, does so only to discover that order has no ontological ground." This "theatrical positivism," he has said, devotes itself to self-canceling games and routines, with which the modern theater reaches its epitome and "seems also to come to an end."[7]

We can be persuaded by such sweeping conclusions, however, only if we somehow exempt Beckett and ourselves from the condition that we say he is expressing. To write or to interpret his plays requires assumptions about the reliability of perception, the communicability of ideas, and the possibility of informed action that could apply to no condition in which we can connect nothing with nothing. Even Vladimir could neither write nor interpret the allusive and shapely dialogue of *Waiting for Godot*, and the speakers of *Play* and *Not I* are much less able to understand the dramatic forms of which they are functions. We can be persuaded by such conclusions, moreover, only if we overlook values that the plays accept as given and proceed to build into their effects. Didi and Gogo are comic in their inadvertence and incompetence and admirable for their wit, fortitude, fraternal affection, and sense of justice. Hamm and Clov, who grudgingly acknowledge a mutual dependence, are portrayed with unsentimental charity as the cold, suffering, and self-destructive narcissists that they are. And the self-obsessed Winnie is surely a marvel of sprightly endurance. One critic has recently argued that *Not I* achieves an extreme condition of human absence by giving us minimal details about an "uneventful life," depriving the present of "immediacy," avoiding any image of "consciousness," and offering "only the text that repeats itself within it."[8] At Lincoln Center in 1972, however, audiences quite rightly found Jessica Tandy's rendering of that old woman's blighted, bitter, and yearning life—articulated only through the hysterically detached medium of her mouth—to be a present experience both poignant and searing.

Such values are communicated, of course, in and through the community event that is theater. In the actual performance of a Beckett play, there can be no serious question of "zero identity," the "imminent collapse of being," or "theatrical positivism." Beckett's reduction of his characters to comic types, partial persons, and disembodied voices can be enacted and understood only by beings who are not so reduced. Indeed, every such reduction derives its theatrical force from the fact that it both requires and resists the medium of live actors and witnesses. No performance of *Endgame* could take place in the world represented or suggested by that play. The roles of the confused and enervated pair who wait for Godot require the precision and brio of skilled comedians. The trapped Winnie is a juicy part for an artist of that oblique form of dialogue with an audience which we call dramatic monologue.

Recognizing such facts of theater, we must admit that, whatever Beckett's ostensible aims, he is an ironic master of the rhetoric of minimalism. His apparent negations heighten many positive theatrical qualities. He invites us to relish the precise articulation of uncertainties and the arduous miming of incapabilities. Every apparent separation of mind from body offers a challenge to the actor's discipline.[9] Every apparent loss occurs in a world of literary and theatrical plenitude without which this performance would be impossible. And every image of solipsism reaches us through a collaboratively shaped event. If the performed action seems to imply despair or vertigo on the edge of the abyss, the action of performance requires of director, actors, and audience the full stretch of our sympathetic and interpretive powers. Through the shared imagination of absence, such plays as *Endgame, Happy Days,* and *Not I* open themselves to the fullness of human presence.

No doubt, Beckett, who is a shrewd rhetorician and a skilled director of his own plays, knows all this quite well. When he was thinking about *That Time,* a play written two years after *Not I,* he jotted down this note: "to the objection visual component too small, out of all proportion with aural, answer: make it smaller on the principle that less is more."[10] And he had earlier written to a young and admiring playwright, Keith Johnstone, that a "stage is an area of maximum verbal presence, and maximum corporeal presence." Johnstone, who taught improvisation at the Royal Court Theatre, was especially delighted by the word "corporeal."[11] Such craftsman's remarks are worth more than all Beckett's talk about the expression that there is nothing to express. Only if we recognize him as a minimalist, an ironic artist of "maximum presence," can we begin to cope with the otherwise incomprehensible fact that this playwright of stasis, sterility, and absence has become such an explosively fertile presence in a theater that still declines to come to an end.

II

For some three decades, as Beckett has pursued his hyperbolic and ironic course, he has nourished directors and playwrights whose strategies may seem at odds with his own but whose transformations of his work acknowledge and help to elucidate its implications. A minor but instructive instance recently occurred in Cambridge, Massachusetts. The American Repertory Theatre began work late in 1984 on a production of *Endgame* that would set the action in a subway

tunnel, give the roles of Hamm and Nagg to black actors, make some
minor textual changes, and add music by Philip Glass. The director
JoAnne Akalaitis wasn't new to the task of opening up or translating
a Beckett script. Several years earlier she had produced for Mabou
Mines an adaptation of the introverted radio play *Cascando* that
struck some viewers as a remarkable experiment in auditory and visual
design. Her proposed *Endgame*, however, aroused Beckett's objec-
tions. Through his United States publisher and agent, he sought to
halt the production. An out-of-court settlement, reached hours before
the opening night curtain, allowed the play to proceed only on condition that the theater withdraw the author's name from all advertis-
ing and print a program insert containing the original stage directions
and a statement by Beckett that disavowed the production "as a complete parody of the play as conceived by me." For Robert Brustein,
the theater's artistic director, Beckett had raised "a serious civil rights
issue, one with First Amendment considerations." He, therefore, also
inserted in the program a rejoinder stating, "Normal rights of interpretation are essential in order to free the full energy and meaning
of the play."[12]

The dispute is not easy to resolve. Akalaitis and Brustein assume
that theater is a collaborative art and that a play can't release its
meaning without the contributions of directors and actors. Beckett
assumes that his legal rights of ownership over the text should enable
him to prevent distortion of its form and meaning by a theatrical
company. Both parties, however, effectively agree that theatrical
meanings are social, embodied, fairly determinate, and subject to
reasonable debate. And neither seems troubled by some universal
crisis of identity, imminent collapse of being, or lack of relation between individual consciousness and external reality. Indeed, their
exchange might have been predicted on the basis of a letter that
Beckett had written in 1957 to his first American director, Alan
Schneider, warning against journalistic attempts to interpret *Endgame*:

My work is a matter of fundamental sounds (no joke intended) made as
fully as possible, and I accept responsibility for nothing else. If people
want to have headaches among the overtones, let them. And provide their
own aspirin. Hamm as stated, and Clov as stated, together as stated, nec
tecum nec sine te, in such a place and in such a world, that's all I can
manage, more than I could.[13]

Excited by some of the ethical and apocalyptic overtones in *Endgame*, Akalaitis no doubt thought to amplify them for an American audience in 1984 by alluding to our tense and ambivalent household of blacks and whites trapped within a terrifying urban devastation. And she couldn't resist asking Philip Glass to add some further harmonies. As a citizen in a capitalist society, Beckett may choose to object, but he seems up against the fact that "maximum presence" is inherently prolific.

A friendlier instance of Beckett's presence in a mode of theater that he could hardly endorse occurred in 1972, when the Old Vic produced Tom Stoppard's *Jumpers*. Stoppard had earlier written an inside-out version of *Hamlet* that drew on the style and situation of *Waiting for Godot* without, as critics often complained, taking its existential predicament quite seriously. Perhaps because Stoppard grasped a paradox in Beckett's work that such critics had missed, he let *Rosencrantz and Guildenstern Are Dead* play rather self-consciously with the notion of ontological "absence" as a means of establishing a lively theatrical presence.[14] *Jumpers*, however, would have seemed to its first audience quite un-Beckettlike despite the fact that its comic hero, the bumbling moral philosopher George Moore, makes an academic career out of Vladimir's talent for worrying over the uncertain grounds for ethical action while ignoring nearby calls for help. Brashly eclectic in style, *Jumpers* uses Orton and Feydeau, Shaw and the circus, Joyce and the TV sitcom to explore the ambiguities of our modern condition. Only at its end does Beckett's presence declare itself. When the exasperated and exhausted George Moore falls into a Joycean dream and delivers a passionate and absurd speech in defense of ethical certainties despite the fact that "nothing is certain," he is answered by his antagonist, the suave and amoral philosopher, Sir Archibald Jumper, who suddenly becomes Stoppard's ironic raissoneur. Archie's jazzy speech plays with yet more specific memories of *Waiting for Godot*: Vladimir's interest in the two thieves, only one of whom was saved; Pozzo's dark summary of how "They give birth astride of a grave, the light gleams an instant, then it's night once more"; and Vladimir's elaboration of that vision: "Astride of a grave and a difficult birth. Down in the hole, lingeringly, the grave-digger puts on the forceps. We have time to grow old. The air is full of our cries."[15] Remembering these things, Archie begins his speech with a kind of riff on the theme of the two thieves:

Do not despair—many are happy much of the time; more eat than starve, more are healthy than sick, more curable than dying; not so many dying as dead; and one of the thieves was saved. Hell's bells and all's well—half of the world is at peace with itself, and so is the other half; vast areas are unpolluted; millions of children grow up without suffering deprivation, and millions, while deprived, grow up without suffering cruelties, and millions, while deprived and cruelly treated, none the less grow up. No laughter is sad and many tears are joyful.

Then, impudently reversing Pozzo's and Didi's dark reflections on the birth astride a grave, he adds: "At the graveside the undertaker doffs his top hat and impregnates the prettiest mourner. Wham, bam, thank you Sam."[16] With that arch translation of death into fertility and "ma'am" into "Sam," Stoppard drives home his play's complex irony. Archie has reason enough to be grateful: the world portrayed in *Jumpers* seems almost as devoid of ontological grounding as that in *Waiting for Godot*, and this sinister Dr. Pangloss is its apologist. But Stoppard himself is also grateful: he has found in Beckett's play not solipsistic games but a precise and inclusive wit, an acute ethical sensibility, and a wry sympathy with the foibles and anxieties of our common humanity. If the worlds represented in *Waiting for Godot* and *Jumpers* seem to deprive our ethical judgments of ontological grounds, Stoppard understands that both plays, nevertheless, rely for their intelligibility on our imperiled capacities for just such judgments. As ironic works, they establish their centers of dramatic understanding not in the worlds they represent but in the present community that plays those worlds.

III

We could usefully spend a good deal of time thinking about Beckett's presence in British theater—and especially in that of Harold Pinter. But perhaps his ethical and even metaphysical presence emerges most clearly, not in such variations on his idiom as Stoppard's *Rosencrantz and Guildenstern Are Dead* or *Jumpers*; or James Saunders's *Next Time I'll Sing to You*; or Edward Bond's *Saved*; or Peter Brook's production of *King Lear*; or Pinter's *The Birthday Party*, *The Caretaker*, *Landscape*, *Old Times*, or *No Man's Land*, but in the quite distinctive work of two African dramatists. The country road of *Waiting for Godot*, which runs across a bare stage from nowhere to nowhere, has had special resonances for both Athol Fugard and Wole Soyinka. The South African road through the great Karroo, that "awesome landscape of nothing" in which Fugard was born, became an insistent motif in his work as early as 1961 with *The Blood Knot*.[17] And the hazardous Nigerian road, littered with carrion and automobile parts, has long been for Soyinka a place of both accidents and essence, ruled by the god of death and creativity and the first actor.[18] Though Fugard and Soyinka have learned much from Beckett, they haven't let his reputation as a playwright of absence distort their own understandings of the theater. Fugard has remained a naturalist who agrees with Albert Camus that a literature of despair is a contradiction in terms. Soyinka has remained an ambivalent poet-satirist who is fascinated by ritual theater. And both have understood that Beckett's road of ontological insecurity must somehow become in the theater a road of ethical and even metaphysical transformation.

During the 1960s, Beckett was central to what Fugard called his own attempts "to understand the possibility of affirmation in an essentially morbid society." Rehearsing a nonwhite production of *Waiting for Godot* in 1962, he told the cast that "Vladimir and Estragon must have read the accounts of the Nuremberg trials—or else they were at Sharpeville or were the first in at Auschwitz. Choose your horror—they know all about it." And he thought that the often unemployed man who was playing Lucky "had his fingers on the pulse" of the action because "*Godot* was all about what had been happening to him for as long as he could remember." But if Fugard could say that Vladimir and Estragon "are Man in a state of Anguish," he didn't find the play itself a depressing sign of that condition. Everything of Beckett's that he had read made him want to work. "I suppose," he said, "it's because I really understand, emotionally, and this cannot but give me power and energy and faith." He rejected a critic's argument that Beckett's writing is an extension of the thought of Descartes. And he defended that writing against a friend's charge of "despairing futility." What did he find in it that was positive? "Love and compassion." But of what? "Man's absurd and bruised carnality."[19]

In producing *Godot*, moreover, Fugard learned once again that a play is fundamentally "an actor before an audience" and that its production may be even more important for what it does to the actors than for what it does to the audience. In any case, he said, the "audience's awareness of the actors and the living moment" is always matched by "the actor's awareness *within* that moment." And he added: "My wholeness as a playwright is that I contain within myself both experiences—I watch and am watched—I examine the experience and I experience." Partly because Beckett could elicit and confirm such insights into the participatory nature of the theatrical events, Fugard thought him a greater "poet in the theatre" than T. S. Eliot "has been or ever will be."[20]

Several years after his production of *Godot*, Fugard began writing a play about a colored and Afrikaans-speaking couple who, having been reduced to "rubbish" by their society, face each other "across the scraps and remnants of their life." Like Didi and Gogo or, indeed, like the Morris and Zach of Fugard's *The Blood Knot*, Boesman and Lena are "tied" together, "victims of a common predicament— and of each other." And like Didi and Gogo, they cling to each other in antagonism, uncertainty, and fidelity. But the level at which their predicament fascinated Fugard was finally, as he said, "neither political nor social but metaphysical . . . a metaphor of the human condition which revolution or legislation cannot substantially change." Like Lena, we are all burdened by those "unanswerable little words: Why? How? Who?" And our ontological insecurity leads us, as it leads her, to ask that our "life be witnessed."[21]

Boesman and Lena is shot through with variations on familiar Beckett themes. "I asked you when we came here last," says the muddled Lena, staring about the empty stage. "Is that nonsense?" "Yes!" snaps Boesman. "What difference does it make? To anything? You're here now!" But Lena won't let the question drop. "From where to where?" she later asks. "All mixed up. The right time on the wrong road, the right road leading to the wrong place."[22] She would understand Gogo's complaint: "I sometimes wonder if we wouldn't have been better off alone," he says to Didi, "each one for himself. We weren't made for the same road."[23] But Lena's husband is not just a South African Vladimir. In his arrogance, disgust, self-hatred, and secret dependence, he is also a Pozzo and a Hamm, just as Lena, in her confused passivity and hard resistance, is also a Lucky and a Clov—and, in her final claim to be worthy of being witnessed, another Vladimir and a Winnie. *Boesman and Lena*, therefore, contains a synthesis of Beckett situations, but it produces a rather different effect. Fugard the naturalist, always concerned with the "intimacy of experience,"[24] has found for these compound characters a rich sub-text. "Only a fraction of my truth," he could rightly say, "is in the words."[25] Any performance, therefore, brings into the open, to a degree impossible in the more stylized action of *Godot, Endgame,* or *Happy Days,* the implicit positives that Fugard found in Beckett's bleak verbal comedy. Watching *Boesman and Lena,* we easily understand that, though its characters seem tied to each other by hatred, abuse, and acceptance, it is really about their hidden love and their imperfectly acknowledged value. And we also understand why Lena's demand to be witnessed by Outa, the dying old black and the ultimate Lucky of this play, constitutes a major clue to the ethical and metaphysical implications of both Fugard's and Beckett's drama.

Vladimir, we recall, says to the Boy, "Tell him . . . tell him you saw us."[26] And in *Happy Days* Winnie fastens her eyes on the audience and says: "Someone is looking at me still. . . . Caring for me still. . . . That is what I find so wonderful. . . . Eyes on my eyes."[27] Fugard's Lena says to Outa: "You be witness for me." And again: "I'll tell you what it is. Eyes, Outa. Another pair of eyes. Something to see you." And she proceeds to share with him her mug of tea and piece of bread. She realizes that the rudimentary witnessing provided by a sick and outcast black who can repeat only one word in her language—"Lena"—can provide the present goal for all her wanderings. "The walks led *here,*" she says to Boesman. "Tonight. And he sees it."[28] But Outa is not Lena's only witness, nor are she and Boesman left on an empty stage as witnesses for each other. Fugard's understanding of the participatory dimension of Beckett's theater and his own implies that the playwright, actors, and audience are also witnesses to this situation, which is also theirs, and that such mutual witnessing is finally more important than the represented deprivations. When Vladimir hears the cries of the blind and fallen Pozzo, he says: "To all mankind they were addressed, those cries for help still ringing in our ears! But at this place, at this moment of time, all mankind is us, whether we like it or not." And a few minutes later Estragon says of Pozzo himself: "He's all humanity."[29] For Fugard, the comedy of that situation does not obliterate its primal truth. In 1971 he could look back on the writing of *Boesman and Lena* as the time when he "moved from 'artifice' to 'witnessing'—with all the compulsion, urgency, moral imperative of that role."[30] And on many occasions—in South Africa in 1969 with Fugard and Yvonne Bryce-

land as Boesman and Lena, in New York in 1970 with James Earl
Jones and Ruby Dee, in London in 1971 with Zakes Mokae and
Bryceland, and even in Paris in 1976 with a cast directed by Roger
Blin, the first director of En attendant Godot—actors and audiences
have found their various walks leading here, tonight, for a renewed
awareness of our human solidarity.[31]

Though never again following Beckett so closely, Fugard has continued to turn the road of emptiness, isolation, and repression into
one of mutual understanding. And he has also continued in surprising ways to suggest Beckett's presence. A recent play, mounted by the
Yale Repertory Theater in 1984, seems firmly in the Ibsen tradition.
The action of The Road to Mecca takes place in a provincial and
Calvinist town. The set is a living room. The dialogue is freighted
with retrospective analysis. The three characters are a narrow-minded
pastor, a desperate young teacher and political activist, and an eccen-
tric widow. Gradually, however, we learn why this widow, who lives
along a road that runs through the vast emptiness of the Karroo, has
for years devoted herself to making a fantastic sculpture garden and
decorating her sometimes candle-lit room with mirrors and bits of
ground-up beer bottles. Helen has sought to transform the dark road
of her life into an illuminated road to Mecca. And in doing so, she
has come to seem a bizarre and poignant image of the modern artist,
an artist rather like Beckett as he is commonly perceived, who keeps
a precarious hold on sanity by withdrawing from the void to create a
tiny but endlessly reflecting play of lights and mirrors and grotesque
creatures. Having shown us this, however, The Road to Mecca proceeds to suggest a more adequate image of dramatic art—whether
Beckett's or Fugard's—one in accord with the process that its actors
and audience have already begun to experience. By showing us the
understanding of Helen's quest attained by the pastor and by the
young teacher, Elsa, it begins to undo the ironies of isolation that
both Ibsen and Beckett had underlined. Somewhat as Fugard had
found in Beckett's work an inspiriting energy and faith, so Elsa now
finds in Helen's a courage that helps her to break out of her own
desperate self-closure. In their moment of mutual understanding,
Helen resolves to learn how to blow out the candles and face the
darkness—and Elsa makes the difficult leap to join her in trust.[32]

The partial image of Beckett as a hermetic master who withdraws
from a landscape of destruction or emptiness to fashion an art almost

indistinguishable from absence or death has been explicated in a very different way by Wole Soyinka. Unlike Fugard, Soyinka has not acknowledged Beckett's work with much sympathy. In *Myth, Literature and the African World*, a book published in 1976, he cited Beckett's oeuvre as an instance of "literary ideology" taking "private hallucinatory forms." Beckett, he said, "gropes incessantly towards the theatrical statement that can be made in one word, a non-too-distant blood-relation of the chimeric obsessions of the Surrealists." He granted that, if we leave the "lunatic fringe of the literary Unilateral Declaration of Independence," we may find that "a literary ideology does occasionally achieve coincidence—and so a value expansion— with a social vision."[33] But he chose not to mention the fact that he himself had already expanded Beckett's "ideology" in just that way.

After studying with G. Wilson Knight at Leeds University, Soyinka had worked at the Royal Court Theatre in the late 1950s as playreader, writer, producer, and actor, along with a remarkable group that included Edward Bond, John Arden, Anne Jellicoe, and Keith Johnstone—the admirer of Beckett's verbal and corporeal "presence" who influenced them all through his teaching of improvisation and the use of masks to unlock the hidden and perhaps Dionysiac energies of the psyche.[34] During the early sixties, Soyinka was back in Ibadan, putting some of this teaching into practice as he wrote and directed Nigerian plays for several acting companies. He returned to London in 1965 to advise on Stage '60's production of his play *The Road* at the Theatre Royal, Stratford East.[35] *The Road* makes it quite clear that he had come to see Beckett as a partial image of his own rather Nietzschean attempt to devise a theater in which characters, actors, and witnesses might enter something like the Yoruba "abyss of transition" and so experience both death and new life.[36]

Just as Beckett, in Soyinka's later phrase, "gropes incessantly towards the theatrical statement that can be made in one word," so Professor in *The Road*, according to an introductory note, is engaged in a "part psychic, part intellectual grope . . . towards the essence of death,"[37] which he understands to be the hidden Word. A defrocked Christian minister of doubtful sanity, he approaches that essence through the accidents of the road. He runs an "Aksident Store" that recycles the parts of wrecked lorries, forges licenses for unskilled truck drivers, and devotes himself to a Yoruba cult of death. Like some demented *symboliste*, he goes about pulling up road signs because the word "BEND," for example, sprouting from the earth, might give him a clue to the ultimate Word. And in his description of a nearby gorge, he seems to have revised Vladimir's meditation on the difficult birth astride of a grave—not, as Stoppard's Archie will revise it, into a celebration of fertility but into a yet harsher comment on sterility: "Below that bridge, a black rise of buttocks, two unyielding thighs and that red trickle like a woman washing her monthly pain in a thin river. So many lives rush in and out between her legs, and most of it a waste."[38] But Professor's grope toward the Word of absence and death is not just a wry version of Beckett's. It is also part of a serious interrogation of Ogun, the death-bringing and creative tutelar spirit of truck drivers and actors.

The rather sprawling shape of The Road, which has nothing to do with Beckett's minimalism, richly expands Professor's ideology so that it coincides with an ethically ambiguous social vision. Its comic and macabre episodes, which cover a daylong stretch of almost continuous action, acquaint us with an entire community of drivers who are haunted or obsessed by death. Drumming, choral dirges, and hypnotic dances are an integral part of the play's effect. In its first major climax in Part Two, the drivers Samson and Kotonu reenact their experience during a Drivers Festival in celebration of Ogun, when a third driver, Murano, had been run down by their truck while bearing the egungun, a mask of hypnotic and deathly power. Since that accident, we know, Murano has been suspended in a state of living death. He has been for us, ever since the play's opening moments, a liminal presence onstage, radiating absence: mute, limping, ready to slash out with a knife. And his incommunicable knowledge has been the most immediate object of Professor's quest. At the end of this day, after bringing the palm wine to Professor for their nightly communion, Murano disappears into the Aksident Store and then seems to reemerge as the egungun. The mask begins a dance of death, accompanied by the drummers who are urged on by Professor in his hope to provoke some direct disclosure of the Word. At the climax of the dance, however, a terrified driver tries to halt this "sacrilege," knifes Professor, and is smashed to death by the egungun. As the mask collapses into nothingness, Professor utters a dying benediction that asks us to identify with the abyss that the play has in so many ways evoked:

Be even like the road itself. Flatten your bellies with the hunger of an unpropitious day, power your hands with the knowledge of death. . . . Spread a broad sheet for death with the length and the time of the sun between you until the one face multiplies and the one shadow is cast by all the doomed. Breathe like the road, be even like the road itself. . . .[39]

A haunting and ironical presence, Professor embodies a death longing that is also a desire to reach a heightened and creative state of life. His full meaning becomes evident if we place The Road in the context of Soyinka's notes on the theater. "The stage," he has said, "is created for the purpose of that communal presence which alone defines it." A play's "essence" must, therefore, be found not in the "printed text" alone but in the arena of performance. Soyinka tells how, in Yoruba ritual drama, the actor shares "the protagonist's foray" into the "psychic abyss of the re-creative energies," and the choric community shares the actor's own "disintegration and re-assembly within the universal womb of origin," and the entire event repeats the primal experience of Ogun, the first actor.[40] Qualified by a distancing but not negating irony, that vision of participatory theater—which rather parallels Nietzsche's account in The Birth of Tragedy—informs The Road. And Beckett's expanded presence in The Road seems finally to come to this: by way of G. Wilson Knight, Nietzsche, Keith Johnstone, and Yoruba lore, Soyinka has understood that Beckett's plays can operate rather like severe European versions of those Yoruba masks and rites of death which may serve to unlock in us a subliminal and transpersonal creative energy.

Fugard and Soyinka shed light on Beckett's ironic minimalism from two sharply different angles. Boesman and Lena invites us to experience an ethic of mutual witnessing that is grounded in an implicit metaphysic of human solidarity. The Road invites us to explore an ethically ambiguous realm that threatens—or promises—to transform our social identities. That exploration is grounded in an implicit metaphysic of participation in a transpersonal energy that can support the risky journey of the ongoing community. From the paradoxical matrix of Beckett's theater of apparent absence, these African playwrights have abstracted and amplified two complementary modes of histrionic presence.

IV

The puzzles that lurk in this double vision of Beckett may be unfolded or at least complicated a bit further if we glance at two American playwrights, David Mamet and Sam Shepard. Here Beckett's presence is again quite evident—as mediated, of course, by Harold Pinter, the American vernacular, the underbelly of Chicago, and salesmen's hype or by jazz, rock culture, Pirandellian theatricalism, Brechtian narrative acting, the myth of the West, and much else. Beckett's empty road, bare room, wheelchair throne, ash cans, urns, rocking chairs, and disappearing characters find their counterparts in such things as Kent's empty silhouette in *La Turista*, the abandoned Chevy in *The Unseen Hand*, the bare room in *Action*, the cosmic throne room in *The Tooth of Crime*, the trashed Resale Shop in *American Buffalo*, the prison cell in *Edmond*, and the reverberating motel room and spectral rocking chair on the edge of the Mojave Desert in *Fool for Love*. Mamet and Shepard invite our identification with characters who seem lost in a pile of junk, making themselves up as they go along, ruminating in an echoing void, or speeding toward an impossible absence. An ethical response to that identification, however, though often encouraged by images of the venality and viciousness of a commercial society, is likely to be blocked or complicated by theatrical strategies that make our usual categories of judgment seem irrelevant. Forcing us toward a more problematic experience, those strategies invoke an aspect of Beckett's theater that is finally more important than his sets, characters, situations, or motifs. Mamet and Shepard seem to have understood the theater as a model of consciousness that is both interpersonal and intrapersonal—and so, in effect, transpersonal. They have, therefore, been able to give American expression to that strange presence-in-absence or intimacy-in-isolation which gains force in Büchner, the later Ibsen, Chekhov, and Strindberg and utterly dominates Beckett's work.

Several dramatic strategies, we may recall, make *Waiting for Godot* and *Endgame* not so much dialogues among distinct selves as the miming of a mind's conversation with itself. Reduced, stylized, and isolate types—Didi and Gogo, Pozzo and Lucky, Hamm and Clov, Nagg and Nell—form patterns of mirroring and complementary pairs. Their balanced actions, stichomythic exchanges, and dreamlike echoings and reversals comprise lyric and meditative wholes beyond their individual intent. *Happy Days* and *Play* go even further to subsume their isolate characters within a larger theatrical field: the offstage alarm clock, stage lights, and audience of *Happy Days* and the spotlight and audience of *Play* are agents within the plays that they seem to control or observe. In such theatrical events the relations among the characters and participants no longer seem simply external: each character, actor, or member of the audience tends to become a spontaneous function of some waking dream that is at once the collaborative act of several minds and the encompassing act of a larger mind or psychic field. Beckett's own rigorous direction of *Endgame* as an almost musical performance is clearly in harmony with this notion.[41] If a Beckett play offers us a model of consciousness, it is one that reflects us in its parts and as a whole and one in which we also participate. Within such a model, the characters and participants can seem both terribly alone and inseparably members of one another.

Mamet's theater approaches that paradoxical condition by way of its most distinctive attribute: the dialogue. In *The Duck Variations* of 1971, Mamet had already transferred the meditative duets of *Waiting for Godot* on isolation and togetherness, nothing and everything, to a Chicago park, where he explored their possibilities for serial elaboration. Didi and Gogo have a lovely duet on "All the dead voices": "They make a noise like wings"; "Like leaves"; "Like sand"; "Like leaves"—and so forth.[42] When the fourteenth Duck Variation has the elderly George and Emil describe the duck's death in antiphonal style—"Living his last"; "Dying"; "Leaving the Earth and sky"; "Dying"; "Lying on the ground"; "Dying"; "Fluttering"; "Dying"; and so forth[43]—Mamet is quietly saying, "Thank you Sam." By 1976, with *American Buffalo*, this verbal music, of which the characters tend to become mere functions, had absorbed some important lessons from Pinter as well as Beckett. The inarticulate mumblings, gropings, backtrackings, and outbursts of Don, Teach, and Bob combine to shape a taut, subtly nuanced, and rhythmically elaborate counterpoint of banality, aggression, evasion, and desperation. These characters—like their more glib and strident cousins in *Glengarry Glen Ross*, of 1983—are really as isolate as Hamm and Clov, though too unself-consciously gregarious to be aware of their own predicament. They seem to have not ambiguity but vacuity as a subtext. As masks of a hollow society, they couldn't meet us on any grounds of mutual understanding, and they seem almost beyond our pity or judgment. But as richly modulated, interwoven, and embodied voices, they compose with us a contrapuntal celebration of the American vernacular.

The main paradoxes of Mamet's theater are clarified in a very different kind of play, *Edmond*, of 1982, which recapitulates a heritage that runs from Büchner through Georg Kaiser to Beckett. *Edmond's* twenty-three elliptical scenes follow the downward course of a wife-hating, black-hating, homosexual-hating, and implicitly self-hating man who abruptly leaps from his middle-class existence into the life of the streets. His story, like that of Büchner's Woyzek, involves the fatality experienced by an enraged and repressed loneliness. Edmond's psychotic career, which leads from a search for prostitutes, a mugging by a pimp, and the murder of a waitress, on to a prison, where he is sodomized by a black cell mate, seems to be in the cards from the beginning. But this play is also a rethinking of Kaiser's *From Morn to Midnight*, which it follows in its "station-drama" form and in some details of plot and character. Kaiser's violently erupting Cashier, who tries for a brief upward mobility, meets his end in a Salvation Army Hall rather like the Mission through which Edmond passes in Scene 17. Both *Woyzek* and *From Morn to Midnight* translate the inverted lyricism of isolation into a jagged scenic form in which we can participate. And for both, a suggestion of fatality seems to make irrelevant the ethical judgments that their portrayals of society obviously invite. But poetic naturalism and expressionism culminate in Beckett's synthesis as Mamet implicitly recognizes in the last scene of *Edmond*. There the protagonist and his cell mate become, in effect, another Vladimir and Estragon as their groping antiphonal meditation moves through questions of destiny, abandonment, self-degradation, and guilt to a strangely peaceful resolution. Their goodnight kiss, which may seem sentimental or outrageous if we see them as two distinct selves who have reached a dead end, appropriately resolves the play's interior or transpersonal exorcism of hatred, an exorcism of which all the characters seem to be functions. Divorced from women, the remaining psychic and physical opposites, destructive and self-destructive in their opposition, have moved to an ironic truce of intimacy and isolation within and beyond us.

Shepard's theater approaches a similar condition by more various means. Very much impressed by *Waiting for Godot*, Shepard was already drawing on Beckett's antiphonal dialogues in his first play, *Cowboys*. But even in the extant rewriting of that play, *Cowboys #2*,[44] it is clear that Shepard would be yet more concerned with some other Beckett strategies: the lyrical or expansively self-conscious solos or arias of his characters; their desperate and virtuoso role playing in order to clothe the emptiness of the self; their obscure twinnings and reciprocities; their potentiality for histrionic transformations and reversals; and the paradoxical fields within which they are established. *La Turista*, of 1967, replays in two acts its protagonist's double desire to go away and to go home, but it does so in the context of two settings and two groups of auxiliary characters—Mexican and American—that replicate each other. As in *Godot*, the more it changes, the more it's the same thing. The doubling plot also operates, through weird transformations, increasingly to exile Kent from the action that he already wants to escape—and from the stage itself. With the help of a swinging rope, he finally leaps from the back of the auditorium through the rear stage wall, becoming the emptiness that both he and his circumstances have wanted him to become. Or has he simply vanished from our theatrical field into the depths of our minds? *The Tooth of Crime*, of 1972, translating Hamm's bare room with its dominating chair into a center of power within some stellar void, also elaborates Hamm's histrionic virtuosity still further through the doomed figure of Hoss, who can say: "Ya know, you'd be O.K., Becky, if you had a self. So would I. Something to fall back on in a moment of doubt or terror or even surprise." In his "style match" with Crow, Hoss necessarily loses to that epitome of the next rock generation, whose "survival kit" is the "image," who can almost always avoid talking "like a person" and who can sing: "But I believe in my mask—the man I made up is me."[45] The play's rock music, as hypnotic as Soyinka's rites of death, sweeps us into a shared celebration of histrionic behavior that we understand to be driven by our suicidal fear of our own absence.

La Turista and The Tooth of Crime, like *Godot*, *Endgame*, *Happy Days*, and *Play*, manage to suggest that the theater itself is both our necessary field of play and our unavoidable prison. *Action*, a play of 1979, is Shepard's most probing exploration of that ambivalence. Jeep's first lines—"I'm looking forward to my life. I'm looking forward to uh—me. The way I picture me"—open a self-analytic and quietly hysterical meditation on the arbitrariness of histrionic action as a prison or desert. It's a meditation that takes place not just within Jeep—who can ask, "What's a community?" or "Could you create some reason for me to move?"—but within a group of characters who inhabit an incoherent and incompletely specified situation, both isolate and banal, and who find it hard to convince themselves that they are other than empty but somehow animate bodies.[46] At the cost of ordinary dramatic coherence and symmetry, Shepard has dared to represent in Action a world for which "zero identity" and "theatrical positivism" might almost be adequate labels—as they still would not be, of course, for the shared action of presenting that world in the theater.

Shepard's True West, of 1980, and Fool for Love, of 1983, make clear that this predicament need not incapacitate the playwright. True West shapes a taut drama out of the shifts of power and identity between characters that seem separate but behave like aspects of a single mind. "I think we're split in a much more devastating way than psychology can ever reveal," Shepard has said.[47] Fool for Love focuses, in its tense drama of incest, both our helpless love for those who are not finally separate from ourselves and our unbridgeable distance from them. The half brother and half sister, Eddie and May, are trapped in another Shepard low-rent motel—unable either to stay or to leave. And the presence of their absent father, a late addition to the script,[48] prevents us from naturalizing its action according to any rational scheme. Rocking in a chair on an extension of the stage, or wandering into the midst of the action, he incarnates the isolate meditation that has either generated this drama or been generated by it. Despite the violence, anguish, and baffling entrapment here, our ethical judgment seems irrelevant. As actors or witnesses, we have become clear-sighted participants in a field of multiplicity and unity, isolation and intimacy, that seems a fatality beyond our understanding. Whenever Eddie tries to break out of this claustral box and the miked door booms, the reverberations of self-conscious imprisonment within the field of our theatrical participation say, in effect: "Wham, bam." Despite Shepard's great distance now from Beckett's aesthetic strategies, he may be, of all the playwrights who have recognized Beckett's presence, the one who has come closest to the irreducible ambiguities in his plays.

Stoppard and Pinter, Fugard and Soyinka, Mamet and Shepard—

it's a remarkable progeny for this ironically absent father of so much contemporary theater. Each seems to have articulated and developed some special aspect of that irreducible original or amplified certain selected overtones of his "fundamental sounds"—so helping us to face a portion of that interpersonal and incompletely rationalizable knowledge which is, I suspect, the secret of drama. In doing so, each has seemed to say, through his distinctive whams and bams, "Thank you Sam."

NOTES

1. John Gruen, "Samuel Beckett Talks About Beckett," *Vogue* (December 1969), p. 210.
2. Samuel Beckett, *Disjecta*, ed. Ruby Cohn (London: John Calder, 1983), p. 139.
3. Samuel Beckett, *Waiting for Godot* (New York: Grove Press, 1954), pp. 7a, 60b; (London: Faber & Faber, 1956). *Endgame* (New York: Grove Press, 1958), pp. 1, 13, 74; (London: Faber & Faber, 1958). Subsequent citations from these plays are from the Grove Press editions.
4. Robert Langbaum, *The Mysteries of Identity* (New York: Oxford University Press, 1977), pp. 7, 137.
5. Alfred Schwarz, *From Büchner to Beckett* (Athens, Ohio: Ohio University Press, 1978), p. 354.
6. J. E. Dearlove, *Accommodating the Chaos: Samuel Beckett's Nonrelational Art* (Durham, N.C.: Duke University Press, 1982), p. 3.
7. Tom Driver, *Romantic Quest and Modern Theory: A History of the Modern Theater* (New York: Delacorte Press, 1970), pp. 387–89.
8. Charles R. Lyons, *Samuel Beckett* (New York: Grove Press, 1983), pp. 155, 157–59. For a more adequate account of the paradoxes of performance, see Paul Lawley, "Counterpoint, Absence, and the Medium in Beckett's *Not I*," *Modern Drama* 26 (1983), 407–13.
9. See William B. Worthen, *The Idea of the Actor* (Princeton, N.J.: Princeton University Press, 1984), pp. 203–14, for a discussion of this aspect of Beckett's plays. Other discussions that are alert to the paradoxes of Beckett's theatrical rhetoric include those by Vivian Mercier, *Beckett/Beckett* (New York: Oxford University Press, 1977), and Ruby Cohn, *Just Play: Beckett's Theater* (Princeton, N.J.: Princeton University Press, 1980). The position taken in these paragraphs has been more fully developed in my own book, *Fields of Play in Modern Drama* (Princeton, N.J.: Princeton University Press,

1977), and "Playing Hell," in *The Yearbook of English Studies*, 9 (1979): 167–87.

10. Quoted in James Knowlson and John Pilling, *Frescoes of the Skull: The Later Prose and Drama of Samuel Beckett* (London: John Calder, 1979), p. 219.

11. Keith Johnstone, *Impro: Improvisation and the Theatre* (New York: Theatre Arts Books, 1979), p. 24. For Johnstone's own perceptive comments on "status transactions" in *Waiting for Godot*, see pp. 72–74.

12. Hilary DeVries, "Playwrights Dispute: Testing Theaters' Collaborative Role," *Christian Science Monitor*, December 19, 1984, pp. 23–24; Samuel G. Freedman, "Who's to Say Whether a Playwright Is Wronged?" *The New York Times*, December 23, 1984, sec. E, p. 6.

13. Beckett, *Disjecta*, p. 109.

14. For an elaboration of this argument, see my book *Tom Stoppard* (New York: Grove Press, 1983), pp. 37–67.

15. Beckett, *Waiting for Godot*, pp. 9b, 57b, 58a–b.

16. Tom Stoppard, *Jumpers* (New York: Grove Press, 1973), p. 87. For an elaboration of the play's ethical implications, see my book *Tom Stoppard*, pp. 85–107.

17. Gitta Honegger, Rassami Patipatpaopong, and Joel Schechter, "An Interview with Athol Fugard," *Theater*, 16:1 (Fall/Winter 1984), 38; Athol Fugard, *Boesman and Lena and Other Plays* (Oxford: Oxford University Press, 1978), pp. 75–76.

18. See Wole Soyinka, "The Fourth Stage," an essay written in 1967, in *Myth, Literature and the African World* (Cambridge: Cambridge University Press, 1976), pp. 140–60.

19. Fugard, *Boesman and Lena and Other Plays*, p. xi; idem, *Notebooks 1960–1977* (New York: Knopf, 1984), pp. 62–63, 102, 67, 68.

20. Fugard, *Notebooks 1960–1977*, pp. 65, 89, 78. See also Fugard, "Introduction," *Statements: Three Plays* (London and Cape Town: Oxford University Press, 1974), pp. vii–xiii.

21. Fugard, *Notebooks 1960–1977*, pp. 181, 155, 168, 167, 173.

22. Fugard, *Boesman and Lena and Other Plays*, pp. 246, 265.

23. Beckett, *Waiting for Godot*, p. 35a.

24. Honegger, Patipatpaopong, Schechter, Interview, p. 36.

25. Fugard, *Notebooks 1960–1977*, p. 171; see also p. 184.

26. Beckett, *Waiting for Godot*, p. 34a.

27. Beckett, *Happy Days* (New York: Grove Press, 1961), pp. 49–50; (London: Faber & Faber, 1962).

28. Fugard, *Boesman and Lena and Other Plays*, pp. 260, 262, 278.

29. Beckett, *Waiting for Godot*, pp. 51a, 54a.

30. Fugard, *Notebooks 1960–1977*, p. 195.
31. For a Fugard chronology, see Stephen Gray, ed., *Athol Fugard* (Johannesburg: McGraw-Hill, 1982), pp. 3–14.
32. For the text of *The Road to Mecca*, see *Theater*, 16:1 (Fall/Winter 1984), 5–32.
33. Soyinka, *Myth, Literature and the African World*, p. 63.
34. Irving Wardle, "Introduction," Johnstone, *Impro*, pp. 9–10.
35. For a Soyinka chronology, see James Gibbs, ed., *Critical Perspectives on Wole Soyinka* (Washington, D.C.: Three Continents Press, 1980), pp. 3–15.
36. For a development of this reading in the context of Soyinka's other plays, see my essay "Soyinka's Elusive Quarry," in *In the House of Osubgo: Essays on Wole Soyinka*, edited by Henry Louis Gates, Jr. (New York: Oxford University Press, 1986). For a somewhat different view of Soyinka's use of Beckett, see Clive T. Probyn, "Waiting for the Word: Samuel Beckett and Wole Soyinka," *Ariel: A Review of International English Literature*, 12:3 (July 1981), 35–48.
37. Soyinka, *Collected Plays 1* (London: Oxford University Press, 1973), p. 149.
38. Ibid., p. 197.
39. Ibid., pp. 228–29.
40. Soyinka, *Myth, Literature and the African World*, pp. 43, 44, 30–31.
41. See Cohn, *Just Play: Beckett's Theater*, pp. 230–79.
42. Beckett, *Waiting for Godot*, p. 40a.
43. David Mamet, *Sexual Perversity in Chicago and The Duck Variations* (New York: Grove Press, 1978), pp. 121–22.
44. For Shepard's own comments on his indebtedness to Beckett and the rewriting of *Cowboys*, see Kenneth Chubb and the editors of *Theatre Quarterly*, "Metaphors, Mad Dogs and Old Time Cowboys" [interview], *American Dreams: The Imagination of Sam Shepard*, edited by Bonnie Marranca (New York: Performing Arts Journal Publications, 1981), pp. 190–91.
45. Sam Shepard, *Seven Plays* (New York: Bantam Books, 1981), pp. 225, 249, 230, 232.
46. Shepard, *Fool for Love and Other Plays* (New York: Bantam Books, 1984), pp. 169, 183, 186, 182–84.
47. Quoted by Ross Wetzsteon, "Introduction" to Shepard, *Fool for Love and Other Plays*, pp. 5–6.
48. I owe this information to David DeRose, who has consulted the script in possession of the Magic Theater, San Francisco.

Contributors

RUBY COHN, called "the doyenne of Beckett criticism" by *The Times Literary Supplement*, teaches in the Department of Dramatic Art at the University of California, Davis. She is the author of *Modern Shakespeare Offshoots, Dialogue in American Drama, Currents in American Drama, New American Dramatists, 1960–1980, Samuel Beckett: The Comic Gamut, Back to Beckett,* and *Just Play: Beckett's Theater.* Her edited work includes *Casebook on "Waiting for Godot," Samuel Beckett: A Collection of Criticism,* and *Disjecta: Miscellaneous Writings and a Dramatic Fragment.*

JOHN RUSSELL BROWN has written *Shakespeare and His Comedies, Shakespeare's Plays in Performance, Effective Theatre, Theatre Language, Free Shakespeare,* and *Discovering Shakespeare.* Chairman of the Department of Theater and Drama at the University of Michigan, he is also associate director of the National Theatre in London, where he has been head of the Script Department. A director as well as a teacher, he is the general editor of *Stratford-upon-Avon Studies* and *Theatre Productions Studies.* He has been chairman of the Drama Advisory Panel (Arts Council of Great Britain) and the Advisory Council of the Theatre Museum, London.

NORMAND BERLIN is the author of *The Secret Cause: A Discussion of Tragedy, The Base String: The Underworld in Elizabethan*

Drama, and has written books on Thomas Sackville and Eugene O'Neill. A founding editor of the journal *Enlish Literary Renaissance*, he teaches in the Department of English, University of Massachusetts, Amherst.

MICHAEL GOLDMAN is professor of English at Princeton University. His published work includes *Shakespeare and the Energies of Drama*, *The Actor's Freedom*, and *Acting and Action in Shakespearean Tragedy*. He is the author of two books of poetry, some of which has also appeared in *The New Yorker*. His plays have appeared off-off Broadway in New York.

CHARLES R. LYONS is chairman of the Department of Drama at Stanford University. His books include *Bertolt Brecht: The Despair and the Polemic*, *Shakespeare and the Ambiguity of Love's Triumph*, *Heinrich Ibsen: The Divided Consciousness*, and *Samuel Beckett*.

ANDREW KENNEDY has written *Six Dramatists in Search of a Language* and *Dramatic Dialogue: The Duologue of Personal Encounter*. He is a senior lecturer in English at the University of Bergen in Norway and an associate of Clare Hall, Cambridge University.

MARTIN ESSLIN joined the BBC in 1940 and was head of Drama (Radio) from 1963 to 1977. He is the author of books on Pinter, Brecht, and Artaud, as well as a seminal book on modern drama, *The Theatre of the Absurd*. He has published two collections of essays, *Brief Chronicles: Essays on Modern Drama* and *Mediations: Essays on Brecht, Beckett and the Media*. His critical articles have appeared regularly in *Plays and Players*, *Encounter*, *The Observer*, *The New Statesman*, and many other periodicals. He is also the author of *An Anatomy of Drama*. A professor of drama at Stanford University, he is, in addition, a respected translator of plays, particularly by German-speaking dramatists.

KEIR ELAM is a lecturer in English at the University of Florence. His books include *The Semiotics of Theatre and Drama* and *Shakespeare's Universe of Discourse*. His studies of individual playwrights have also appeared in *Modern Drama* and other important journals.

BERNARD BECKERMAN was professor of English and comparative literature at Columbia University. He is the author of *Dynamics of Drama: Theory and Method of Analysis* and other highly praised studies in the field.

KATHARINE WORTH is professor of drama and theatre studies at the University of London and head of the Department of Drama and Theatre Studies at Royal Holloway College. Her published works include *Oscar Wilde, The Irish Drama of Europe,* and *Revolutions in Modern English Drama.* She has edited *Beckett the Shape Changer* and has been the producer of three of Beckett's radio plays for the University of London Audio-Visual Centre. She is chairman of the Consortium for Drama and Media in Higher Education.

JAMES KNOWLSON teaches in England in the Department of French Studies at the University of Reading, the home of the Beckett Archive, which he helped found. His published works include *Light and Darkness in the Theatre of Samuel Beckett, Krapp's Last Tape: Theatre Notebook I,* and *Frescoes of the Skull: the Later Prose and Drama of Samuel Beckett* (coauthored).

THOMAS R. WHITAKER is professor of English at Yale University. His books include *Tom Stoppard* and *Fields of Play in Modern Drama.*

ENOCH BRATER teaches modern drama at the University of Michigan, Ann Arbor, and is president of the Samuel Beckett Society. A well-known essayist, he is also the author of *Beyond Minimalism: Beckett's Late Style in the Theater.*

Index

235